Houghton
Mifflin
Harcourt

S0-BZG-190

TEXAS
SCIENCE
Fusion

fusion [FYOO • zhuhn] a combination of two or more things that releases energy

This Write-In Student Edition belongs to

_____

Teacher/Room

_____

Consulting Authors

Michael A. DiSpezio
Global Educator
North Falmouth, Massachusetts

Marjorie Frank
*Science Writer and Content-Area Reading
    Specialist*
Brooklyn, New York

Michael Heithaus
*Executive Director, School of Environment, Arts, and
    Society*
*Associate Professor, Department of Biological
    Sciences*
Florida International University
North Miami, Florida

Donna Ogle
Professor of Reading and Language
National-Louis University
Chicago, Illinois

Program Advisors

Paul D. Asimow
Professor of Geology and Geochemistry
California Institute of Technology
Pasadena, California

Bobby Jeanpierre
Associate Professor of Science
Education
University of Central Florida
Orlando, Florida

Gerald H. Krockover
Professor Emeritus of Earth,
Atmospheric, and Planetary Science
Education
Purdue University
West Lafayette, Indiana

Rose Pringle
Associate Professor
School of Teaching and Learning
College of Education
University of Florida
Gainesville, Florida

Carolyn Staudt
Curriculum Designer for Technology
KidSolve, Inc.
The Concord Consortium
Concord, Massachusetts

Larry Stookey
Science Department
Antigo High School
Antigo, Wisconsin

Carol J. Valenta
Associate Director of the Museum and
Senior Vice President
Saint Louis Science Center
St. Louis, Missouri

Barry A. Van Deman
President and CEO
Museum of Life and Science
Durham, North Carolina

Texas Reviewers

Max Ceballos
District Science Specialist
Edinburg, Texas

Tamara L. Cryar
Cook Elementary
Austin, Texas

Heather Domjan
University of Houston
Houston, Texas

Ashley D. Golden
Washington Elementary
Big Spring, Texas

Linda Churchwell Halliman
Cornelius Elementary School
Houston, Texas

Ellen Lyon
Hays Consolidated ISD
Kyle, Texas

Stephanie McNeil
Bastian Elementary
Houston, Texas

Sue Mendoza
District Science Coach
El Paso ISD
El Paso, Texas

Christine L. Morgan
Emerson Elementary
Midland, Texas

Genaro Ovalle III
Elementary Science Dean
Laredo ISD
Laredo, Texas

Hilda Quintanar
Science Coach
El Paso ISD
El Paso, Texas

Power Up with Texas Science Fusion!

Grade 3

Your program fuses . . .

e-Learning & Virtual Labs

Labs & Explorations

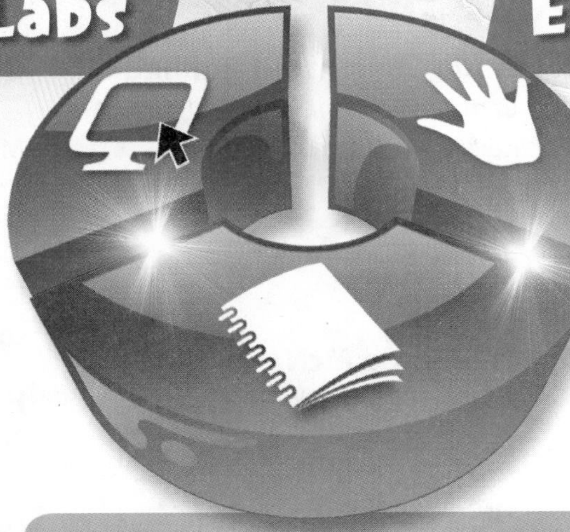

Write-In Student Edition

. . . to generate new energy
for today's science learner— *you.*

Write-In Student Edition

Be an active reader and make this book your own!

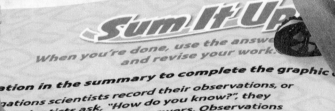

Sum It Up!

When you're done, use the answe... and revise your work.

...tion in the summary to complete the graphic ...

...ring ...nations scientists record their observations, or
...a. Whe... ...r scientists ask, "How do you know?", they
...ain how ...data supports their answers. Observations
...e shared ... ...ny ways. Data in the form of numbers
...e shown in ... tables and bar graphs. Data can also be
... as models, ... or in writing.

1 ...etail: Scientists...

Write your ideas, answer questions, make notes, and record activity results right on these pages.

...ain ... data
Scientist... ...data
to answer ...stions,
and they r... ...it in
different w...

3 ...tail:

Learn science concepts and skills by interacting with every page.

Find...

1 Data
- to...
- ste...
- pie...

2 Evidenc...
- a ki...
- how
- the f...
  is co...

3 Data tabl...
- a char...
- the nu...
- a piec...

4 Bar graph
- a chart ...
- a graph ...
- a graph t...

5 Communicat...
- take a ph...
- share dat...
- collect and...

e-Learning & Virtual Labs

Digital lessons and virtual labs provide e-learning options for every lesson of *Texas Science Fusion*.

Let's do it!

Click the Reset button and run the experiment again if you missed anything.

Use the camera to take a photo of water particles in the gas state.
Click the Reset button and run the experiment again if you missed anything.

Unit 9 Lesson 4 · What are the States of Matter?

Volume is a measure of how much space matter takes up.
By looking at these ice cubes, it is clear how much space they take up.

On your own or with a group, explore science concepts in a digital world.

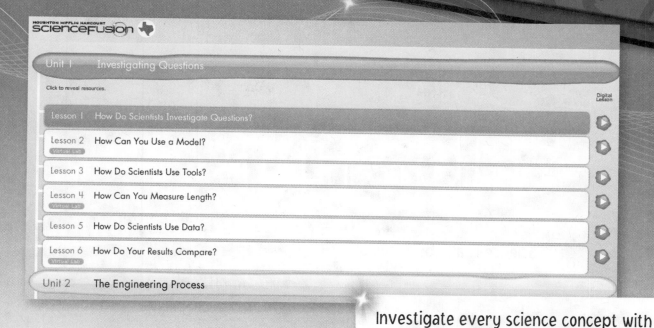

Unit 1   Investigating Questions

Click to reveal resources.

Digital Lesson

Lesson 1   How Do Scientists Investigate Questions?

Lesson 2   How Can You Use a Model?
Virtual Lab

Lesson 3   How Do Scientists Use Tools?

Lesson 4   How Can You Measure Length?
Virtual Lab

Lesson 5   How Do Scientists Use Data?

Lesson 6   How Do Your Results Compare?
Virtual Lab

Unit 2   The Engineering Process

Investigate every science concept with multiple virtual labs in every unit.

Continue your science explorations with these online tools:

→ **ScienceSaurus**   → **People in Science**

→ **NSTA Scilinks**   → **Media Gallery**

→ **Video-based Projects**   → **Vocabulary Cards**

→ Science Readers for Texas with complete AUDIO!

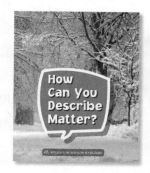

How Can You Describe Matter?

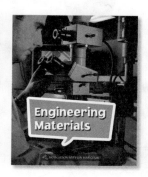

Engineering Materials

Labs & Explorations

Science is all about doing.

Exciting investigations for every lesson.

Ask questions and test your ideas.

Draw conclusions and share what you learn.

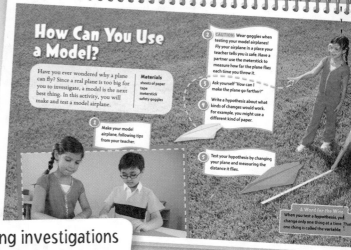

How Can You Use a Model?

Have you ever wondered why a plane can fly? Since a real plane is too big for you to investigate, a model is the next best thing. In this activity, you will make and test a model airplane.

Materials
sheets of paper
tape
meterstick
safety goggles

1. Make your model airplane, following tips from your teacher.

2. CAUTION: Wear goggles when testing your model airplanes! Fly your airplane in a place your teacher tells you is safe. Have a partner use the meterstick to measure how far the plane flies each time you throw it.

3. Ask yourself "How can I make the plane go farther?"

4. Write a hypothesis about what kinds of changes would work. For example, you might use a different kind of paper.

5. Test your hypothesis by changing your plane and measuring the distance it flies.

Word for the Wise
When you test a hypothesis, you change only one thing at a time. That one thing is called the variable.

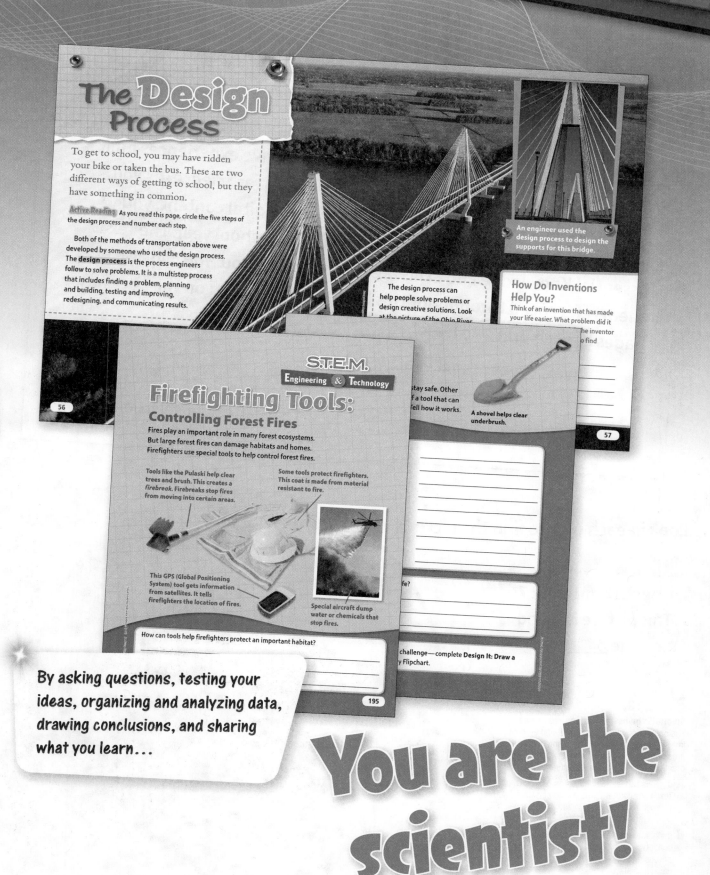

The Design Process

To get to school, you may have ridden your bike or taken the bus. These are two different ways of getting to school, but they have something in common.

Active Reading As you read this page, circle the five steps of the design process and number each step.

Both of the methods of transportation above were developed by someone who used the design process. The **design process** is the process engineers follow to solve problems. It is a multistep process that includes finding a problem, planning and building, testing and improving, redesigning, and communicating results.

An engineer used the design process to design the supports for this bridge.

The design process can help people solve problems or design creative solutions. Look at the picture of the Ohio River...

How Do Inventions Help You?

Think of an invention that has made your life easier. What problem did it ... the inventor ... to find

56

57

A shovel helps clear underbrush.

S.T.E.M.
Engineering & Technology

Firefighting Tools:
Controlling Forest Fires

Fires play an important role in many forest ecosystems. But large forest fires can damage habitats and homes. Firefighters use special tools to help control forest fires.

Tools like the Pulaski help clear trees and brush. This creates a *firebreak*. Firebreaks stop fires from moving into certain areas.

Some tools protect firefighters. This coat is made from material resistant to fire.

...tay safe. Other ...f a tool that can ...ell how it works.

This GPS (Global Positioning System) tool gets information from satellites. It tells firefighters the location of fires.

Special aircraft dump water or chemicals that stop fires.

How can tools help firefighters protect an important habitat?

195

...fe?

...challenge—complete **Design It: Draw a** ... **Flipchart.**

By asking questions, testing your ideas, organizing and analyzing data, drawing conclusions, and sharing what you learn...

You are the scientist!

Texas Essential Knowledge and Skills

Dear Students and Family Members,

The *ScienceFusion* Student Edition, Inquiry Flipchart, and Digital Curriculum provide a full year of interactive experiences built around the Texas Essential Knowledge and Skills for Science. As you read, experiment, and interact with print and digital content, you will be learning what you need to know for this school year. The Texas Essential Knowledge and Skills are listed here for you. You will also see them referenced throughout this book. Look for them on the opening pages of each unit and lesson.

Have a great school year!

Sincerely,
The HMH *ScienceFusion* Team

Look in each unit to find the picture.

Check it out: Unit 7
This picture is found on page _____.

TEKS 3.1

Scientific investigation and reasoning. The student conducts classroom and outdoor investigations following school and home safety procedures and environmentally appropriate practices. The student is expected to:

A demonstrate safe practices as described in the Texas Safety Standards during classroom and outdoor investigations, including observing a schoolyard habitat; and

B make informed choices in the use and conservation of natural resources by recycling or reusing materials such as paper, aluminum cans, and plastics.

x

Check it out: Unit 1
This picture is found on page _____.

Check it out: Unit 2
This picture is found on page _____.

Check it out: Unit 1
This picture is found on page _____.

TEKS 3.2

Scientific investigation and reasoning.
The student uses scientific inquiry methods during laboratory and outdoor investigations. The student is expected to:

A plan and implement descriptive investigations, including asking and answering questions, making inferences, and selecting and using equipment or technology needed, to solve a specific problem in the natural world;

B collect data by observing and measuring using the metric system and recognize differences between observed and measured data;

C construct maps, graphic organizers, simple tables, charts, and bar graphs using tools and current technology to organize, examine, and evaluate measured data;

D analyze and interpret patterns in data to construct reasonable explanations based on evidence from investigations;

E demonstrate that repeated investigations may increase the reliability of results; and

F communicate valid conclusions supported by data in writing, by drawing pictures, and through verbal discussion.

TEKS 3.3

Scientific investigation and reasoning.
The student knows that information, critical thinking, scientific problem solving, and the contributions of scientists are used in making decisions. The student is expected to:

A in all fields of science, analyze, evaluate, and critique scientific explanations by using empirical evidence, logical reasoning, and experimental and observational testing, including examining all sides of scientific evidence of those scientific explanations, so as to encourage critical thinking by the student;

B draw inferences and evaluate accuracy of product claims found in advertisements and labels such as for toys and food;

C represent the natural world using models such as volcanoes or Sun, Earth, and Moon system and identify their limitations, including size, properties, and materials; and

D connect grade-level appropriate science concepts with the history of science, science careers, and contributions of scientists.

TEKS 3.4

Science investigation and reasoning.
The student knows how to use a variety of tools and methods to conduct science inquiry. The student is expected to:

A collect, record, and analyze information using tools, including microscopes, cameras, computers, hand lenses, metric rulers, Celsius thermometers, wind vanes, rain gauges, pan balances, graduated cylinders, beakers, spring scales, hot plates, meter sticks, compasses, magnets, collecting nets, notebooks, sound recorders, and Sun, Earth, and Moon system models; timing devices, including clocks and stopwatches; and materials to support observation of habitats of organisms such as terrariums and aquariums; and

B use safety equipment as appropriate, including safety goggles and gloves.

Answer Key: page 35, page 77, page 18

Check it out: Unit 3
This picture is found on page _____.

Check it out: Unit 4
This picture is found on page _____.

Check it out: Unit 6
This picture is found on page _____.

TEKS 3.5

Matter and energy. The student knows that matter has measurable physical properties and those properties determine how matter is classified, changed, and used. The student is expected to:

A measure, test, and record physical properties of matter, including temperature, mass, magnetism, and the ability to sink or float;

B describe and classify samples of matter as solids, liquids, and gases and demonstrate that solids have a definite shape and that liquids and gases take the shape of their container;

C predict, observe, and record changes in the state of matter caused by heating or cooling; and

D explore and recognize that a mixture is created when two materials are combined such as gravel and sand and metal and plastic paper clips.

TEKS 3.6

Force, motion, and energy. The student knows that forces cause change and that energy exists in many forms. The student is expected to:

A explore different forms of energy, including mechanical, light, sound, and heat/thermal in everyday life;

B demonstrate and observe how position and motion can be changed by pushing and pulling objects to show work being done such as swings, balls, pulleys, and wagons; and

C observe forces such as magnetism and gravity acting on objects.

TEKS 3.7

Earth and space. The student knows that Earth consists of natural resources and its surface is constantly changing. The student is expected to:

A explore and record how soils are formed by weathering of rock and the decomposition of plant and animal remains;

B investigate rapid changes in Earth's surface such as volcanic eruptions, earthquakes, and landslides;

C identify and compare different landforms, including mountains, hills, valleys, and plains; and

D explore the characteristics of natural resources that make them useful in products and materials such as clothing and furniture and how resources may be conserved.

Answer Key: page 120, page 155, page 286

Check it out: Unit 9
This picture is found on page _____.

Check it out: Unit 10
This picture is found on page _____.

Check it out: Unit 11
This picture is found on page _____.

TEKS 3.8

Earth and space. The student knows there are recognizable patterns in the natural world and among objects in the sky. The student is expected to:

A observe, measure, record, and compare day-to-day weather changes in different locations at the same time that include air temperature, wind direction, and precipitation;

B describe and illustrate the Sun as a star composed of gases that provides light and heat energy for the water cycle;

C construct models that demonstrate the relationship of the Sun, Earth, and Moon, including orbits and positions; and

D identify the planets in Earth's solar system and their position in relation to the Sun.

TEKS 3.9

Organisms and environments. The student knows that organisms have characteristics that help them survive and can describe patterns, cycles, systems, and relationships within the environments. The student is expected to:

A observe and describe the physical characteristics of environments and how they support populations and communities within an ecosystem;

B identify and describe the flow of energy in a food chain and predict how changes in a food chain affect the ecosystem such as removal of frogs from a pond or bees from a field; and

C describe environmental changes such as floods and droughts where some organisms thrive and others perish or move to new locations.

TEKS 3.10

Organisms and environments. The student knows that organisms undergo similar life processes and have structures that help them survive within their environments. The student is expected to:

A explore how structures and functions of plants and animals allow them to survive in a particular environment;

B explore that some characteristics of organisms are inherited such as the number of limbs on an animal or flower color and recognize that some behaviors are learned in response to living in a certain environment such as animals using tools to get food; and

C investigate and compare how animals and plants undergo a series of orderly changes in their diverse life cycles such as tomato plants, frogs, and lady bugs.

Contents

Levels of Inquiry Key ■ DIRECTED ■ GUIDED ■ INDEPENDENT

Safety in Science . . . . **xxiii**
Inquiry Flipchart pp. 1–2—Safety in Science

THE NATURE OF SCIENCE AND S.T.E.M.

Unit 1—Investigating Questions 1

Lesson 1 **How Do Scientists Investigate Questions?** 3
Inquiry Flipchart p. 3—Mystery Box/Magnet Mysteries

Inquiry Lesson 2 **How Can You Use a Model?** 15
Inquiry Flipchart p. 4— How Can You Use a Model?

Lesson 3 **How Do Scientists Use Tools?** 17
Inquiry Flipchart p. 5—I Can See Clearly Now/Talented Tools

Inquiry Flipchart pp. 6–9—Science Tools Activities

Inquiry Lesson 4 **How Can You Measure Length?** 27
Inquiry Flipchart p. 10—How Can You Measure Length?

Lesson 5 **How Do Scientists Use Data?** 31
Inquiry Flipchart p. 11—Data Two Ways/Raise the Bar

Inquiry Lesson 6 **How Do Your Results Compare?** 45
Inquiry Flipchart p. 12— How Do Your Results Compare?

Careers in Science: Meteorologist 47

Unit 1 Review 49

Unit 2—The Engineering Process 53

Lesson 1 **How Do Engineers Use the Design Process?** 55
Inquiry Flipchart p. 13—Chill Out/Science Solutions

Inquiry Lesson 2 **How Can You Design a Tree House?** 67
Inquiry Flipchart p. 14— How Can You Design a Tree House?

Lesson 3 **How Are Technology and Society Related?** 69
Inquiry Flipchart p. 15—Modes of Transportation/You are the Target!

Inquiry Lesson 4 **How Can We Improve a Design?** 83
Inquiry Flipchart p. 16— How Can We Improve a Design?

Careers in Science: Civil Engineer 85

Unit 2 Review 87

PHYSICAL SCIENCE

Unit 3—Properties of Matter 91

Lesson 1 **What Are Some Physical Properties?** 93
Inquiry Flipchart p. 17—Will It Float or Sink?/Sort Some Matter

Inquiry Lesson 2 **How Can We Measure Magnetism?** 107
Inquiry Flipchart p.18— How Can We Measure Magnetism?

Careers in Science: Metallurgist 109

Inquiry Lesson 3 **What Physical Properties Can We Observe?** 111
Inquiry Flipchart p. 19— What Physical Properties Can We Observe?

Inquiry Lesson 4 **How Is Temperature Measured?** 113
Inquiry Flipchart p. 20— How Is Temperature Measured?

Lesson 5 **What Are the States of Matter?** 115
Inquiry Flipchart p. 21—Temperature Takes a Dive!/The Shape of Different States

Lesson 6 **What Are Some Changes to Matter?** 127
Inquiry Flipchart p. 22—Break It Up!/Coming Apart

S.T.E.M. **Engineering and Technology:** Resources on the Road 141
Inquiry Flipchart p. 23— Design It: Float Your Boat

Unit 3 Review 143

Unit 4—Energy 147

Lesson 1 **What Are Some Forms of Energy?** 149
Inquiry Flipchart p. 24—Energy in Motion/Make It Move

People in Science: Ben Franklin 159

Lesson 2 **What Is Sound?** 161
Inquiry Flipchart p. 25—See Changes in Vibrations/Change the Sound

Inquiry Lesson 3 **How Are Sounds Changed?** 173
Inquiry Flipchart p. 26— How Are Sounds Changed?

S.T.E.M. **Engineering and Technology:** Telephone Timeline 175
Inquiry Flipchart p. 27— Design It: Make a Musical Instrument

Lesson 4 **How Does Light Move?** 177
Inquiry Flipchart p. 28—Explore How Light Travels/Refraction

Lesson 5 **What Are Some Heat Sources?** 189
Inquiry Flipchart p. 29—Heat Race/Where There's Light...

Inquiry Lesson 6 **Where Can Heat Come From?** 201
Inquiry Flipchart p. 30— Where Can Heat Come From?

Unit 4 Review 203

Unit 5—Forces and Work 207

Lesson 1 **What Are Simple Machines?** 209
Inquiry Flipchart p. 31—Machines and Forces/Change It!

S.T.E.M. **Engineering and Technology: Reach for the Sky** 221
Inquiry Flipchart p. 32—Design It: Working Elevator Model

Lesson 2 **What Are Some Other Simple Machines?** 223
Inquiry Flipchart p. 33—Wrap It Up/Everyday Machines

Inquiry Lesson 3 **How Do Simple Machines Affect Work?** 235
Inquiry Flipchart p. 34—How Do Simple Machines Affect Work?

People in Science: Helen Greiner and Dean Kamen 237

Lesson 4 **What Is Gravity?** 239
Inquiry Flipchart p. 35—Measure the Force/Forces Acting on a Compass

Unit 5 Review 251

EARTH SCIENCE

Unit 6—Earth's Surface 255

Lesson 1 **What Are Some Landforms?** 257
Inquiry Flipchart p. 36—Folding Up Mountains/Making Other Landforms

Lesson 2 **How Does Earth's Surface Change Slowly?** 269
Inquiry Flipchart p. 37—The Power of Water/Find Some Erosion!

S.T.E.M. **Engineering and Technology: Erosion Technology** 279
Inquiry Flipchart p. 38— Improvise It: Reducing Erosion

Inquiry Lesson 3 **How Can We Model Erosion?** 281
Inquiry Flipchart p. 39—How Can We Model Erosion?

Lesson 4 **How Does Earth's Surface Change Quickly?** 283
Inquiry Flipchart p. 40—A Model Volcano/Simulate an Earthquake

People in Science: Hugo Delgado Granados and Waverly Person 295

Unit 6 Review 297

Unit 7—People and Resources 301

Lesson 1 What Are Some Natural Resources? 303
Inquiry Flipchart p. 41—Polluted Plants/Clean It Up!

Inquiry Lesson 2 How Can We Conserve Resources? 317
Inquiry Flipchart p. 42—How Can We Conserve Resources?

Lesson 3 What Is Soil? 319
Inquiry Flipchart p. 43—Forming Soil/Compost It!

Careers In Science: Geologist 333

S.T.E.M. Engineering and Technology: Problems and Fixes 335
Inquiry Flipchart p. 44—Redesign It: Reduce Packaging

Unit 7 Review 337

Unit 8—Water and Weather 341

Lesson 1 What Is the Water Cycle? 343
Inquiry Flipchart p. 45—Weather in a Box/A Salty Change!

Careers in Science: Hydrologist 355

Lesson 2 What Is Weather? 357
Inquiry Flipchart p. 46—Measuring Wind Speed/Check the Weather

Inquiry Lesson 3 How Can We Measure Weather? 369
Inquiry Flipchart p. 47—How Can We Measure Weather?

S.T.E.M. Engineering and Technology: Keeping Dry: Raincoat vs. Poncho 371
Inquiry Flipchart p. 48— Design It: Build a Wind Streamer

Unit 8 Review 373

Unit 9—Space 377

Lesson 1 How Do Earth and the Moon Move? 379
Inquiry Flipchart p. 49—Tilted Earth/Darkness Falls

People in Science: Katherine Johnson and Amanda Nahm 393

Inquiry Lesson 2 How Can We Model the Moon's Phases? 395
Inquiry Flipchart p. 50—How Can We Model the Moon's Phases?

Lesson 3 What Are the Sun and Stars? 397
Inquiry Flipchart p.51—Starry Lights/Let's Cook!

Lesson 4 What Are the Planets in Our Solar System? 409
Inquiry Flipchart p. 52—How Can We Model the Orbit of Comets and Planets?/Planet Map

Inquiry Lesson 5 How Can We Model the Sun and Planets? 423
Inquiry Flipchart p. 53—How Can We Model the Sun and Planets?

S.T.E.M. Engineering and Technology: How It Works: Keck Observatory 425
Inquiry Flipchart p. 54—Owner's Manual: Using a Telescope

Unit 9 Review 427

LIFE SCIENCE

Unit 10—Ecosystems and Interactions 431

Lesson 1 **What Are Ecosystems?** 433
Inquiry Flipchart p. 55—Take a Closer Look/Study an Ecosystem

Inquiry Lesson 2 **What's in an Ecosystem?** 445
Inquiry Flipchart p. 56—What's in an Ecosystem?

People in Science: Dení Ramírez and Cassandra Nichols 447

Lesson 3 **What Is a Food Chain?** 449
Inquiry Flipchart p. 57—Break It Down/Make a Food Chain

Inquiry Lesson 4 **What Are Some Food Chains?** 461
Inquiry Flipchart p. 58—What Are Some Food Chains?

Lesson 5 **How Do Environmental Changes Affect Living Things?** .. 463
Inquiry Flipchart p. 59—Too Much Water!/Not Enough Water!

S.T.E.M. **Engineering and Technology:** Controlling Forest Fires 477
Inquiry Flipchart p. 60— Design It: Draw a Safari Backpack

Unit 10 Review 479

Unit 11—Living Things Grow and Change 483

Lesson 1 What Are Some Plant Life Cycles? 485
  `Inquiry Flipchart` p. 61—Make It Germinate!/Flowers and Cones

Lesson 2 What Are Some Animal Life Cycles? 495
  `Inquiry Flipchart` p. 62—Model a Life Cycle/Plan a Life Cycle Observation

Inquiry Lesson 3 How Do Living Things Change? 507
  `Inquiry Flipchart` p. 63—How Do Living Things Change?

Lesson 4 What Are Structural Adaptations? 509
  `Inquiry Flipchart` p. 64—Show and Tell/Adapted to Survive

People in Science: Miriam Rothschild and Charles Henry Turner 521

Inquiry Lesson 5 How Can We Model a Physical Adaptation? 523
  `Inquiry Flipchart` p. 65—How Can We Model a Physical Adaptation?

Lesson 6 What Are Behavioral Adaptations? 525
  `Inquiry Flipchart` p. 66—Instinct or Learned Behavior?/Plan a Lesson

S.T.E.M. Engineering and Technology: Save It For Later 537
  `Inquiry Flipchart` p. 67—Solve It: Helping Animals Migrate

Unit 11 Review 539

Interactive Glossary R1
Index R19

Safety in Science

Indoors Doing science is a lot of fun. But a science lab can be a dangerous place. Falls, cuts, and burns can happen easily. When you are doing a science investigation, you need to be safe. Know the safety rules and listen to your teacher.

Adult scientists have to follow lab safety rules, too.

Pay attention to these safety rules.

1 **Think ahead.** Study the investigation steps so you know what to expect. If you have questions, ask your teacher. Be sure you understand all caution and safety reminders.

2 **Be neat and clean.** Keep your work area clean. If you have long hair, pull it back so it doesn't get in the way. Roll or push up long sleeves to keep them away from your activity.

3 **Oops!** If you spill or break something, or get cut, tell your teacher right away.

4 **Watch your eyes.** Wear safety goggles anytime you are directed to do so. If you get anything in your eyes, tell your teacher right away.

5 **Yuck!** Never eat or drink anything during a science activity.

6 **Don't get shocked.** Be careful if an electric appliance is used. Keep electric cords in a safe place where you can't trip over them. Never pull a plug out by the cord.

7 **Keep it clean.** Always clean up afterward. Put everything away and wipe your work area. Wash your hands.

8 **Play it safe.** Always know where to find safety equipment, such as fire extinguishers. Know how to use the safety equipment around you.

Outdoors

Lots of science research happens outdoors. It's fun to explore the wild! But you need to be careful. The weather, the land, and the living things can surprise you.

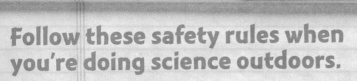

This scientist has to protect his eyes.

Follow these safety rules when you're doing science outdoors.

1 **Think ahead.** Study the investigation steps so you know what to expect. If you have any questions, ask your teacher. Be sure you understand all caution statements and safety reminders.

2 **Dress right.** Wear appropriate clothes and shoes for the outdoors. Cover up and wear sunscreen and sunglasses for sun safety.

3 **Clean up the area.** Follow your teacher's instructions for when and how to throw away waste.

4 **Oops!** Tell your teacher right away if you break something or get hurt.

5 **Watch your eyes.** Wear safety goggles when directed to do so. If you get anything in your eyes, tell your teacher right away.

6 **Yuck!** Never taste anything outdoors.

7 **Stay with your group.** Work in the area as directed by your teacher. Stay on marked trails.

8 **"Wilderness" doesn't mean go wild.** Never engage in horseplay, games, or pranks.

9 **Always walk.** No running!

10 **Play it safe.** Know where safety equipment can be found and how to use it. Know how to get help.

11 **Clean up.** Wash your hands with soap and water when you come back indoors.

Investigating Questions

©Houghton Mifflin Harcourt Publishing Company (bg) ©Peter Arnold, Inc./Alamy; (inset) ©Arco Images GmbH/Alamy; (border) ©NDisc/Age Fotostock

Big Idea

Scientists raise questions about Earth and the universe and seek answers to some of them by careful investigation.

TEKS 3.2A, 3.2B, 3.2C, 3.3A, 3.3D, 3.4A

I Wonder Why

Scientists work on the beach as well as many other places. How do scientists help animals survive? *Turn the page to find out.*

Here's Why Scientists get their hands dirty! They use tools such as tags, cameras, notes, and maps to help animals survive.

In this unit, you will explore the Big Idea, the Essential Questions, and the Investigations on the Inquiry Flipchart.

Levels of Inquiry Key ■ DIRECTED ■ GUIDED ■ INDEPENDENT

Big Idea Scientists raise questions about Earth and the universe and seek answers to some of them by careful investigation.

Essential Questions

Lesson 1 How Do Scientists Investigate Questions? 3
Inquiry Flipchart p. 3—Mystery Box/Magnet Mysteries

Inquiry Lesson 2 How Can You Use a Model? 15
Inquiry Flipchart p. 4—How Can You Use a Model?

Lesson 3 How Do Scientists Use Tools? 17
Inquiry Flipchart p. 5—I Can See Clearly Now/Talented Tools
pp. 6–9—Science Tools Activities

Inquiry Lesson 4 How Can You Measure Length? 27
Inquiry Flipchart p. 10—How Can You Measure Length?

Lesson 5 How Do Scientists Use Data? 31
Inquiry Flipchart p. 11—Data Two Ways/Raise the Bar

Inquiry Lesson 6 How Do Your Results Compare? 45
Inquiry Flipchart p. 12—How Do Your Results Compare?

Careers in Science: Meteorologist 47

Unit 1 Review 49

Now I Get the Big Idea!

Track Your Progress

Science Notebook

Before you begin each lesson, be sure to write your thoughts about the Essential Question.

TEKS **3.2A** plan and implement descriptive investigations, including asking and answering questions, making inferences, and selecting and using equipment or technology needed, to solve a specific problem in the natural world **3.2B** collect data by observing and measuring using the metric system and recognize differences between observed and measured data

Essential Question

How Do Scientists Investigate Questions?

Engage Your Brain!

Find the answer to the following question in this lesson and record it here.

How is this student acting like a scientist?

_____

_____

_____

Active Reading

Lesson Vocabulary

List the terms. As you learn about each one, make notes in the Interactive Glossary.

_____ _____

_____ _____

_____ _____

_____

Use Headings

Active readers preview, or read, the headings first. Headings give the reader an idea of what the reading is about. Reading with a purpose helps active readers understand what they are reading.

What Is Science?

Science is about Earth and everything beyond it. What does a scientist look like? To find out, take a look in the mirror!

Active Reading As you read these two pages, underline the main idea.

Why do volcanoes erupt?

Ask a Question

You can ask questions too! Write a question of your own about the natural world that you could answer by doing a descriptive investigation.

_____

_____

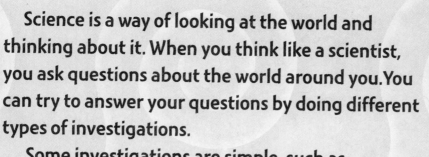

Science is a way of looking at the world and thinking about it. When you think like a scientist, you ask questions about the world around you. You can try to answer your questions by doing different types of investigations.

Some investigations are simple, such as watching animals play. Other investigations take planning. You need to gather and set up materials. Then you write down what happens.

You can think like a scientist on your own or in a group. Sharing what you learn is part of the fun. So get started!

Why does a compass point north?

What do stars look like through a telescope?

What Do You See?

So you want to think like a scientist? Let's get started. Try making some observations and inferences!

Active Reading As you read these two pages, find and underline the definition of *observe*.

Look at the pictures on this page. What do you see? When you use your senses to notice details, you **observe**.

Things you observe can start you thinking. Look at the picture of the small sailboat. You see that it has more than one sail. The sails are different shapes and sizes. Information that you collect when you observe is called *data*.

You might infer that the shape or size of the sails affects how the boat moves. When you **infer**, you offer an explanation of what you observed. You might infer that each sail helps the boat move in a different way.

Collect data about this boat by observing it.

_____

_____

_____

6

Collect data about this ship by observing it.

_____

_____

CONTAINER SHIP

Collect data about this boat.

_____

_____

623   U.S. COAST GUARD

Make an inference based on this observation: "I can see the wind blowing this sail."

_____

_____

Getting Answers!

People ask questions all day long. But not all questions are science questions. Science questions can be answered in many ways.

Active Reading As you read these two pages, underline the definition of *investigation*.

Exploring

Some science questions can be answered by exploring. Say you see a leaf float by on the water. You wonder what else can float on water. You find an eraser in your pocket. You **predict**, or use what you know to tell if it will sink or float. When you know which items float and which don't, you can **classify**, or group, them.

Predict

Think about each item pictured. Then circle the ones you predict will float. Mark an X on those you predict will sink.

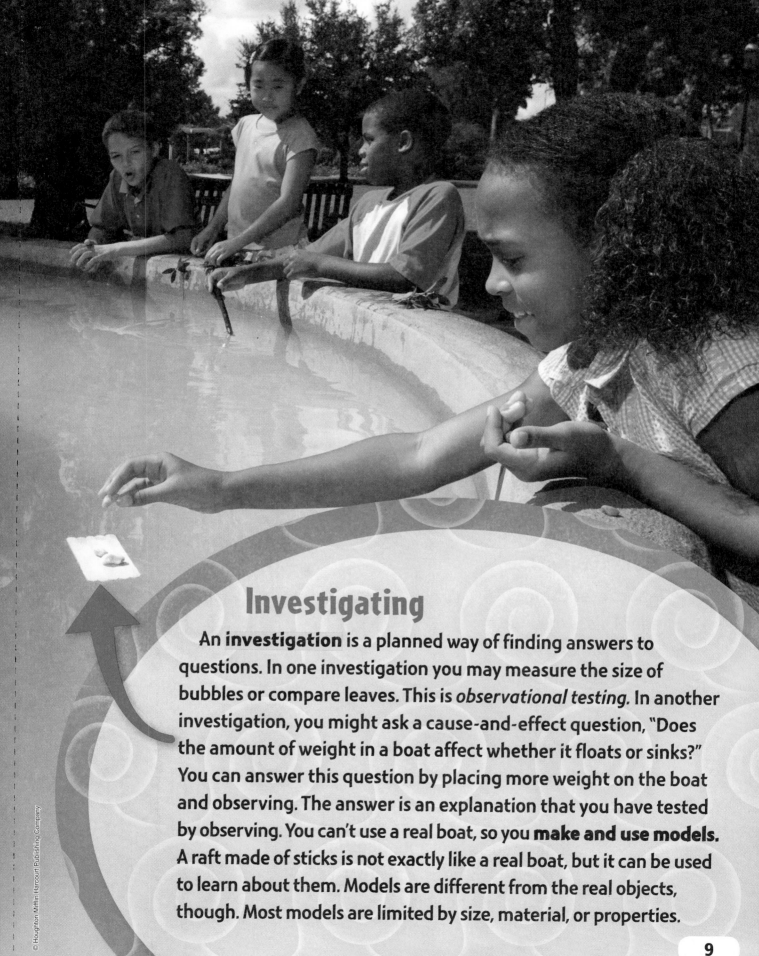

Investigating

An **investigation** is a planned way of finding answers to questions. In one investigation you may measure the size of bubbles or compare leaves. This is *observational testing*. In another investigation, you might ask a cause-and-effect question, "Does the amount of weight in a boat affect whether it floats or sinks?" You can answer this question by placing more weight on the boat and observing. The answer is an explanation that you have tested by observing. You can't use a real boat, so you **make and use models.** A raft made of sticks is not exactly like a real boat, but it can be used to learn about them. Models are different from the real objects, though. Most models are limited by size, material, or properties.

Experimental Testing

There are many steps a scientist may take during an investigation. Some do all five described here.

Active Reading As you read these two pages, number the sentences that describe Onisha's experiment to match the numbered steps in the circles.

1 **Ask a Question**
What causes things to change? This is the kind of question you can answer with an investigation.

2 **Hypothesize**
A **hypothesis** is a statement that could answer your question. A good hypothesis explains why. You must be able to test a hypothesis.

3 **Predict and Plan an Investigation**
Predict what you will observe if your hypothesis is correct. **Identify the variable** to test, and keep other variables the same.

10

What Onisha Did ...

Onisha thought about rafts floating down a river. She asked a question, "Does the size of a raft affect the amount of weight it can carry?"

Onisha **hypothesizes** that a bigger raft can carry more weight. Then she predicted, "I should be able to add more weight to a bigger raft than to a smaller raft." Onisha planned an investigation called an experiment. An **experiment** is a test done to gather empirical evidence. The evidence might support the hypothesis, or it might not. In her experiment, Onisha built three model rafts that differed only in their number of planks. She carefully put one penny at a time onto each raft until it sank. She repeated her experiment several times to be sure her results were accurate. She recorded her results and drew a conclusion.

Variable

The factor that is changed in an experiment is called a **variable**. It's important to change only one variable at a time.

Draw Conclusions

Analyze your results, and **draw a conclusion.** Ask yourself, "Do the results support my hypothesis? How well does my hypothesis explain the data?" Share your conclusion with others.

4 Experiment

Now do the experiment to test your hypothesis.

5

Beyond the Book

Use what you've learned in this lesson to plan and implement a descriptive investigation. Begin by asking a specific question about a problem in the natural world. Select and use the equipment or technology you will need. Make inferences as needed to arrive at an answer.

Sum It Up!

When you're done, use the answer key to check and revise your work.

Write words from the lesson that match the pictures.

1. _____

2. _____

3. _____

4. _____

The small plane will fly farther.

Use what you learned from the lesson to fill in the sequence below.

observe → 5. _____

6. _____ → 7. _____

12

Name _____

Word Play

1 Use the words in the box to complete the puzzle.

Across

1. You do this when you make a conclusion after observing.
5. the one factor you change in an experiment
6. to make a guess based on what you know or think
8. something that is like the real thing—but not exactly
9. a statement that will answer a question you want to investigate

Down

1. Scientists plan and carry one out to answer their questions.
2. Scientists ask these about the world around them.
3. You do this when you use your five senses.
4. an investigation in which you use variables
7. You draw this at the end of an investigation.

experiment*   infer*   **questions**   investigation*   variable*   hypothesis*

predict*   **model**   observe*   **conclusion**

*Key Lesson Vocabulary

Apply Concepts

2 This bridge is over the Mississippi River. Select materials you could use to make a model of it.

_____

_____

3 Greyson wants to know what plants need in order to survive. He places one plant in a window. He places another plant in a dark closet. What question is he trying to answer?

_____

4 Jared looks carefully at a young turtle in his hand. Label each of his statements _observation_ or _inference_.

Its front legs are longer than its back legs. _____

It has sharp toenails. _____

It uses its toenails to dig. _____

It can see me. _____

Its shell feels cool and dry against

my hand. _____

Take It Home!

Share what you have learned about observations and inferences with your family. With a family member, make observations and inferences about items in or near your home.

Inquiry Flipchart page 4

TEKS 3.2C construct maps, graphic organizers, simple tables, charts, and bar graphs using tools… to organize, examine, and evaluate measured data 3.4A collect, record, and analyze information using tools, including…metric rulers…meter sticks…timing devices, including clocks and stopwatches…

Name _____

Essential Question

How Can You Use a Model?

Set a Purpose

What is the question you will try to answer with this investigation?

_____

_____

_____

State Your Hypothesis

Write your hypothesis, or idea you will test.

_____

_____

_____

Think About the Procedure

What is the variable you plan to test?

_____

_____

How will you know whether the variable you changed worked?

_____

_____

Record Your Results

Construct a chart using tools to organize, examine, and evaluate your data. Include changes to your model, distance it flew and time in the air.

Draw Conclusions

Which changes to your model worked best?

_____

_____

_____

_____

Was your hypothesis supported by the results? How do you know?

_____

_____

_____

Analyze and Extend

1. How is your model the same as a real airplane?

_____

_____

_____

2. Analyze the data from the stopwatch and meterstick. What is the relationship between how long the plane stayed in the air and how far it flew?

_____

_____

_____

3. What did you learn about real airplanes from using a model?

_____

_____

_____

4. What were some of the limitations of your model airplane?

_____

_____

_____

5. What can't you learn about real airplanes by using a paper airplane?

_____

_____

_____

6. Think of another question you would like to answer about airplane models.

_____

_____

_____

TEKS **3.2B** collect data by observing and measuring using the metric system and recognize differences between observed and measured data **3.4A** collect, record, and analyze information using tools, including microscopes, cameras, computers, hand lenses, metric rulers, Celsius thermometers, wind vanes, rain gauges, pan balances, graduated cylinders, beakers…

Essential Question

How Do Scientists Use Tools?

🧠 Engage Your Brain!

A hand lens can make a bug look bigger.

What other tools make objects look bigger?

_____

_____

_____

Active Reading

Lesson Vocabulary
List the terms. As you learn about each one, make notes in the Interactive Glossary.

_____

_____

_____

Compare and Contrast
Ideas in parts of this lesson explain comparisons and contrasts—they tell how things are alike and different. Active readers focus on comparisons and contrasts when they ask questions such as, How are measuring tools alike and different?

Inquiry Flipchart p. 5 — I Can See Clearly Now/Talented Tools
pp. 6–9 — Science Tools Activities

Make It Clear!

Scientists use tools to give them super-vision! These tools help scientists observe objects and collect information about them.

Active Reading As you read these two pages, circle words or phrases that signal when things are alike and different.

> Light microscopes let you see tiny objects by using a light source and lenses or mirrors inside the microscope.

> A magnifying box has a lens in its lid.

> A hand lens has one lens with a handle.

> Use forceps to pick up tiny objects to view with magnifiers.

> Use a dropper to move small amounts of liquids for viewing.

Close, Closer, Closest!

Magnifying tools make objects look larger. Hold a hand lens close to one eye. Then move the hand lens closer to the object until it looks large and sharp. A magnifying box is like a hand lens in that it also has one lens. You can put things that are hard to hold, such as an insect, in it.

A **microscope** magnifies objects that are too tiny to be seen with the eye alone. Its power is much greater than that of a hand lens or magnifying box. Most microscopes have two or more lenses that work together. All of these tools help you observe to collect data. Observed data are collected using the five senses, but they are not measured data.

Pond water as seen with your eyes alone.

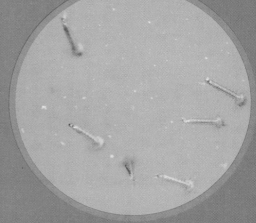

Pond water as seen through a hand lens.

▶ Draw a picture of how something you see might look if it was magnified.

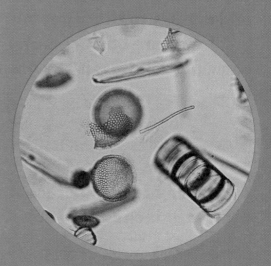

Pond water as seen through a microscope.

Measure It!

Measuring uses numbers to describe the world around you. Many kinds of data are measured.

Active Reading As you read the next page, circle the main idea.

A balance has a pan on either side. Put the object you want to measure on one pan and add masses to the other pan until they are balanced. The basic unit of mass is the gram.

The units on measuring tapes can be centimeters and meters or inches and feet.

ruler

Length, Mass, and Volume

A graduated cylinder has units of volume marked on its side.

Every tool has its purpose! You can **measure** length with rulers and tape measures. Mass is measured with a pan balance. The volume of a liquid can be measured with a **graduated cylinder** or a measuring cup or spoon. You can also use these tools to find the volume of solids that can be poured, such as sugar or salt.

Data that include units of measurement are measured data. Length, mass, and volume all have units of measurement, such as meters, grams, and liters. You **use numbers** to report measurements and **compare** objects. You can also **order** things using measurements. You can put pencils in order from shortest to longest.

Measuring cups and spoons also measure volume.

Do the Math!
Subtract Units

Use the frog above to measure its parts using a metric ruler.

1. How many centimeters is the frog's longest front leg?

_____

2. How many centimeters is the frog's longest back leg?

_____

3. Now find the difference.

_____

4. Compare your measurements to those of other students.

_____

_____

Time and Temperature

How long did that earthquake shake? Which freezes faster, hot water or cold water? Time and temperature are also measured data!

Time

When you count the steady drip of a leaky faucet, you are thinking about time. You can **use time and space relationships.** Clocks and stopwatches are tools that measure time. The base unit of time is the second. One minute is equal to 60 seconds. One hour is equal to 60 minutes.

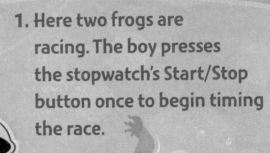

1. Here two frogs are racing. The boy presses the stopwatch's Start/Stop button once to begin timing the race.

START!

Temperature

When you say that ovens are hot or freezers are cold, you are thinking about **temperature**. A thermometer is the tool used to measure temperature. The base units of temperature are called degrees, but all degrees are not the same. Scientists usually measure temperature in degrees Celsius. Most people around the world use Celsius, too. In the United States, however, degrees Fahrenheit are used to report the weather, body temperature, and in cooking.

2. He presses the Start/Stop button again when a frog finishes. He can read the winning time in minutes and seconds.

▶ You can recognize the difference between observed and measured data. Think about the frog race. Give an example of each kind of data that could be gathered from the race.

_____

_____

_____

Sum It Up!

When you're done, use the answer key to check and revise your work.

The idea web below summarizes this lesson. Complete the web.

How Scientist Use Tools

1 They use hand lenses and microscopes to make things look

_____.

They use tools to measure.

2 Length is measured with

_____

_____.

3 A graduated cylinder measures

_____.

4 Pan balances measure

_____.

5 They measure time with clocks and

_____.

Answer Key: 1. bigger, 2. rulers and measuring tapes, 3. volume, 4. mass, 5. stopwatches

Name _____

Word Play

1 Write each term after its definition. Then find each term in the word search puzzle.

A. A tool used to measure mass _____

B. A temperature scale used by scientists _____

C. A tool used to pick up tiny objects _____

D. A tool used to measure volume _____

E. A tool you hold against your eye to make objects look bigger

_____

F. How hot or cold something is _____

G. A tool that measures temperature _____

H. Something you measure with a stopwatch _____

I. How much space something takes up _____

L	T	E	M	P	E	R	A	T	U	R	E	R	M	Y	O	L
U	H	R	P	A	M	I	L	C	E	L	S	I	U	S	V	W
K	E	E	A	V	S	U	N	B	O	W	L	M	A	X	Y	M
N	R	V	N	U	O	M	Z	O	O	L	I	S	S	T	F	O
G	M	C	B	E	U	L	I	H	T	M	A	Y	T	L	O	K
Y	O	Y	A	B	L	U	U	M	I	M	M	Y	O	R	R	J
F	M	S	L	K	K	Z	W	M	M	X	Q	I	P	Z	C	D
K	E	H	A	R	O	O	R	L	E	A	F	S	I	M	E	E
E	T	N	N	R	U	C	L	M	K	P	I	U	T	X	P	H
S	E	N	C	F	I	L	L	H	A	N	D	L	E	N	S	S
J	R	U	E	M	M	U	V	L	V	I	G	T	H	M	I	T
G	R	A	D	U	A	T	E	D	C	Y	L	I	N	D	E	R

Apply Concepts

In 2–5, tell which tool(s) you would use and how you would use them.

 thermometer

measuring spoons

 measuring tape

ruler

 magnifying box

2 Find out how long your dog is from nose to tail.

_____

_____

_____

3 Examine a ladybug and count its legs without hurting it.

_____

_____

_____

4 Make a bubble bath that has just the right amount of bubbles and is not too hot or too cold.

_____

_____

_____

_____

5 In the box above, circle the tool(s) for collecting and analyzing observed data. Place an X on the tool(s) for collecting and analyzing measured data.

Take It Home!

Share what you have learned about measuring with your family. With a family member, identify examples of objects you could measure in or near your home.

26

TEKS 3.2C construct maps, graphic organizers, simple tables, charts, and bar graphs using tools and current technology to organize, examine, and evaluate measured data

Name _____

Essential Question

How Can You Measure Length?

Set a Purpose
What will you be able to do at the end of this investigation?

_____

_____

_____

_____

Think About the Procedure
What will you think about when choosing the measurement tool for each item?

_____

_____

_____

How will you choose the units that are best for each item?

_____

_____

_____

Record Your Results
In the space below, construct a simple table using tools to organize your measured data.

Draw Conclusions

How does choosing the best tool make measuring length easier?

_____

_____

_____

_____

_____

How do units affect the quality of a measurement?

_____

_____

_____

_____

Evaluate the data on your map. Which classroom wall is the longest? Which two classroom objects are farthest apart?

_____

_____

_____

Analyze and Extend

1. Did groups who used the same tools as your group get the same results as you? Explain why or why not.

_____

_____

_____

2. Why was it important to communicate your results with other groups? Explain.

_____

_____

_____

3. Think of another question you would like to ask about making a map.

_____

_____

4. **REVIEW** How did the map help you examine data?

_____

_____

_____

_____

5. **REVIEW** Evaluate the data on your map. List two conclusions you can draw.

_____

_____

_____

_____

_____

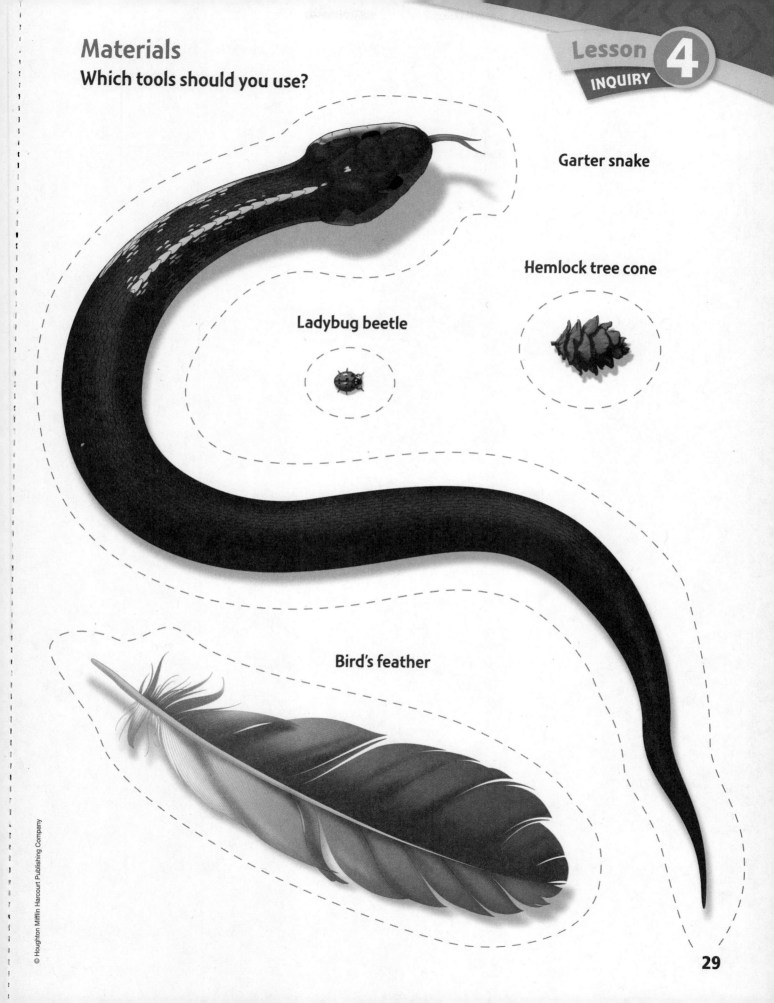

Garter snake

Hemlock tree cone

Ladybug beetle

Bird's feather

TEKS **3.2C** construct…bar graphs using tools…to organize, examine, and evaluate measured data **3.3A** in all fields of science, analyze, evaluate, and critique scientific explanations by using empirical evidence, logical reasoning, and experimental and observational testing, including examining all sides of scientific evidence of those scientific explanations…

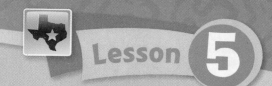

Essential Question

How Do Scientists Use Data?

Engage Your Brain!

People sometimes make statues out of blocks. If you could count how many blocks of each color there are, how would you record this information?

_____

_____

_____

Active Reading

Lesson Vocabulary

List each term. As you learn about each one, make notes in the Interactive Glossary.

_____ _____

_____ _____

_____ _____

_____

Main Ideas

The main idea of a section is the most important idea. The main idea may be stated in the first sentence, or it may be stated elsewhere. Active readers look for main ideas by asking themselves, What is this section mostly about?

Show Me the Evidence

Evidence helps us answer science questions.

Active Reading As you read these two pages, find and underline the definitions of *data* and *empirical evidence*.

My data are my *evidence*. The data show that a raft with six planks floats twice as much weight as a raft with three planks.

Onisha, how do you know that a bigger raft can float more weight than a smaller one?

— I put the pennies on the raft with three planks. It sank with fewer pennies than the other raft did.

Each measurement and science observation from experimental or observational testing is a piece of **data**. For example, the number of pennies on a raft is data. We use collected data as **empirical evidence**. This evidence is used to show whether a hypothesis is or is not supported. Scientists look for patterns in evidence to help explain the world around them.

It is important to review scientific explanations to see if they are correct. We can use *logical reasoning* when we review these explanations. Using logic means that you use the facts you know to decide if something makes sense. Personal opinions are not a part of using logical reasoning.

▶ Sam is testing the flavor of apples. He tastes a yellow and a red apple. Based on his results, he says that red apples taste better because they are red. Use logical reasoning to analyze his explanation.

_____

_____

_____

_____

_____

_____

_____

_____

Communicating Data

Scientists record and display data so others can understand the results. There are many ways to do this.

How can I communicate my results?

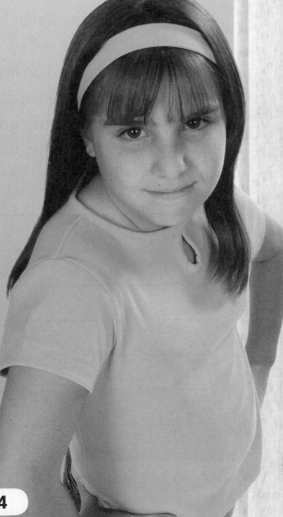

Models can help us understand things that are too big, small, or dangerous to do or observe.

▶ You want to find how high different kinds of balls bounce. You test each ball 20 times. How will you record and display your measurements?

_____

_____

After you **gather data**, you can share, or **communicate**, the results with others in different ways. How can you **record data**? To show how birds get seeds from a feeder, you can use a camera. If you observe how a dog cares for her puppies, write in a journal.

Sometimes scientists use charts and graphs to help **interpret** and **display data**. A **chart** is a display that organizes data into rows and columns. A **data table** is a kind of chart for recording numbers. A **bar graph** is used to compare data about different events or groups. Bar graphs make it easier to see patterns or relationships in data.

These students made a bar graph and a data table to compare results.

▶ You want to show kinds of weather in different places. How could you display this information?

_____

_____

Maps, like this world map, help to show the relationships between different objects or ideas. Maps also organize measured data, such as distance. You can examine the distance data on a map, then evaluate the data to find the shortest way. People make maps with simple tools such as a pencil, a ruler, and a compass or with technology such as computer programs.

How to Do It!

What are some ways to display data? You can use data tables, bar graphs, and line graphs. How can students display data they collected about plant growth?

Active Reading As you read these two pages, draw boxes around clue words that signal a sequence, or order.

DATA TABLE

Day	Plant Height (cm)
Mon.	5
Wed.	6
Fri.	9
Sun.	14

BAR GRAPH

Plant Growth

How do you create a graph? First, look at the data table. Each column has a heading telling what information is in that column. Now, look at the graphs. Did you notice that the same headings are used to name the parts of the graphs?

On the graphs, look at the line next to the heading "Plant Height (cm)." It looks like a number line, starting at zero and getting larger. It shows the height of the plants.

To complete the bar graph, find the name of a day along the bottom. Then, move your finger up until you reach the height of the plant for that day. Draw a bar to that point. To complete the line graph, draw points to show the height of the plant for each day. Then, connect the points.

LINE GRAPH

Plant Growth

Do the Math!

Construct Bar and Line Graphs

Use a tool, such as a pencil, to construct the rest of the bar graph and the line graph using the measured data in the data table. After you organize the data in the bar graph, examine and evaluate the data. What do the data tell you?

_____

_____

_____

_____

Critical Thinking

Scientists check scientific explanations in all fields of science. They do this by using critical thinking. You can also think critically.

As you read these two pages, underline the definitions of *analyze*, *evaluate*, and *critique*.

Before we can check an explanation, we have to know what critical thinking is. There are three main things people do when they use critical thinking. First, they *analyze*, or think about all the parts of, the explanation. Next, they *evaluate* the explanation. This means that they decide if the explanation is valuable. Finally, they *critique* the explanation. When a person critiques something, they judge it based on the available information and their beliefs.

Now let's check Onisha's explanation based on the evidence from her testing. Remember that Onisha said a larger boat will always be able to float more weight than a smaller one. Is this accurate?

Analyze, Evaluate, and Critique

Analyze, evaluate, and critique Onisha's explanation using logical reasoning and empirical evidence from her testing. Answer each question to help you decide if you agree with her explanation.

Start by thinking about the parts of Onisha's explanation:
Does her evidence support every part of her explanation?
Were the variables in her experiment controlled properly?

Decide if Onisha's explanation is valuable:
Is there any disagreement between her explanation and evidence?
Was her procedure the best way to test her hypothesis?

Judge the explanation:
Does it agree with other things you know to be true?
Does the explanation make sense for every boat?

▶ Based on your answers above, tell whether you agree with Onisha. Explain your answer.

_____

_____

_____

Beyond the Book

Think of ways you could use observational and experimental testing to find out which boats float more weight. Carry out your tests. Use the evidence you collect to analyze, evaluate, and critique Onisha's explanation.

Other Explanations

Thinking like a scientist takes practice! Read how these children are thinking critically.

Active Reading As you read this page, underline the empirical evidence used in the example.

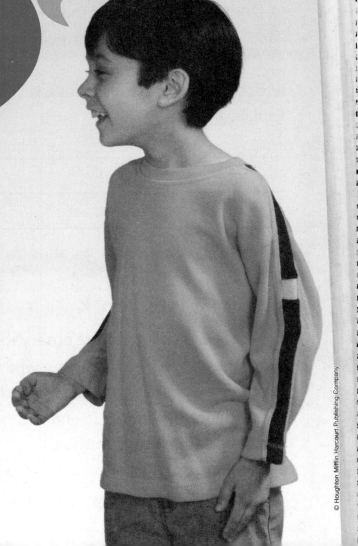

Why does your explanation say that violets grow best in full sunshine?

I planted one violet plant in the sunshine and one under a tree. Two weeks later, the one that got the most light was taller.

Mike asked Emily how she knew that violets grow better in the sun. She described her evidence. But sometimes other explanations are equally valid. Mike said the violet under the tree also got less rainfall, so it grew less than the other violet did. When you examine all sides of the scientific evidence, first you think of all the possible explanations. Then you analyze and evaluate those explanations. You decide which one makes the most scientific sense. Finally, you critique. To critique is to give feedback. A scientific critique uses evidence to tell the ways an explanation is good or bad.

Read the example. Examine all sides of the scientific evidence. Analyze and evaluate the explanation. Were the variables controlled? Is their any disagreement between their explanation and the evidence?

Carol and Maria designed an investigation about composting. They put food scraps into each of two bins. Bin *A* was placed in the sun. Bin *B* was placed in the shade. They waited a few weeks. They observed that the scraps in bin *A* decayed more than the scraps in bin *B*. They explained that scraps decay more quickly in sunlight. Think critically about their explanation. Do you agree? Explain.

_____

_____

_____

Critique the explanation. Does it make sense based on the evidence and what you know to be true?

_____

_____

_____

_____

Sum It Up!

When you're done, use the answer key to check and revise your work.

Use information in the summary to complete the graphic organizer.

During investigations scientists record their observations, or data. When other scientists ask, "How do you know?", they explain how their empirical evidence supports their answers. Observations can be shared in many ways. Data in the form of numbers can be shown in data tables and bar graphs. Data can also be shared as models, maps, or in writing.

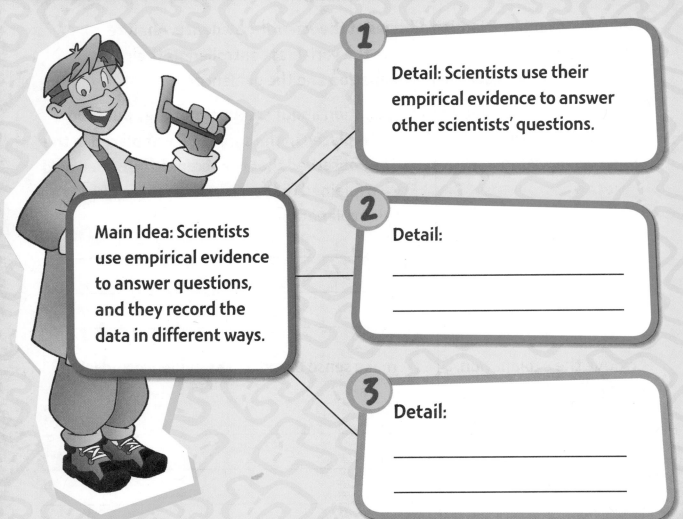

1

Detail: Scientists use their empirical evidence to answer other scientists' questions.

Main Idea: Scientists use empirical evidence to answer questions, and they record the data in different ways.

2

Detail:

_____

_____

3

Detail:

_____

_____

Answer Key: 2. Data can be shown in data tables and bar graphs. 3. Data can also be shared as models, maps, or in writing.

Name _____

Word Play

Find the correct meaning of each word and underline it.

1 Data
- tools used to measure
- steps in an investigation
- pieces of scientific information

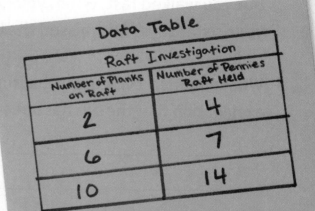

Data Table

Raft Investigation

Number of Planks on Raft	Number of Pennies Raft Held
2	4
6	7
10	14

2 Empirical evidence
- a kind of graph
- how much space something takes up
- the facts that show if a hypothesis is correct

3 Data table
- a chart for recording numbers
- the number of planks on a raft
- a piece of furniture used by scientists

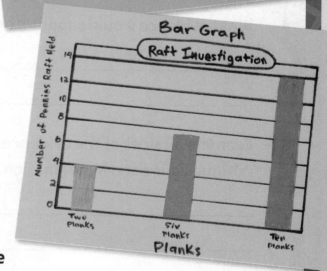

Bar Graph

Raft Investigation

4 Bar graph
- a chart for recording numbers
- a graph in the shape of a circle
- a graph that shows how things compare

5 Communicate
- take a photograph
- share data with others
- collect and record data

43

Apply Concepts

Read the paragraph and look at the picture. Then use logical reasoning to answer the questions.

One morning, your dad walks you and your sister to the school bus stop. You left a few minutes late, but you walked fast. When you get there, your sister says, "We missed the bus!"

6 What empirical evidence would support the explanation that the bus has not arrived yet?

_____

_____

_____

7 What evidence would support the explanation that the bus had already come?

_____

_____

8 Examine all sides of the evidence. Think about your answers to 6 and 7. Then, critique your sister's explanation.

_____

_____

_____

Take It Home!

Share with your family what you have learned about testing explanations. With a family member, identify an explanation to test. Then decide how to observe and record your data.

Lesson **6**

INQUIRY

TEKS **3.2C** construct maps, graphic organizers, simple tables, charts, and bar graphs using tools and current technology to organize, examine, and evaluate measured data

Name _____

Essential Question

How Do Your Results Compare?

Set a Purpose
What will you learn from this investigation?

_____

_____

State Your Hypothesis
Tell how you think the height of bubbles in water relates to the amount of dishwashing liquid used.

_____

_____

_____

Think About the Procedure
List the things you did that were the same each time.

_____

_____

_____

Describe the one variable you changed each time.

_____

_____

_____

Record Your Results
Construct a simple table using tools to organize, examine, and evaluate your measured data.

Draw Conclusions

Construct a bar graph using current technology to organize your data. Use the bar graph to examine and evaluate your data. How did the data change among containers *A, B,* and *C?* Which container had the highest bubble layer? The lowest?

_____

_____

_____

Based on the data you collected, did your results support your hypothesis? Explain your answer.

_____

_____

_____

Analyze and Extend

1. Why is it helpful to compare results with others?

_____

_____

_____

2. What would you do if you found out that your results were very different from those of others?

_____

_____

3. The bar graph below shows the height of the column of bubbles produced by equal amounts of three brands of dishwashing liquid. What do these data show?

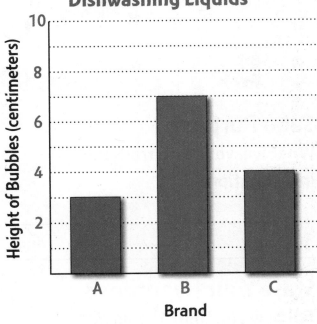

Bubbles Made by Dishwashing Liquids

_____

_____

_____

_____

_____

4. Think of other questions you would like to ask about bubbles.

_____

_____

_____

46

TEKS **3.3D** connect grade-level appropriate science concepts with the history of science, science careers, and contributions of scientists

Careers *in* Science

6 THINGS You Should Know About Meteorologists

1
A meteorologist is a person who studies weather.

2
Meteorologists use tools to measure temperature, wind speed, and air pressure.

3
Meteorologists use data they collect to forecast the weather.

4
Computers help meteorologists share weather data from around the world.

5
Keeping good records helps meteorologists see weather patterns.

6
Meteorologists' forecasts help people stay safe during bad weather.

Be a Meteorologist

Answer the questions below using the Weather Forecast bar graph.

1 What was the temperature on Thursday? _____

2 Which day was cloudy and rainy? _____

3 How much cooler was it on Tuesday than Thursday?
_____

4 Which day was partly cloudy? _____

5 Compare the temperatures on Tuesday and Friday. Which day had the higher temperature?
_____

6 In the forecast below, which day has the highest temperature _____? The lowest?
_____

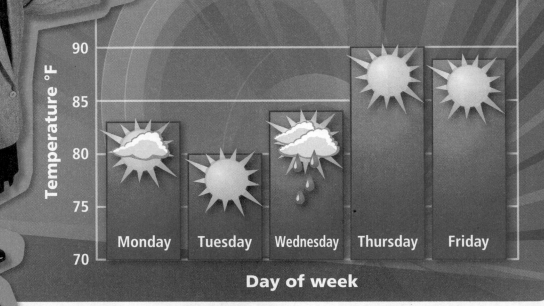

WEATHER FORECAST

Temperature °F

90
85
80
75
70

Monday Tuesday Wednesday Thursday Friday

Day of week

Name _____

Vocabulary Review

Use the terms in the box to complete the sentences.

> bar graph
> empirical evidence
> experiment
> hypothesis
> variable

TEKS 3.2C

1. You can share the results of an investigation with others by using a(n) _____.

TEKS 3.2A

2. An observation often leads to a testable statement known as a(n) _____.

TEKS 3.2A

3. A planned study meant to answer a question is called a(n) _____.

TEKS 3.2A

4. In an investigation, it is very important to test only one _____.

TEKS 3.3A

5. A hypothesis should be supported by _____.

Science Concepts

Fill in the letter of the choice that best answers the question.

TEKS 3.4A

6. Tami is using a compass to find direction.

   In which direction is the compass needle pointing?

   Ⓐ west

   Ⓑ northeast

   Ⓒ southeast

   Ⓓ south

TEKS 3.3A

7. Samuel's friend says that smaller dogs always have a higher-pitched bark. What is an observational test that Samuel could carry out in order to critique his friend's explanation?

(A) listen to barking from a wide variety of dogs

(B) listen to barking from several small dogs

(C) listen to barking from several large dogs

(D) listen to barking from a large and a small dog

TEKS 3.2B

8. Which of the following explains how observed data differs from measured data?

(A) You use models to observe data. You use bar graphs to measure data.

(B) You use your senses to observe data. You use tools to measure data.

(C) You use experiments to observe data. You use hypotheses to measure data.

(D) You use variables to observe data. You use empirical evidence to measure data.

TEKS 3.4A

9. A tool often used in science to collect and analyze information is shown below.

For which task would this tool most likely be used?

(A) observing bread mold closely

(B) observing the color of a leaf

(C) observing planets in the solar system

(D) observing the texture of a rock

TEKS 3.2A, 3.4A

10. Gabe is interested in snakes that live in the desert. He wants to know how fast the snakes move. Which of these could Gabe use to collect data in his investigation?

(A) balance

(B) graduated cylinder

(C) hand lens

(D) stopwatch

TEKS 3.3A

11. Alix did an experiment to test a scientific explanation about how fertilizer affects plants. Plant A had fertilizer. Plant B did not. All other conditions were kept the same. Plant A grew taller and was greener in color. Analyze and evaluate Alix's empirical evidence. What is the best explanation for what happened?

Ⓐ Fertilizer does not affect the growth of bean plants.

Ⓑ Fertilizer causes bean plants to grow more quickly.

Ⓒ Fertilizer causes bean plants to grow more slowly.

Ⓓ The same fertilizer would make all plants grow more quickly.

TEKS 3.4A

12. Ranjit wants to build shelves in a closet. The closet is 2 meters wide. The wooden boards he wants to use are more than 2 meters long. He will need to measure the boards, then use a saw to cut the correct length. What tool should Ranjit use to collect and analyze measurements to find the correct length of the boards?

Ⓐ a balance

Ⓑ a pedometer

Ⓒ a meterstick

Ⓓ a graduated cylinder

TEKS 3.2C

13. Martina is investigating how different types of soil affect radish seed germination. She plans to plant the same number of radish seeds in three different types of soil. At the end of a week, she will count the number of radish seeds that have emerged from the soil. What should Martina construct, using a computer, to organize, examine, and evaluate her data?

Ⓐ a map

Ⓑ a bar graph

Ⓒ a model

Ⓓ a thermometer

TEKS 3.4A

14. Zane is doing an experiment in which he measures the temperature of the water in three different tanks. Which of the following tools would he use to collect and analyze information?

Ⓐ a Celsius thermometer

Ⓑ a pan balance

Ⓒ a microscope

Ⓓ a stopwatch

Apply Inquiry and Review the Big Idea

Write the answers to these questions.

TEKS 3.3D

15. A meteorologist measured overnight temperatures in Dallas, Texas. The bar graph shows her data.

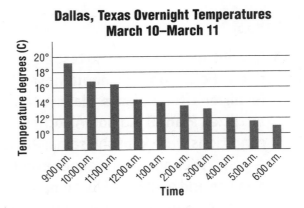

Dallas, Texas Overnight Temperatures March 10–March 11

What is the difference between the highest temperature and the lowest temperature?

_____

TEKS 3.2F, 3.4A

16. Luisa was studying whether certain tropical flowers would bloom even when temperatures dropped below 15 degrees Celsius. She placed the blooming plants outside. She measured the temperature outside each day for seven days. She observed that the plants bloomed each day of the week. The graph shows the data she collected.

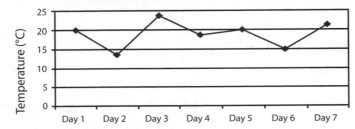

Communicate in writing one conclusion Luisa could draw based on the data in her graph.

_____

_____

TEKS 3.3A

17. Two teams measured the mass and the volume of the same rubber duck. One team found the mass to be 65 g and the volume to be 150 mL. The other team found that the mass was 63 g and the volume was 149 mL. Evaluate the results and use logical reasoning to explain these differences.

_____

_____

UNIT 2

The Engineering Process

Big Idea

Technology is all around us. The design process is used to develop new types of technology to meet people's needs.

TEKS 3.2A, 3.2F, 3.3B, 3.3D

I Wonder Why

This building was built in 1894. How has the building process changed since then? How has it stayed the same? *Turn the page to find out.*

Here's Why In 1894, tools were less complex than they are today. The tools were not electric. Today's builders still have to draw plans, choose materials, and make sure the building is safe to use.

In this unit, you will explore the Big Idea, the Essential Questions, and the Investigations on the Inquiry Flipchart.

Levels of Inquiry Key ■ DIRECTED ■ GUIDED ■ INDEPENDENT

Track Your Progress

Big Idea Technology is all around us. The design process is used to develop new types of technology to meet people's needs.

Essential Questions

Lesson 1 How Do Engineers Use the Design Process?.....55
Inquiry Flipchart p. 13—Chill Out/Science Solutions

Inquiry Lesson 2 How Can You Design a Tree House? 67
Inquiry Flipchart p. 14—How Can You Design a Tree House?

Lesson 3 How Are Technology and Society Related?....69
Inquiry Flipchart p. 15—Modes of Transportation/You Are the Target!

Inquiry Lesson 4 How Can We Improve a Design? 83
Inquiry Flipchart p. 16—How Can We Improve a Design?

Careers in Science: Civil Engineer 85

Unit 2 Review 87

Now I Get the Big Idea!

Science Notebook

Before you begin each lesson, be sure to write your thoughts about the Essential Question.

TEKS **3.2A** plan and implement descriptive investigations, including asking and answering questions, making fliferences, and selecting and using equipment or technology needed, to solve a problem in the natural world

Essential Question

How Do Engineers Use the Design Process?

Engage Your Brain!

Designs solve problems. What problem does the bridge solve?

_____

_____

Active Reading

Lesson Vocabulary

List the term. As you learn about it, make notes in the Interactive Glossary.

_____

Problem-Solution

Ideas in this lesson may be connected by a problem-solution relationship. Active readers mark a problem with a *P* to help them stay focused on the way information is organized. When solutions are described, active readers mark each solution with an *S*.

The Design Process

To get to school, you may have ridden your bike or taken the bus. These are two different ways of getting to school, but they have something in common.

Active Reading As you read this page, circle the five steps of the design process and number each step.

Both of the methods of transportation above were developed by someone who used the design process. The **design process** is the process engineers follow to solve problems. It is a multistep process that includes finding a problem, planning and building, testing and improving, redesigning, and communicating results.

The William H. Natcher Bridge makes crossing the Ohio River easy and fast!

ton Mifflin Harcourt Publishing Company   (bkgd) ©David Sailors/Corbis

An engineer used the design process to design the supports for this bridge.

The design process can help people solve problems or design creative solutions. Look at the picture of the Ohio River between Rockport, Indiana, and Owensboro, Kentucky. In the past, only one bridge connected these cities. Over time, the bridge got very crowded. In this lesson, you'll see how the design process was used to design a solution to this problem.

How Do Inventions Help You?

Think of an invention that has made your life easier. What problem from the natural word did it solve? How do you think the inventor used the design process to find the solution?

_____

_____

_____

_____

_____

Finding a Problem

The design process starts with finding a problem in the natural world. An engineer can't design a solution without first knowing what the problem is!

Active Reading As you read these two pages, put brackets [ ] around sentences that describe the problem, and write *P* in front of the brackets. Put brackets around sentences that describe the steps toward a solution, and write *S* in front of the brackets.

A team of scientists and engineers worked together. They saw there was a lot of traffic on the old bridge. People of both cities needed another way to cross the Ohio River. The team studied the best way to get the most people and cars across the river.

Engineers used tools to measure the width and depth of the river. They also may have measured how fast the river runs and how high the water rises. After the team measured, it kept good records of its work.

Selecting the right equipment or technology is important. This tool helps the surveyor measure exact distances and angles.

▶ What problem do you think the surveyor is trying to solve? How might the design process help him?

_____

_____

_____

_____

Planning and Building

The team decided the best solution would be to build another bridge across the Ohio River.

Active Reading As you read these two pages, underline the sentences that describe steps in the design process.

The next steps in the design process are to develop, test, and improve a prototype. The engineers gather data about important features of the bridge design, such as how stable it is and how much weight it can support. The team may modify minor aspects of the design based on this data.

If the data show that the prototype has significant flaws, the team must start over again. They redesign the bridge by making major changes to their initial plan.

Engineers carefully evaluated and tested the safety of the William H. Natcher Bridge. They made sure that builders followed the plans and used the correct materials.

The last step in the design process is to communicate the solution. Bridge inspectors used their findings, or evidence, to write reports. They used mathematical representations, such as graphs, tables, and drawings, to explain that the bridge was safe to open. Engineers could now use this information to make improvements and build bridges in other places!

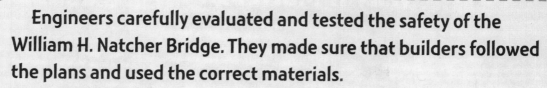

The prototype helped builders know how wide, tall, and long to make the bridge.

Communication Is Key!

List three other ways you might communicate the results of a project to others.

_____

_____

How Do Designs Get Better Over Time?

An engineer's work is never done! Every invention can be improved. For example, instead of building a fire in a wood stove or turning on a gas or electric oven, you can use a microwave to cook your food.

Just as with stoves, engineers have come up with newer and better designs for cell phones. Forty years ago, cell phones were bulky and heavy. Today, the smallest cell phone is not much bigger than a watch!

Martin Cooper invented the first cell phone in 1973. It was 13 inches long, weighed about 2 pounds, and allowed only 30 minutes of talk time.

▶ What might happen if cell phones get too small?

_____

_____

_____

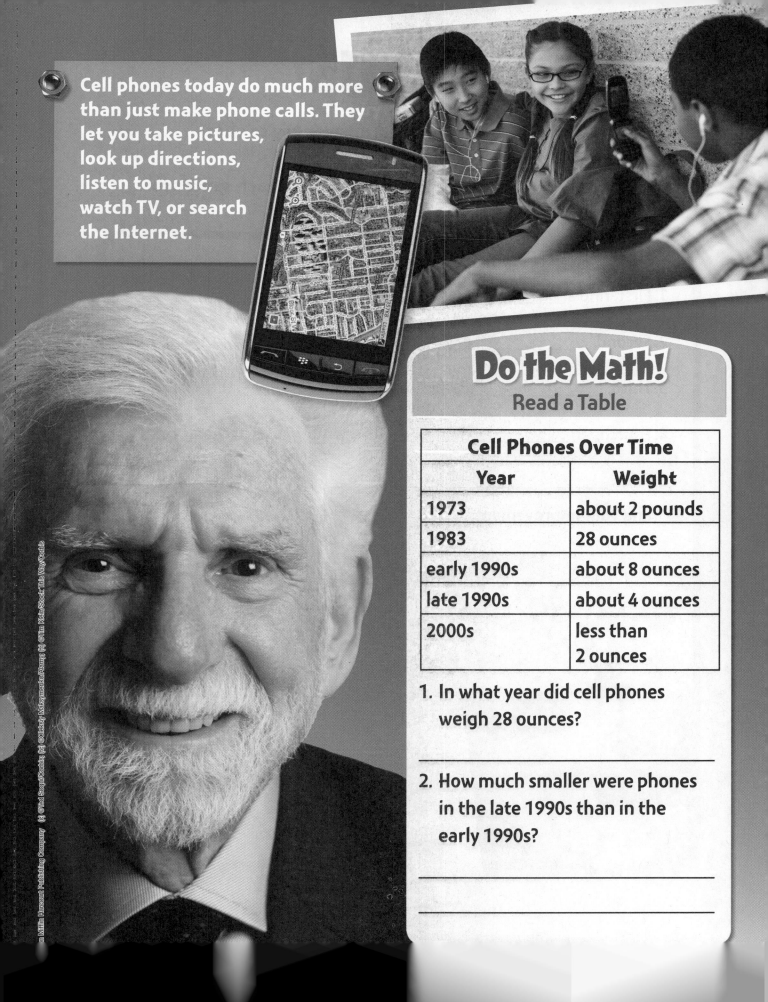

Cell phones today do much more than just make phone calls. They let you take pictures, look up directions, listen to music, watch TV, or search the Internet.

Do the Math!
Read a Table

Cell Phones Over Time	
Year	**Weight**
1973	about 2 pounds
1983	28 ounces
early 1990s	about 8 ounces
late 1990s	about 4 ounces
2000s	less than 2 ounces

1. In what year did cell phones weigh 28 ounces?

_____

2. How much smaller were phones in the late 1990s than in the early 1990s?

_____

_____

Sum It Up!

When you're done, use the answer key to check
and revise your work.

Complete the step of the design process in each sentence.

1

1. First, find a _____.

2. Second, _____ and _____ a prototype.

3. Third, _____ and _____ the prototype.

4. Fourth, _____ the prototype as necessary.

5. Fifth, _____ the solution, test data,

and your improvements.

Name _____

Word Play

1 Use these words to complete the puzzle.

Across

2. A plan for a solution that may use many drawings

6. A way of letting people know about a design

Down

1. Something that needs a solution

3. The steps engineers follow to solve problems

4. To judge how well a design works

5. The outcome of the design process

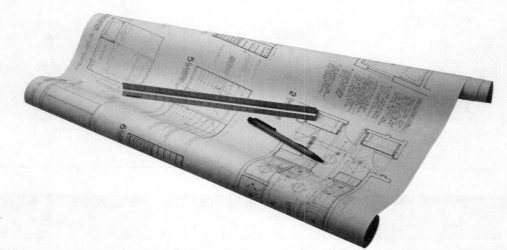

| problem | process | solution | design | evaluate | communicate |

Apply Concepts

2 Kyle's pet hamster is curious! It always finds a way out of its cage. Use the design process to help Kyle solve this problem.

_____

_____

_____

_____

_____

3 Label each of the following as a problem or a solution.

_____ _____ _____ _____

Take It Home!

Share what you have learned about the design process with your family. With a family member, identify products that are good examples of the design process. What problems do they solve?

TEKS **3.2A** plan and implement descriptive investigations, including asking and answering questions, making inferences, and selecting and using equipment or technology needed, to solve a specific problem in the natural world **3.2F** communicate valid conclusions supported by data in writing, by drawing pictures...

Name _____

Essential Question

How Can You Design a Tree House?

Set a Purpose
What will you do in this activity?

_____

_____

_____

_____

State Your Hypothesis
What parts of the design process will you use in this activity?

_____

_____

_____

_____

Think About the Procedure
Why is it important to have a plan before you start building the tree house?

_____

_____

_____

_____

_____

_____

_____

What problems do you identify? How might you solve these problems?

_____

_____

_____

_____

_____

_____

_____

Record Your Data

Draw a picture to communicate your final design.

[drawing box]

Draw Conclusions

Why do you think it is important to build a prototype for your plan before you start building the actual tree house?

_____

_____

_____

_____

Analyze and Extend

1. Suppose you were going to use the design process to build the tree house you've designed. What more would you need to do before you began building?

_____

_____

_____

_____

2. As you look at your prototype and think about it, is there any part you would want to redesign? Why?

_____

_____

_____

_____

_____

_____

_____

_____

3. What other things would you like to know about how the design process is used to plan projects like your tree house?

_____

_____

_____

_____

_____

_____

_____

TEKS **3.3B** draw inferences and evaluate accuracy of product claims found in advertisements and labels such as for toys and food

Essential Question

How Are Technology and Society Related?

Engage Your Brain!

Find the answer to the following question in this lesson and record it here.

Where is the technology in this picture?

_____

_____

_____

_____

_____

Active Reading

Lesson Vocabulary

Write the term. As you learn about it, make notes in the Interactive Glossary.

_____

Signal Words: Details

Signal words show connections between ideas. *For example* signals examples of an idea. *Also* signals added facts. Active readers remember what they read because they are alert to signal words that identify examples and facts about a topic.

Technology

What is technology? Look at this train station. Nearly everything you see is an example of technology.

Active Reading As you read these two pages, circle two clue words or phrases that signal a detail such as an example or an added fact.

Technology is anything that people make or do that changes the natural world. Technology meets people's wants or needs. Technology is not just computers and cell phones. Think about the things in a train station. They all have a purpose. The technology in a train station helps people travel easily. Can you imagine how different the world would be without technology?

Suitcase

A suitcase contains a traveler's needs. For example, it can carry clothing, shoes, pajamas, a hairbrush, a toothbrush, and toothpaste. All of these items are examples of technology.

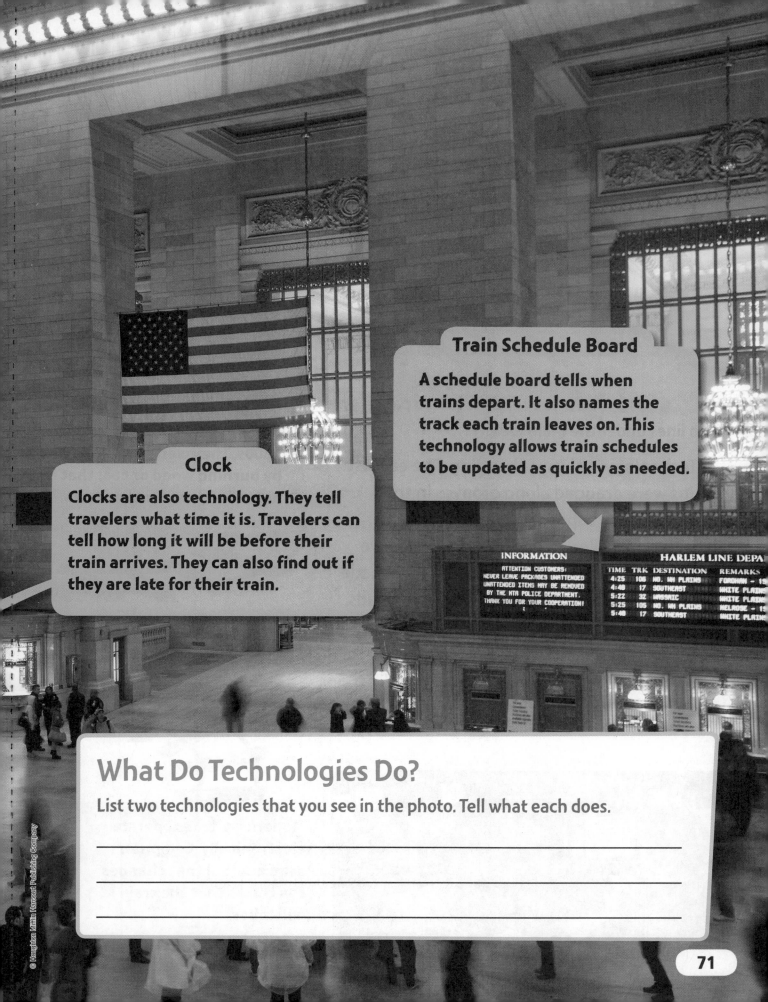

Train Schedule Board

A schedule board tells when trains depart. It also names the track each train leaves on. This technology allows train schedules to be updated as quickly as needed.

Clock

Clocks are also technology. They tell travelers what time it is. Travelers can tell how long it will be before their train arrives. They can also find out if they are late for their train.

INFORMATION

ATTENTION CUSTOMERS:
NEVER LEAVE PACKAGES UNATTENDED
UNATTENDED ITEMS MAY BE REMOVED
BY THE MTA POLICE DEPARTMENT.
THANK YOU FOR YOUR COOPERATION!

HARLEM LINE DEPA

TIME	TRK	DESTINATION	REMARKS
4:25	106	NO. WH PLAINS	FORDHAM - 19
4:40	17	SOUTHEAST	WHITE PLAIN
5:22	32	WASSAIC	WHITE PLAIN
5:25	105	NO. WH PLAINS	MELROSE - 1
5:40	17	SOUTHEAST	WHITE PLAIN

What Do Technologies Do?

List two technologies that you see in the photo. Tell what each does.

_____

_____

_____

Technology Through Time

A train today is different from a train from 100 years ago or even 50 years ago!

Active Reading As you read these two pages, draw two lines under the main idea.

Technology is always changing. The earliest trains were dragged along grooves in the ground. Today, super-fast trains can travel hundreds of miles an hour. Train tracks have changed over time, too. New technology made tracks of iron. These could carry heavier loads. Trains could be larger and also travel faster. These improvements made trains more useful to people. Improvements in technology make trains work better, faster, and more easily.

Steam locomotive 1800s

Steam locomotives were developed in the early 1800s. They were powered by burning wood or coal that heated water to make steam.

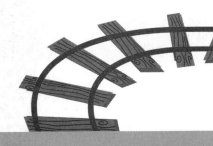

Modern switches operate electronically. Computers send a signal that changes the tracks that the train will follow.

The earliest track switches were moved by hand.

Diesel engine 1900s

By the mid-1900s, the diesel engine had replaced the steam locomotive. Diesel is a type of fuel.

Maglev train 2000s

The fastest trains don't run on tracks anymore. Maglev trains ride on powerful magnets.

Do the Math!
Interpret a Table

Look at the table. How much faster is the Maglev train than the steam locomotive at maximum speed?

Train Speeds	
Train	Maximum speed (mph)
Steam locomotive	126
Diesel engine	100
Bullet train	275
Maglev	361

_____

_____

_____

Technology and Society

Technology and society are connected. Technology affects how people live and what they do. People also affect technology by inventing new things.

Active Reading As you read these two pages, put brackets [ ] around the sentence that describes a problem and write *P* next to it. Underline the sentence that describes the solution and write *S* next to it.

Trains are an example of technology's connection to society. Trains carry people and cargo long distances. Resources, such as coal, can be carried long distances in a few days. Before trains, people in California may not have been able to get coal easily. People affect new train technology by finding ways for trains to cross high bridges or to tunnel through mountains. New technology helps trains meet people's needs and wants.

Some cities are far away from where coal is found and steel is produced. Train technology helps resources reach people in faraway cities.

Although trains through the Swiss Alps are safer than trucks on a road, only small trains can pass. The cars, roads, trains, and tracks are all transportation technologies that help people and goods move around the globe.

This new tunnel is beneath the Swiss Alps. The machine behind the workers is a technology that was used to help drill the tunnel. Large trains will be able to use the tunnel. Now people will be able to save more time traveling between cities.

Trains of the Future?

How would you change trains in the future? How would your changes affect society?

_____

_____

_____

_____

_____

Freight trains have refrigerator cars for keeping food fresh. This technology means that food can then be carried safely over long distances.

Advertisements and Labeling

Companies make products for people to buy. Sometimes, the products do not do what the seller says. Smart shoppers learn about products before they buy them.

Active Reading As you read these two pages, circle claims on the ads and labels that you can evaluate for accuracy.

An *advertisement*, or ad, is used to sell goods. An ad tells about the product. Sometimes, claims about the product are not *accurate*, or true. Always read the whole ad. You can *evaluate*, or judge, an advertisement by reading labels or using logical reasoning. A label may tell you a lot about the product. Logical reasoning can help you evaluate an ad. Does the claim made in the advertisement make sense? Is it something you can test?

Sensational new space-age ball is made from Astronaut-approved rubber! The Apollo Space Ball can bounce to the moon! Amaze your friends! Be the first to own the Apollo Space Ball!

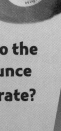

The ad says this ball can bounce to the moon. The label says "Highest Bounce Ever!" Are these statements accurate?

▶ You can make wise buying choices! Choose one product from these pages. Draw inferences and evaluate the accuracy of that product's claims in its advertisement and label.

_____
_____
_____
_____
_____
_____
_____
_____
_____
_____
_____
_____

Moms and Kids Agree!

Super Crunch Cereal is the best! Kids love its great taste. Moms love that it's low in sugar. Super Crunch Cereal provides your daily allowance of vitamins and minerals. *

*As part of a complete breakfast.

You can infer whether this cereal really is good for you by comparing the nutrition facts label to the ad.

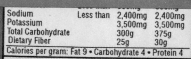

Sodium	Less than	2,400mg	2,400mg
Potassium		3,500mg	3,500mg
Total Carbohydrate		300g	375g
Dietary Fiber		25g	30g

Calories per gram: Fat 9 • Carbohydrate 4 • Protein 4

INGREDIENTS: MILLED CORN, SUGAR, HONEY, MALT FLAVORING, HIGH FRUCTOSE CORN SYRUP, SALT.
VITAMINS AND IRON: IRON, NIACINAMIDE, SODIUM ASCORBATE AND ASCORBIC ACID (VITAMIN C), PYRIDOXINE HYDROCHLORIDE (VITAMIN B6), RIBOFLAVIN (VITAMIN B2), THIAMIN HYDROCHLORIDE (VITAMIN B1), VITAMIN A PALMITATE, FOLIC ACID, VITAMIN B12 AND VITAMIN D. TO MAINTAIN QUALITY, BHT HAS BEEN ADDED TO THE PACKAGING.

CORN USED IN THIS PRODUCT CONTAINS TRACES OF SOYBEANS

Exchange: 1½ Carbohydrates
The dietary exchanges are based on the *Exchange Lists for Meal Planning*, ©2003 by the American Diabetes Association, Inc. and the American Dietetic Association.

Look at the ingredients in this cereal. Sugar, honey, and high fructose corn syrup are all types of sweeteners.

The label on the front of the box says this cereal is low in sugar. Is it?

How Does Technology Affect You?

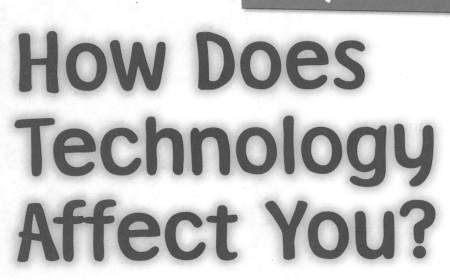

Technologies are always changing. Cars replaced horse-drawn carriages, and maybe someday flying cars will replace the cars we drive today!

Active Reading As you read this page, draw boxes around the names of the things that are being compared.

Think about the technology you use at school and at home. Have you noticed how they have changed? New televisions look different from older ones. Newer computers look much different, too. These newer technologies also do more than their older versions. Technology keeps improving with the goal of making life better.

Cell phone
Do you think when your grandparents were children they had the technology this boy has today?

Technology Changes

This camera uses film, which can store only about 20 images on a roll.

Digital cameras store hundreds of images. Images can be deleted for more space.

Cars in the 1960s used a lot of oil and gas and caused air pollution.

Hybrid cars use both electricity and gas to operate. They cause less air pollution.

Then and Now

Look at the technologies below. What can you do with these technologies today that people couldn't do 50 years ago?

Earlier telephones had rotary dials and were connected to the wall.

_____

_____

You could not easily edit your work on this typewriter.

_____

_____

Sum It Up!

When you're done, use the answer key to check and revise your work.

Complete the summary. Use the information to complete the graphic organizer.

Summarize

Technology is all around you. It can be very simple, like (1) _____.
At a train station, you may see a (2) _____ or a (3) _____.
If you live in a city, you may see (4) _____ and (5) _____.
Even in your classroom at school you have a (6) _____, and you may even have a (7) _____. You can draw inferences and evaluate the accuracy of product (8) _____ and (9) _____.

Main Idea: Technology can be as simple as a fence or as complex as a space station. Companies try to sell new products to people using ads.

(10) Detail:	(11) Detail:	(12) Detail:
Technology can be complex like a	Technology can be simple like a	Companies try to sell products.
_____	_____	_____
_____	_____	_____
_____	_____	_____

Name _____

Word Play

1 Write five words from the box that are examples of technology.

fence	giraffe	cell phone	toy
horse	car	leaf	stove

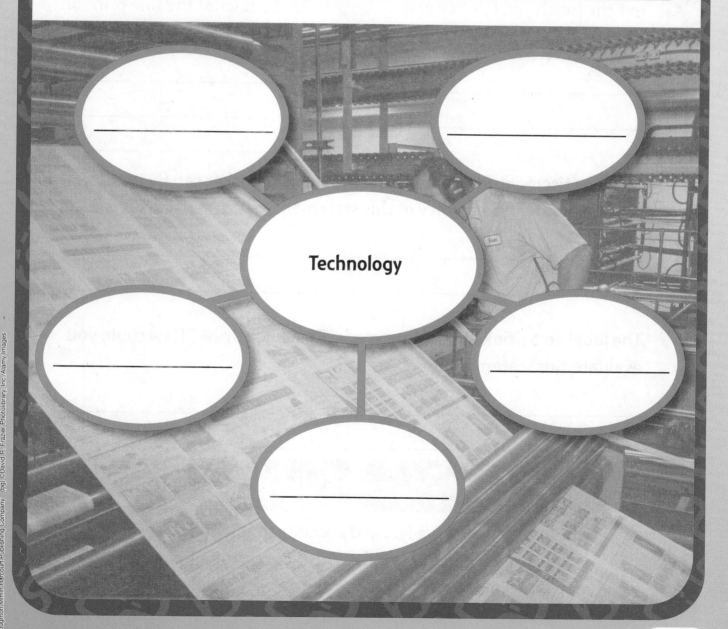

Technology

Apply Concepts

In 2–5, tell which technology you would use and how you would use it.

cell phone

magnifying glass

train

2 Get the lunch you left at home

_____

_____

_____

3 Find out what the fine print on an advertisement says

_____

_____

_____

4 An advertisement for a toy rocket says that the rocket can fly to the stars. Evaluate the accuracy of this statement.

_____

_____

5 The label on a drink at the store reads "Real Juice Drink." How could you evaluate this statement for accuracy?

_____

_____

Take It Home!

Share what you have learned about technology and advertising with your family. With a family member, evaluate and draw inferences about the accuracy of an ad or a label.

TEKS **3.2A** plan and implement descriptive investigations, including asking and answering questions, making inferences, and selecting and using equipment or technology needed, to solve a specific problem in the natural world **3.2F** communicate valid conclusions supported by data... through verbal discussion

Name _____

Essential Question

How Can We Improve a Design?

Set a Purpose
What will you discover in this activity?

_____

_____

Think About the Procedure
How could you and your partner redesign the bridge to make it stronger?

_____

_____

_____

_____

Do you and your partner have different ideas for changing the bridge? Explain.

_____

_____

_____

_____

Record Your Data

Sketch your plan for a new bridge design to solve the problems of the first bridge. Include the equipment you will use in your sketch. Tell how it differs from the first bridge.

Draw Conclusions

What were the best features of your design? What were the worst features? Explain.

_____

_____

_____

_____

_____

Analyze and Extend

1. Look at the bridges that other students made. What did all the new bridges that worked have in common?

_____

_____

_____

_____

2. What were the main reasons that the first bridge collapsed?

_____

_____

_____

_____

3. Communicate your valid conclusions about the features of your design by discussing them with other students. How could the conclusions of other students help you redesign your own bridge?

_____

_____

_____

_____

_____

_____

4. What other questions do you have about how things can be redesigned?

_____

_____

_____

_____

_____

TEKS **3.3D** connect grade-level appropriate science concepts with the history of science, science careers, and contributions of scientists

Careers in Science

1
Civil engineers plan the structures that are built in cities and towns. Roads and bridges are some of the things they plan.

DETOUR

2
The projects that civil engineers build need to be safe. They must hold up to daily use.

3
Civil engineers improve how we live. They help people get the things they need.

4
Civil engineers are important to a growing city or town. They look at the need for new structures.

8 Things
YOU SHOULD
KNOW ABOUT
Civil Engineers

5
Civil engineers keep cars and trucks moving. They fix roads that are no longer safe.

6
Civil engineers make drawings called construction plans.

7
Civil engineers use tools, such as compasses and rulers. Many engineers use computers.

8
Some civil engineers measure the surface of the land. They use this data to plan buildings.

Engineering Emergency!

Connect science concepts with science careers. Match the problems that can be solved by a civil engineer with its solution in the illustration. Write the number of the problem in the correct triangle on the picture.

1 We have an energy shortage! We can harness the river's energy to generate electricity.

2 The city is getting crowded! More people are moving here. They need more places to live and work.

3 The streets are always jammed. We have a transportation crisis!

4 The nearest bridge is too far away. We need a faster and easier way to get across the river.

Think About It!

If you were a civil engineer, what kind of changes would you make where you live?

_____

_____

Unit 2 Review

Vocabulary Review

Use the terms in the box to complete the sentences.

> design process
> technology

TEKS 3.2A

1. When Ms. Simm's third graders designed a tunnel, they

   followed steps in a _____.

TEKS 3.2A

2. A dishwasher is an example of something that makes a family's

   life easier and is a kind of _____.

Science Concepts

Fill in the letter of the choice that best answers the question.

TEKS 3.3B

3. You are in the grocery store buying whipped cream. Next to the whipped cream, you see a product called Liten Up! brand creme whip. The law says that Liten Up! cannot say "whipped cream" on the label. It has to be called "creme whip." What does that tell you about the product?

   Ⓐ It is not actually whipped.

   Ⓑ It does not actually contain cream.

   Ⓒ The government likes to misspell words on labels.

   Ⓓ The government thinks that "creme" sounds more appetizing.

TEKS 3.2A

4. Stewart will be working with a team to design an improved outdoor light.

   What should they do before beginning improvements?

   Ⓐ improve their new design

   Ⓑ keep the old design just as it is

   Ⓒ test their new design

   Ⓓ test the old design

TEKS 3.2A

5. What is the **main** goal of the design process?

   Ⓐ to find solutions to problems

   Ⓑ to give scientists something to do

   Ⓒ to make charts and graphs

   Ⓓ to write articles for magazines

TEKS 3.3B

6. *Silly School Bus* is the second book in the Wacky Wanda series. An ad says that half the people who read the first Wacky Wanda book also bought *Silly School Bus*. What can you infer from that statement?

Ⓐ *Silly School Bus* is an expensive book.

Ⓑ Everybody who read the first book liked it.

Ⓒ *Silly School Bus* is not as good as the first Wacky Wanda book.

Ⓓ Half the people who read the first book did not buy *Silly School Bus*.

TEKS 3.3B

7. The label on a box of toy jacks says, "People have been playing jacks for over a hundred years. The rules are simple and easy to learn. Everything you need is in this box. Everyone loves to play jacks!"

Which statement is probably not accurate?

Ⓐ Everyone loves to play jacks!

Ⓑ Everything you need is in this box.

Ⓒ The rules are simple and easy to learn.

Ⓓ People have been playing jacks for over a hundred years.

TEKS 3.2A

8. This is a technology that helped John's grandmother.

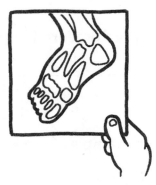

How did this technology most likely help John's grandmother?

Ⓐ It showed his grandmother that she was wearing the wrong size shoe.

Ⓑ It showed his grandmother what type of socks she should wear.

Ⓒ It showed that his grandmother's foot did not have bones.

Ⓓ It showed his grandmother's broken bones.

TEKS 3.2A

9. Scientists notice a problem with an engine. It is getting too hot after it runs for a long time. What should the scientists do next?

Ⓐ pour water on the engine

Ⓑ plan and build a new engine

Ⓒ test and improve the new engine design

Ⓓ communicate results of the new engine design

TEKS 3.2A

10. An engineer designs a new engine, but one of the parts keeps melting. The engine can get hotter than 240 °C. Look at the table.

Material	Melting Point (°C)
potassium	64
plastic	120
tin	232
aluminum	660

Which material would you suggest the engineer use in the next design?

Ⓐ aluminum

Ⓑ plastic

Ⓒ potassium

Ⓓ tin

TEKS 3.2A

11. Suppose you are digging a stone out of the ground with a shovel. You have a problem after you dig all the dirt around the stone. The stone is too heavy to lift. What is your best option in solving this problem?

Ⓐ continue to try lifting it yourself

Ⓑ start over and pick a smaller rock

Ⓒ use a bigger shovel

Ⓓ use a tractor to pull it out of the ground

TEKS 3.2A

12. Suppose you are in a tree house you built. You notice that one of the boards is broken and could cause an accident. How could you improve your design?

Ⓐ paint the board with a bright color

Ⓑ replace the board with stronger wood

Ⓒ replace the entire floor

Ⓓ tear down the tree house

TEKS 3.3B

13.

Moms! Wobbly-Os meet your child's daily needs of 12 important nutrients.

*As part of this complete breakfast.

Based on this ad, which is true about Wobbly-Os?

Ⓐ Wobbly-Os provide all the nutrients mentioned in the ad.

Ⓑ Wobbly-Os provide some of the nutrients while the toast, milk, and juice provide the rest.

Ⓒ The toast, milk, and juice provide all the nutrients mentioned in the ad.

Ⓓ Neither the Wobbly-Os nor the toast, milk, and juice provide any of the nutrients mentioned in the ad.

Apply Inquiry and Review the Big Idea

Write the answers to these questions.

TEKS 3.2A

14. You are working on an engineering team that will design a better type of car air conditioning. The first question the group addresses is: "What problem does car air conditioning solve?" What answer do you record in your notebook?

_____

TEKS 3.2A

15. You move to a new home with a doghouse in the backyard. Your small dog cannot get into the doghouse easily because it is raised up off the ground.

What is the problem? What can you do to solve this problem?

_____

_____

_____

TEKS 3.2A

16. Imar plans a descriptive investigation. He asks a question about which cars use the least amount of gas. He records the results of his investigation in a chart. The chart shows the number of miles per gallon of gas used by some models of cars. The models that use the least gas travel more miles per gallon. How many models use the least amount of gas?

Gas Mileage Per Gallon of Gasoline

Miles Per Gallon	Tally of Car Models
9–12	I
13–16	III
17–20	IIII
21–25	III
26–30	IIII II
31–34	IIII IIII
35–40	II

Each tally mark represents one car model.

_____

UNIT 3
Properties of Matter

Big Idea

Matter has properties that can be observed, described, and measured. Matter can change.

TEKS 3.2C, 3.2D, 3.3D, 3.4A, 3.5A, 3.5B, 3.5C, 3.5D, 3.7D

I Wonder Why

The colors of coral and fish can help us learn how to use properties of matter. Why is this so? *Turn the page to find out.*

Here's why Color is a physical property of matter. You can use color to sort coral and fish into groups.

In this unit, you will explore the Big Idea, the Essential Questions, and the Investigations on the Inquiry Flipchart.

Levels of Inquiry Key ■ DIRECTED ■ GUIDED ■ INDEPENDENT

Track Your Progress

Big Idea Matter has properties that can be observed, described, and measured. Matter can change.

Essential Questions

Lesson 1 **What Are Some Physical Properties?**........93
Inquiry Flipchart p. 17—Will It Float or Sink?/Sort Some Matter

Inquiry Lesson 2 **How Can We Measure Magnetism?** .107
Inquiry Flipchart p. 18—How Can We Measure Magnetism?

🔬 **Careers in Science:** Metallurgist 109

Inquiry Lesson 3 **What Physical Properties Can We Observe?**.......................111
Inquiry Flipchart p. 19—What Physical Properties Can We Observe?

Inquiry Lesson 4 **How Is Temperature Measured?**.....113
Inquiry Flipchart p. 20—How Is Temperature Measured?

Lesson 5 **What Are the States of Matter?** 115
Inquiry Flipchart p. 21—Temperature Takes a Dive!/The Shape of Different States

Lesson 6 **What Are Some Changes to Matter?**........127
Inquiry Flipchart p. 22—Break It Up!/Coming Apart

S.T.E.M. **Engineering & Technology:** Resources on the Road 141
Inquiry Flipchart p. 23—Design It: Float Your Boat

Unit 3 Review 143

Now I Get the Big Idea!

Science Notebook
Before you begin each lesson, be sure to write your thoughts about the Essential Question.

TEKS **3.4A** collect, record, and analyze information using tools, including microscopes, cameras, computers, hand lenses, metric rulers, Celsius thermometers, wind vanes, rain gauges, pan balances, graduated cylinders, beakers, spring scales... **3.5A** measure, test, and record physical properties of matter, including temperature, mass, magnetism, and the ability to sink or float

Lesson **1**

Essential Question

What Are Some Physical Properties?

Engage Your Brain!

Find the answer to the question in this lesson and record it here.

How can you compare these beach umbrellas?

_____

_____

_____

Active Reading

Lesson Vocabulary
List the terms, and make notes in the Interactive Glossary as you learn more.

_____

_____

_____

_____

Compare and Contrast
Many ideas in this lesson are connected because they explain comparisons and contrasts—how things are alike and different. Active readers stay focused on comparisons and contrasts when they ask themselves, How are things alike? How are they different?

It's Everything!

What is matter? Everything you see on this page is matter. All the "stuff" around you is matter.

Active Reading As you read the next page, draw a line under each main idea.

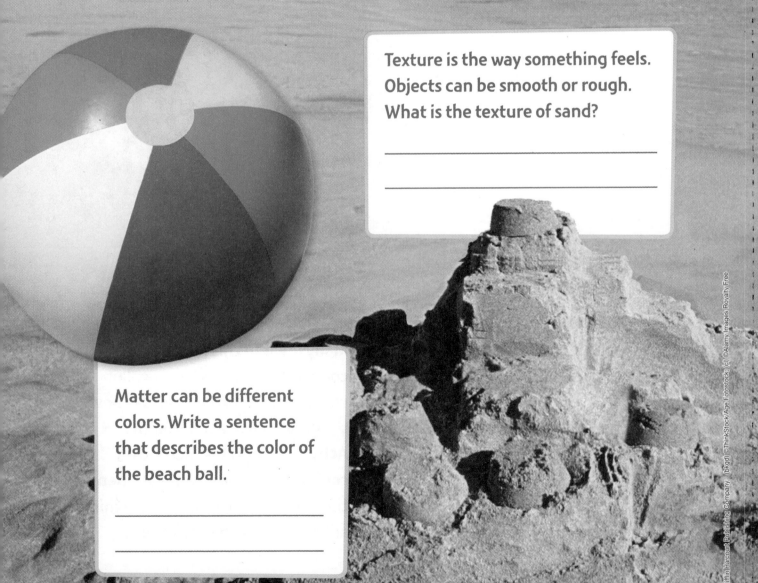

Texture is the way something feels. Objects can be smooth or rough. What is the texture of sand?

_____

_____

Matter can be different colors. Write a sentence that describes the color of the beach ball.

_____

_____

94

Matter is anything that takes up space. Your science book takes up more space than your pencil does. Did you know that no two things can take up the same space?

You describe matter by naming its physical properties. A **physical property** is a characteristic of matter that you can observe or measure directly. Look in the boxes to learn about some properties of matter.

Even we are made of matter!

Hardness describes how easily an object's shape can be changed. Name hard objects you see.

_____

_____

_____

_____

Size is how big something is. Which object is the biggest and takes up the most space?

_____

_____

Shape is the form an object has. What words can you use to describe the two smallest shells?

_____

_____

_____

How Much Mass?

Why is it so difficult to lift a bucket full of water? Would it be easier to carry the water in smaller containers instead?

As you read these two pages, find and underline the definition of *mass*. Then circle the name of the tool we use to measure mass.

Mass is the amount of matter an object has. Mass is also a measure of how hard it is to move an object. The more mass an object has, the harder it is to move the object.

How can you measure the mass of sand, water, or other materials in a bucket? Check out the next page.

Measure It!

We use a pan balance to measure mass. The pan balance measures mass in grams (g). How can you measure the mass of the contents of a bucket? To find the mass, you collect and analyze information from the pan balance.

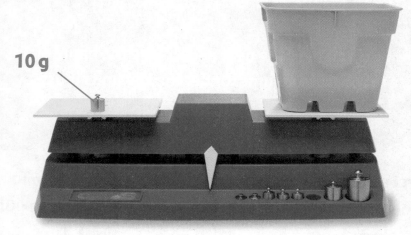

Find the mass of the container alone. _____

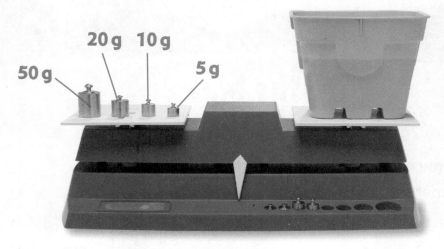

Find the mass of the container + contents. _____

Analyze the information by subtracting to find the mass of the contents.

Mass of the container + contents	-	Mass of the container	=	Mass of the contents
_____		_____		_____

What's the Volume?

Matter takes up space. How can you measure the amount of space an object takes up?

Active Reading As you read the next page, circle the name of a tool you can use to measure volume. Underline the units it uses.

An object's **volume** is the amount of space it takes up. To find the volume of a cube or a rectangular [rek•TAN•gyuh•luhr] solid, multiply its length by its width and its height. The length, width, and height of the small cube below are one centimeter.

Do the Math!
Find the Volume

This cube's volume is one cubic centimeter.

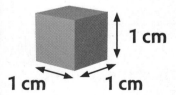

1 cm

1 cm   1 cm

Find the volume of this cube.

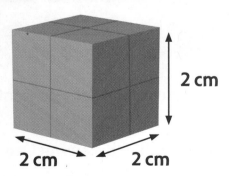

2 cm

2 cm   2 cm

_____ x _____ x _____ = _____ cubic centimeters

L   W   H

Use a graduated cylinder to measure the volume of a liquid. The units are in milliliters (mL). You can also use it to find the volume of a solid.

Measure It!

Collect information by reading the level of the water in the graduated cylinder. This is the volume of the water.

_____

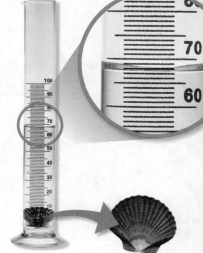

Add a shell and collect information again. What is the volume of the water + the shell?

_____

Now analyze the information. Subtract to find the volume of the shell. The volume of a solid is measured in cubic centimeters. 1 milliliter equals 1 cubic centimeter, so just change _milliliters_ to _cubic centimeters_.

volume of water + shell		volume of water		volume of shell
_____	-	_____	=	_____

Sink or Float

Some things have the ability to float on water. Other things sink. How can you test the ability of matter to sink or float?

Active Reading As you read these two pages, draw two lines under the main idea.

One physical property is the ability to sink or float. Some objects float on water, but others sink. You can test the ability of something to sink or float by placing it in water. Objects that float will stay at the water's surface. Objects that sink will go to the bottom of the water. Some objects that sink in water will float in other liquids. Also, objects float more easily in salt water than they do in freshwater. This boy is testing the ability of these items to sink or float in freshwater.

Record It!

Observe each object to test whether it sinks or floats in water. Record your answers on the lines.

Surfboard _____

Ducks _____

Anchor _____

Hot and Cold

Temperature is a property of matter. You can test the temperature of matter by touching it. How can you measure temperature?

Active Reading As you read this page, circle the names of the temperature scales that are being compared.

Temperature is a measure of how warm something is. You use a thermometer to measure temperature.

Thermometers use a scale of numbers to show temperature. There are two scales that are frequently used.

Most weather reports use the Fahrenheit [FAIR•uhn•hyt] scale. On this scale, water becomes ice at 32 degrees. Water boils at 212 degrees.

The other scale is the Celsius [SEL•see•uhs] scale. On this scale, water becomes ice at 0 degrees. Water boils at 100 degrees.

> What temperature does the thermometer show?
>
> _____
>
> _____

Measure It!

Measure the temperatures of the air and the water. Record your answers on the lines. Then color the thermometer to show the temperature of the sand.

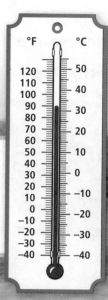

Air Temperature

_____ degrees Celsius

_____ degrees Fahrenheit

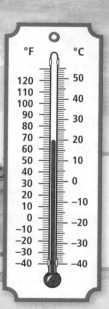

Analyze the data from the Celsius thermometers. Which is warmer—the air or the water?

Water Temperature

_____ degrees Celsius

_____ degrees Fahrenheit

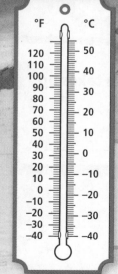

Sand Temperature

The sand's temperature is 37 degrees Celsius. Show that temperature on the thermometer.

Sum It Up!

When you're done, use the answer key to check and revise your work.

Write the vocabulary term that matches the picture and caption.

1

This crab takes up space and has mass.

_____

2

The blue color is a characteristic of the kite.

_____

3

This manatee has a large amount of matter.

_____

4

This umbrella takes up a lot of space.

_____

5

This thermometer tells how hot it is today.

_____

Answer Key: 1. matter 2. physical property 3. mass 4. volume 5. temperature

Name _____

Word Play

1 Write four words from the box to complete this word web about the physical properties of matter.

mass   sink   thermometer   float   milliliters   temperature

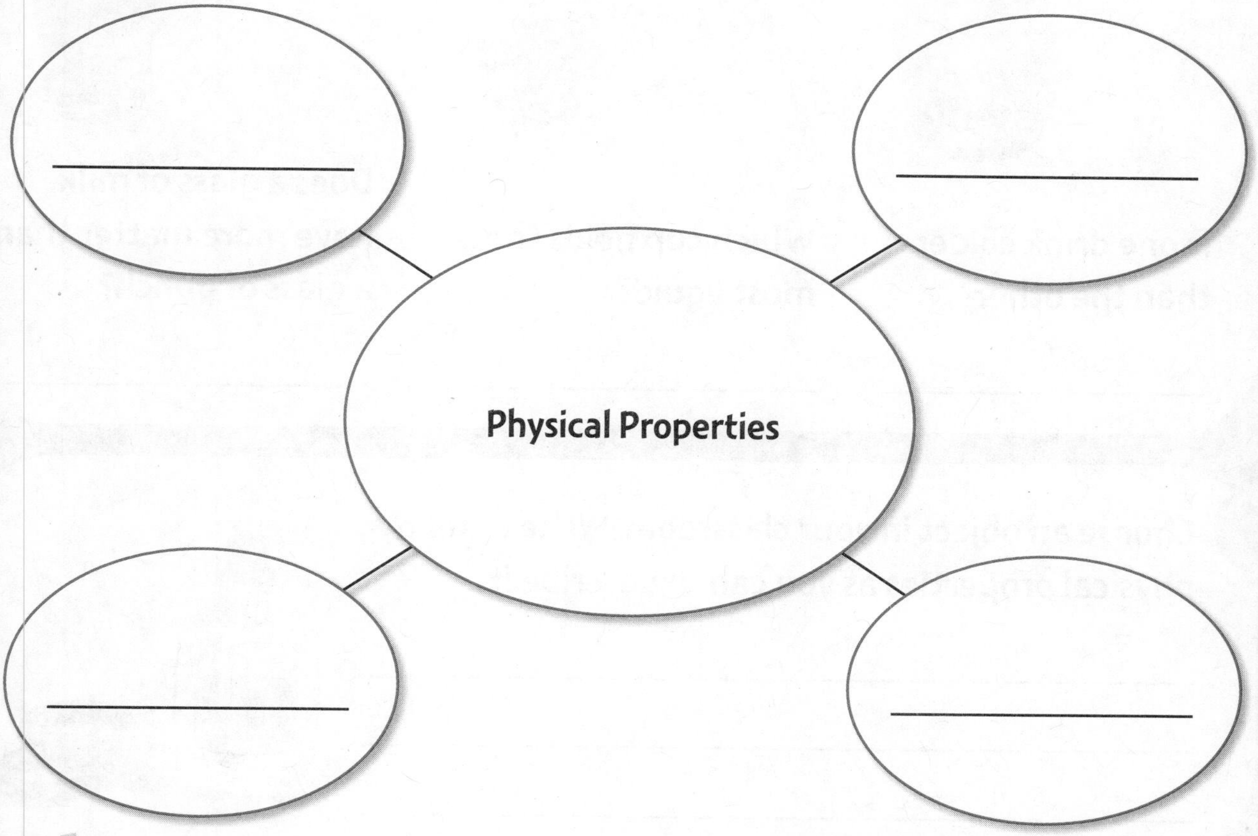

_____

_____

Physical Properties

_____

_____

Apply Concepts

In questions 2–4, write the name of the measurement tool you would use.

 2 **Degrees Celsius**

 3 **Milliliters**

4 **Grams**

Is one drink colder than the other?

_____

Which cup holds the most liquid?

_____

Does a glass of milk have more matter than a glass of punch?

_____

5 Choose an object in your classroom. Write as many physical properties as you can to describe it.

_____

_____

_____

Take It Home!

Share what you have learned about properties of matter with your family. With a family member, test, measure and record properties of matter in places in your home.

Inquiry Flipchart page 18

TEKS **3.2C** construct…graphic organizers, simple tables…using tools and current technology to organize, examine, and evaluate measured data **3.2D** analyze and interpret patterns in data to construct reasonable explanations… **3.4A** …analyze information using tools, including… magnets… **3.5A** measure, test, and record physical properties of matter, including…magnetism…

Name _____

Essential Question

How Can We Measure Magnetism?

Set a Purpose

What will you learn from this experiment?

_____

_____

Think About the Procedure

Which objects do you think are magnetic? Which magnet is the strongest? State your predictions.

_____

_____

_____

How will you test and measure magnetism in this activity?

_____

_____

_____

_____

Record Your Data

In the space below, use tools, such as a pencil, to construct a graphic organizer in which you organize, examine, and evaluate the results of the magnetism tests from Step 1.

Now construct a graphic organizer using technology, such as the classroom computer, to organize, examine, and evaluate your tested data for each object.

Draw Conclusions

Analyze and interpret the patterns in your data. Explain how the objects responded to the magnets. Construct a reasonable explanation based on the evidence.

_____

_____

_____

_____

Analyze and Extend

1. Which objects did you predict would be magnetic? What did you base that prediction on?

_____

_____

_____

2. Analyze the information collected with the magnet. Which objects were magnetic? Was your prediction correct?

_____

3. Which magnet did you predict would be strongest? What did you base that prediction on?

_____

_____

4. Analyze the information collected with the magnet. Which magnet was the strongest? Was your prediction correct?

_____

5. **REVIEW** How does a graphic organizer help you evaluate data?

_____

_____

6. **REVIEW** How did you use a magnet to collect and analyze information?

_____

_____

_____

7. **REVIEW** How do patterns in data help you explain cause and effect relationships involving magnets?

_____

_____

Careers in Science

Ask a Metallurgist

gold bars

aluminum foil

Now It's Your Turn!

What properties make steel a good material to use for building bridges?

_____

_____

_____

Q. What is a metallurgist?

A. A metallurgist is a scientist who works with metals. Iron, aluminum, gold, and copper are just some of these metals. They also combine different metals to make a new metal.

Q. Why do they combine different metals?

A. Metals may have different weights, strengths, and hardnesses. They combine metals to change their properties. The new metal may be stronger, harder, or a different color.

Q. How do they use the properties of metals in their work?

A. They look at the properties of metals and how metals can be used. Iron is strong. Mixed with other materials it becomes steel. Steel is a hard and strong metal. Copper can conduct electricity. It's a good metal to use for electrical wires.

copper pennies

This Leads to That

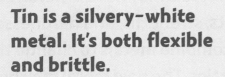

Copper is a soft, red metal. It can be shaped into things and over time turns green.

Tin is a silvery-white metal. It's both flexible and brittle.

Bronze is made by mixing tin and copper. The gold metal is hard and strong. Over time bronze turns green.

Compare the properties of copper and bronze. Then complete the table.

Properties of copper	Properties of both	Properties of bronze

Bronze is shaped to make sculptures and bells.

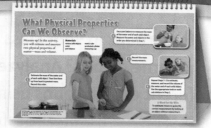

TEKS **3.4A** collect, record, and analyze information using tools, including microscopes, cameras, computers…pan balances, graduated cylinders, beakers, spring scales… **3.5A** measure, test, and record physical properties of matter, including temperature, mass, magnetism, and the ability to sink or float

Name _____

Essential Question

What Physical Properties Can We Observe?

Set a Purpose
What skills will you use in this activity?

_____

_____

Think About the Procedure
How can you test the mass of the objects and water to enable you to place them in the correct order?

_____

_____

_____

How can you test the volumes of the objects and water to enable you to place them in the correct order?

_____

_____

Record Your Data
List the objects and water in the order you placed them when you tested their mass and volume. Then record their actual measurements.

Mass	
Object	Measurement

Volume	
Object	Measurement

Draw Conclusions

When you used water to find the volume of one or more of the objects, why did the volume of the water have to be greater than the volume of the object?

_____

_____

_____

_____

Analyze and Extend

1. Were your estimates correct? Why?

_____

_____

_____

_____

2. Suppose you have two cubes. They are made of the same material, but one has a greater volume than the other. Does the larger cube have more mass? Explain your answer.

_____

_____

_____

_____

3. Did all the groups in your class have the same results? Analyze any different explanations using your experimental testing results.

_____

_____

_____

_____

_____

_____

4. **REVIEW** How did the pan balance and graduated cylinder help you collect information?

_____

_____

_____

5. **REVIEW** How did analyzing information from the pan balance and graduated cylinder help you to compare the objects?

_____

_____

_____

_____

Name _____

TEKS **3.2C** construct maps, graphic organizers, simple tables, charts... **3.4A** collect, record, and analyze information using tools, including...Celsius thermometers... **3.5A** measure, test, and record physical properties of matter, including temperature, mass, magnetism, and the ability to sink or float

Essential Question

How Is Temperature Measured?

Set a Purpose
What skills will you learn from this investigation?

_____

_____

_____

_____

Think About the Procedure
How can you find the temperature of a solid?

_____

_____

_____

_____

Record Your Data
Construct a simple table to organize and examine your temperature data.

Analyze the data from your recorded measurements to list the substances in order from coolest to warmest.

_____

_____

Draw Conclusions

Some of the objects you tested felt warm and some felt cool. How did this compare with the temperatures you measured?

_____

_____

_____

Analyze and Extend

1. How did the temperatures you measured compare with the temperatures measured by other students? Why?

_____

_____

_____

_____

_____

2. Why is it important to put the thermometer bulb all the way into the liquid or directly in contact with the solid you are measuring?

_____

_____

_____

3. Why do you think cooks use thermometers in the kitchen?

_____

_____

_____

_____

4. How could you find out if the air temperature given in your local weather report is correct?

_____

_____

_____

5. Think of other questions you would like to ask about measuring temperature.

_____

_____

_____

_____

6. **REVIEW** Suppose you repeat this investigation. How could you use a clock to collect and analyze information?

_____

_____

_____

_____

Essential Question

What Are the States of Matter?

Engage Your Brain!

Find the answer to the following question in this lesson and record it here.

How does heating this frozen treat affect it?

_____

_____

Active Reading

Lesson Vocabulary
List the terms, and make notes in the Interactive Glossary as you learn more.

_____

_____

_____

_____

_____

Signal Words: Cause and Effect
Signal words show connections between ideas. Words signaling a cause include *because* and *if*. Words signaling an effect include *so* and *thus*. Active readers remember what they read because they are alert to signal words that identify causes and effects.

What's the State?

What a party! You can eat a piece of solid cake, drink a cold liquid, or play with a gas-filled balloon.

Active Reading As you read these two pages, draw circles around the names of the three states of matter that are being compared.

There are three common states of matter. They are solid, liquid, and gas. Water can be found in all three states.

A **solid** is matter that takes up a definite amount of space. A solid also has a definite shape. Your science book is a solid. Ice is also a solid.

A **liquid** is matter that also takes up a definite amount of space, but it does not have a definite shape. Liquids take the shape of their containers. Drinking water is a liquid.

A **gas** is matter that does not take up a definite amount of space. Gases spread out to fill their containers. The air around you is a gas.

curtains _____

ribbon _____

ice cubes _____

orange drink _____

116

▶ Classify the matter in the picture as a solid, liquid, or gas by writing *S*, *L*, or *G* in each box.

air in balloon _____

bubbles _____

Describe Samples of Matter

Give one example of a solid, a liquid, and a gas.

solid _____.

liquid _____.

gas _____.

Cool! It's Freezing!

Water freezes at 0 °C.

When matter cools, it loses energy.
How does cooling affect water?

Active Reading As you read these two pages, draw circles around the clue words that signal a cause-and-effect relationship.

All the pictures show water at a temperature lower than 0 degrees Celsius (0 °C) or 32 degrees Fahrenheit (32 °F). How do we know this? If liquid water cools to that temperature, it freezes. Below that temperature, water exists as a solid—ice. Freezing is the change of state from a liquid to a solid.

How would this igloo be different if its temperature was 10 °C?

_____

_____

How can you tell that the temperature of the snow is below 0 °C?

_____

_____

Hail is water that falls to Earth as small balls of ice.

This snowball holds together because the water in it is frozen into a solid.

This girl can skate on ice because ice is a solid.

Do the Math!

Solve a Story Problem

The temperature of a puddle of water is 10 °C. The water cools by two degrees every hour. Predict how cooling will change the state of matter. How long will this take? Explain how you got your answer.

_____

_____

_____

_____

_____

Just Add Heat!

When matter is heated, it gains energy.
How can heating affect water?

Water is a liquid between the temperatures of 0 °C and 100 °C.

If the sun heats this ice sculpture enough, it will begin to melt.

What happens to an ice cube after you take it from the freezer? As it warms, it begins to melt. Melting is the change of state from a solid to a liquid. Ice melts at the same temperature that liquid water freezes—0 °C (32 °F). Melting is the opposite of freezing.

If you heat a pot of water on the stove, the temperature of the water increases until it reaches 100 °C (212 °F). At 100 °C, water boils, or changes rapidly to a gas called *water vapor*. You can't see water vapor. It's invisible.

Water boils at 100 °C.

Predict Changes in State

Place numbers beneath the images to order them from coldest to hottest.

garden hose

_____

ice cube

_____

boiling water

_____

Predict the changes to an ice cube as it is heated to 100 °C.

_____

_____

_____

_____

_____

_____

Now You See It...

Liquid water can change to a gas without boiling. Look at the drawings of a puddle. What changes do you see?

Water can evaporate at temperatures below 100 °C.

Active Reading As you read these two pages, draw a line under each main idea.

Liquid water does not have to boil to become a gas. When you sweat on a hot day, the water on your skin disappears. The liquid water turns into a gas. This is called **evaporation** [ee•vap•uh•RAY•shuhn]. Water can evaporate from other places, such as a puddle.

The sun's heat makes the water in the puddle change to water vapor, which goes into the air.

The puddle gets smaller as the water disappears. Most of the liquid water has changed to a gas.

A gas can change back to a liquid. This is called **condensation** [kahn•duhn•SAY•shuhn]. Water vapor condenses as it cools and loses energy. Water vapor in the air condenses on a cold car window. The outside of a cold soft drink can becomes wet on a hot day. The grass on a cool morning may have dew on it. These are all condensation.

▶ Observe this picture. Record what happened to the water vapor in the girl's breath as it cooled on the cold window?

_____

_____

_____

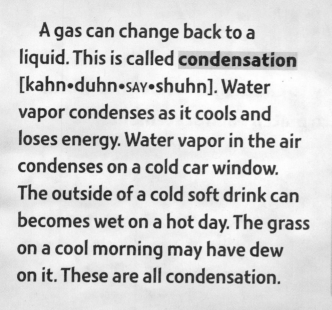

Sum It Up!

When you're done, use the answer key to check and revise your work.

Read the statements. Then draw a line to match each statement with the correct picture.

1 This state of matter does not have a definite size or shape.

2 This state of matter has a definite size and takes the shape of its container.

3 During this process, a liquid changes to a gas.

4 This state of matter has a definite size and shape.

5 During this process, a gas changes to a liquid.

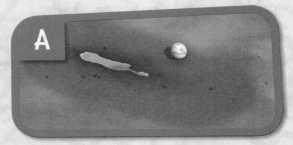

A

B

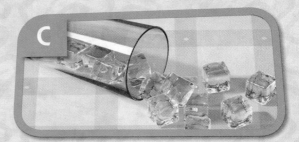

C

D

E

Answer Key: 1. E, 2. B, 3. A, 4. C, 5. D

Name _____

Word Play

1 Use the words in the box to complete the puzzle.

solid*   liquid*   gas*   evaporation*   condensation*

*Key Lesson Vocabulary

Across

2. Boiling changes liquid water to this state.

4. At 0 °C, ice can change to this state if heat is added.

5. The water in a puddle changes to a gas through this process.

Down

1. A gas changes to a liquid through this process.

3. Ice is water in this state.

Apply Concepts

2 Make a list of solids, liquids, and gases in your school.

_____

_____

_____

3 Think about what happens to a glass of cold water outside on a hot day. Use the words *evaporation* and *condensation* to describe what happens to the water inside the glass and what happens on the outside of the glass.

_____

_____

_____

_____

4 Which picture shows solid water? Which shows liquid water? Label the pictures. Circle the picture that shows water that has been cooled.

_____   _____

Take It Home! Share what you have learned about the states of matter with your family. With a family member, name states of matter that are present at mealtime or in places in your home.

Essential Question

What Are Some Changes to Matter?

Engage Your Brain!

Find the answer to the following question in this lesson and record it here.

How have these foods been changed to make a salad?

_____

_____

_____

Active Reading

Lesson Vocabulary

List the terms. As you learn about each one, make notes in the Interactive Glossary.

_____ _____

_____ _____

_____

Compare and Contrast

Many ideas in this lesson are connected because they explain comparisons and contrasts—how things are alike and different. Active readers stay focused on comparisons and contrasts when they ask themselves, How are these things alike? How are they different?

Physical Changes

A change to matter can be either physical or chemical. In physical changes, substances keep their identity. No new matter is formed.

Active Reading As you read these two pages, underline examples of physical changes.

A firefighter folds a piece of paper in half. She tears along the fold. Then she cuts out the shape of a truck.

Two physical properties have changed—size and shape. The cut-out truck is still paper. The scraps are still paper. In a **physical change**, the kind of matter stays the same. Folding, tearing, and cutting are all physical changes.

Many objects are made of one or more kinds of matter. A fire hose contains rubber and fabric. Cutting, bending, and shaping these materials to make the hose are all physical changes. The shapes and sizes of the materials have changed, but they are still the same materials.

Inside a fire hose

Make a Change!

Draw two pictures that show a hose before and after a physical change. Label your pictures to tell how the hose was changed.

The firefighter's sponge is torn. The big piece is a sponge. The little piece is also a sponge. The kind of matter stayed the same. A physical change took place.

MOUNT DORA

MOUNT DORA FIRE/RESCUE

Mixtures and Solutions

Yum! Cool lemonade is a tasty mixture that tastes good in a hot firehouse. Let's explore how a mixture is made!

Active Reading As you read these two pages, find an example of a solution. Circle the word that names the solution and the picture that shows it.

Fruit salad is a mixture. A **mixture** is two or more substances that are combined without changing any of them. Because no new matter is formed, making a mixture is a physical change.

A box of paints and markers is a mixture. So is a chest of toys. Can you name another mixture?

Many different kinds of fruit have been cut and put into the bowl. Each kind of fruit in this mixture has kept its identity.

A **solution** [suh•LOO•shuhn] is a mixture in which all the substances are evenly mixed. Salt water is a solution. So is tea. To make a solution, you completely mix, or **dissolve**, one substance in another.

All solutions are mixtures. Lemonade is a mixture of water, sugar, and lemon juice. It is also a solution because the sugar and lemon juice have dissolved in the water.

Each kind of matter in a solution keeps its identity. It may not seem that way because you cannot see all the different substances. All their tiniest parts are evenly mixed together.

Recognize the Mixture!

Circle each item below that is a mixture.

1. lemonade
2. sand and gravel
3. rice
4. fruit punch
5. metal and plastic paper clips
6. lemons
7. sugar
8. orange juice with pulp
9. paper

Properties Matter!

You can separate a mixture using its properties.

Active Reading As you read this page, draw two lines under the main idea.

Blueberries remain blueberries when you put them in a salad. Sugar is still sugar when you stir it into tea. Each kind of matter keeps its identity. Because making a mixture is a physical change, you can separate a mixture using the physical properties of its parts.

The firefighters' boat and the rescue ring float. Floating is a physical property. You can use it to separate some mixtures. Just add water, and scoop off the objects that float.

Matter that is smaller than the holes passes through the sieve [SIV]. Matter that is larger than the holes stays on top.

A magnet picks up matter that contains iron. This giant magnet separates iron from plastic and other materials in a junkyard.

As the sun heats this saltwater lake, the water evaporates. The salt is left behind. The salt and the water have been separated.

Take It Apart

How could you separate each of the mixtures below?

_____   _____   _____

_____   _____   _____

Chemical Changes

Can you unmix a fruit salad? Sure. Can you uncook an egg? No! How does an egg change when you cook it?

Active Reading As you read these two pages, draw boxes around the two kinds of changes that are being compared.

Uh oh. Someone forgot to clean up after a picnic. Fresh fruit and hardboiled eggs were left in the sun. The bananas have turned black. The strawberries are covered in white fuzz. The eggs are rotting—and they stink!

Chemical changes have taken place in the foods. How are chemical changes different from physical changes? In a **chemical change**, new kinds of matter are formed. Some chemical changes can be reversed using chemical means. But most of the chemical changes you see, such as the changes to food mentioned above, cannot be reversed.

A new mailbox is made from strong metal. Over time, metal can rust. It changes color and becomes weaker. These are signs of a chemical change.

Chemical changes happen all around you. They cause the green leaves on some trees to turn red, orange, and yellow. After the leaves fall, they begin to decompose, or break down, forming new kinds of matter.

Chemical changes happen in your body. After a scraped knee stops bleeding, a scab begins to form. The scab is a new kind of matter. Suppose you eat a pear. As your body digests the pear, chemical changes break it up into simpler substances that your body can use.

Wood burns. New kinds of matter—smoke, ash, and charcoal—are formed.

What's Cooking?

Your dad fries an egg. That's a chemical change. Name one more chemical change you could see at breakfast. How can you tell it's a chemical change?

_____

_____

_____

_____

This small fire burns off wood and leaves, which could fuel a big fire. The firefighter sprays water on the flames. He controls the burn to keep the fire from causing harm.

Making Bagels

Wow, take a look inside this kitchen! It's filled with changes in matter as bagels are made. Hands and kitchen tools cause physical changes. Yeast and heat cause chemical changes.

1 The bakers put yeast, sugar, and flour in warm water to make dough. This causes a chemical change. Then they shape the dough into rings. That's a physical change.

2 Plop! Heat from the boiling water causes the yeast to give off a gas. This makes the bagels puff up. The water changes the crust and makes it chewy!

3 What's your favorite kind of bagel? Adding a tasty topping like these sesame [SES•uh•mee] seeds is a physical change.

Do the Math!
Solve a Two-Step Problem

You can make 100 bagels with 10 pounds of flour. How many bagels can you make with 20 pounds of flour? Show your work.

_____

_____

_____

_____

4 Can you unbake a bagel and get back the original ingredients? No! Their identities have changed.

Sum It Up!

When you're done, use the answer key to check and revise your work.

Fill in the blank in each sentence. Then draw a line to the matching picture.

1 Tearing an object is a _____ change.

2 You cannot see the individual _____ in a solution.

3 The parts of a saltwater solution can be _____.

4 Foods undergo _____ changes as they cook.

5 When you make a salad, the physical _____ of the ingredients stay the same.

Answer Key: 1. physical; sponge **2.** substances; lemonade **3.** separated; lake **4.** chemical; bagels **5.** properties; salad

🧠 Brain Check

Name _____

Word Play

Underline the correct meaning or description of each term.

1 physical change
- a change in which the type of matter stays the same
- a change in which nothing is different
- a change in which a new kind of matter is formed

2 mixture
- substances are cooked
- substances keep their identities
- substances can't be separated

3 solution
- some parts float
- parts are evenly mixed
- parts are unevenly mixed

4 dissolve
- become unmixed
- become evenly mixed
- become unevenly mixed

5 chemical change
- matter is cut into smaller pieces
- matter is neatly folded
- new kinds of matter are formed

Apply Concepts

6 **Tell whether each picture below shows a physical change or a chemical change and explain how you know.**

_____   _____

_____   _____

_____   _____

_____   _____

_____   _____

7 **Look at the picture below. Is it a mixture? Explain how you know.**

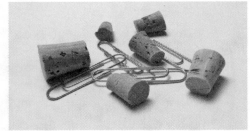

_____

_____

_____

_____

_____

Take It Home!

Share with your family what you have learned about changes in matter. With a family member, name changes in matter that you observe at mealtimes in your home.

TEKS **3.7D** explore the characteristics of natural resources that make them useful in products and materials such as clothing and furniture and how resources may be conserved

S.T.E.M.
Engineering & Technology

Resources on the Road

Machines are made using natural resources. The resources are selected based on their characteristics. Read about the natural resources used to make a car.

Glass is made from minerals. This glass is coated in plastic. It is hard to recycle.

Seats are cotton and plastic. Cotton comes from plants. Plastic is made from oil. Seats often end up in landfills.

Steel makes up the car's frame. Steel is a mixture of metals and can be recycled.

Tires are made from rubber and metal. Rubber comes from trees. Tires can be recycled.

Think about the characteristics of the natural resources used to make this car. Select one material and tell why it is useful for the product it makes.

_____

_____

_____

Change the Design

The supply of many natural resources is limited. Tell what natural resources make up the bicycle parts.

A bike helmet is a technology that uses cloth and plastic.

cotton and plastic

_____

_____

Pick one part of the bicycle. Tell how you could change the design to conserve these resources.

_____

_____

Build On It!

Rise to the engineering design challenge—complete **Design It: Float Your Boat** on the Inquiry Flipchart.

Unit 3 Review

Name _____

Vocabulary Review

Use the terms in the box to complete the sentences.

| gas |
| liquid |
| mass |
| mixture |
| temperature |
| physical properties |

TEKS 3.5D

1. If you combine flour and sugar in a bowl, you will form a _____.

TEKS 3.5A

2. You can use a pan balance to measure and test an object's _____.

TEKS 3.5B

3. A substance that has a definite volume but takes the shape of the container it is put in can be described as a _____.

TEKS 3.5A

4. Magnetism and the ability to sink or float are two of an object's _____.

TEKS 3.5C

5. A sample of water has a temperature of 80 °C. You can predict that if the sample is heated enough, it will turn into a _____.

TEKS 3.5A

6. The physical property that is measured with a thermometer is _____.

Science Concepts

Fill in the letter of the choice that best answers the question.

TEKS 3.5C

7. Kenny demonstrates that a substance changes shape and volume depending on the container it is put into. What do you predict will happen if the substance is then cooled?

(A) It will melt into a solid.

(B) It will melt into a liquid.

(C) It will condense into a solid.

(D) It will condense into a liquid.

TEKS 3.5A

8. Salih is placing various objects in a bin filled with water. Which physical property is he testing?

(A) mass

(B) hardness

(C) boiling point

(D) ability to float

TEKS 3.5C

9. Lysette demonstrates that a substance has a definite shape and volume. What do you predict she will do to change the state of that substance?

(A) place the substance in a freezer

(B) place the substance in a warm oven

(C) place the substance in a dark closet

(D) place the substance on a high shelf

TEKS 3.5A

10. You measure the mass of a pumpkin.

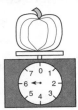

When you record your measurement, what do you write?

(A) 6 g   (C) 6 mL

(B) 6 kg   (D) 6 L

TEKS 3.5C

11. Observe the change of state in the picture below.

If you were to record the change of state shown here, what would you write?

(A) solid to gas

(B) liquid to gas

(C) solid to liquid

(D) liquid to solid

TEKS 3.5A

12. Stephanie observes the color of a liquid. Then she uses a Celsius thermometer to measure the temperature of the liquid. Finally, she uses a graduated cylinder to find the volume of a liquid. What type of properties did Stephanie observe?

Ⓐ physical properties

Ⓑ chemical properties

Ⓒ temporary properties

Ⓓ permanent properties

TEKS 3.4A, 3.5A

14. Darshana puts a toy car on a pan balance and balances it at 50 g. She places a toy dinosaur next to the car. She observes that the balance now levels at 63 g. What can Darshana conclude by analyzing the information?

Ⓐ The mass of the dinosaur is 13 g.

Ⓑ The mass of the dinosaur is 63 g.

Ⓒ The volume of the dinosaur is 13 g.

Ⓓ The volume of the dinosaur is 63 g.

TEKS 3.4A, 3.5A

13. Collect information from these graduated cylinders. Analyze the information.

dish soap

maple syrup

water

dish soap

Based on your analysis of the graduated cylinders, which of the following is true?

Ⓐ Maple syrup will float on water.

Ⓑ Water will float on maple syrup.

Ⓒ The mass of the water is greater than the mass of the dish soap.

Ⓓ The mass of the dish soap is greater than the mass of the maple syrup.

TEKS 3.5A

15. If you were to record the physical properties of the plastic paper clip, what could you write?

Ⓐ It is green.

Ⓑ It is round.

Ⓒ It has the ability to float.

Ⓓ It has a high melting point.

Apply Inquiry and Review the Big Idea

Write the answers to these questions.

TEKS 3.2C

16. Noemi collected the following data during an investigation:

Sample 1: 22 °C, Sample 2: 45 °C, Sample 3: 31 °C, Sample 4: 28 °C

a. First construct a simple table to organize Noemi's data. Then use the table to construct a bar graph to organize Noemi's data.

b. Examine the data on the table and on the bar graph. Which presentation makes the data easier for you to analyze? Why?

_____

_____

TEKS 3.5D

17. Paper clips, salt, and gravel are mixed in a pile. Josh wants to separate the parts of this mixture. What should he do to separate all three parts?

_____

_____

_____

TEKS 3.4A

18. There are four lab tables in the classroom, and each table has two beakers on it. Mr. Tomback pours 25 mL of liquid into each beaker. How much liquid does Mr. Tomback distribute?

_____

Energy

Big Idea

You use many different forms of energy every day. One form of energy can be changed to another.

TEKS 3.2C, 3.2F, 3.3D, 3.6A

I Wonder Why

Many people like to go to concerts. Why can everyone in this large audience hear the music? *Turn the page to find out.*

Here's Why The arena uses electrical energy to make the sound louder. The sound then travels through the air to all the members of the audience.

In the unit, you will explore the Big Idea, the Essential Questions, and the Investigations on the Inquiry Flipchart.

Levels of Inquiry Key ■ DIRECTED ■ GUIDED ■ INDEPENDENT

Track Your Progress

Big Idea You use many different forms of energy every day. One form of energy can be changed to another.

Essential Questions

Lesson 1 **What Are Some Forms of Energy?**............149
Inquiry Flipchart p. 24—Energy in Motion/Make It Move

People in Science: Ben Franklin........................159

Lesson 2 **What Is Sound?**........................161
Inquiry Flipchart p. 25—See Changes in Vibrations/Change the Sound

Inquiry Lesson 3 **How Are Sounds Changed?** 147
Inquiry Flipchart p. 26—How Are Sounds Changed?

S.T.E.M. Engineering & Technology: Call Me: Telephone Timeline 175
Inquiry Flipchart p. 27—Design It: Make a Musical Instrument

Lesson 4 **How Does Light Move?**.....................177
Inquiry Flipchart p. 28—Explore How Light Travels/Refraction

Lesson 5 **What Are Some Heat Sources?**...............189
Inquiry Flipchart p. 29—Heat Race/Where There's Light...

Inquiry Lesson 6 **Where Can Heat Come From?**..........201
Inquiry Flipchart p. 30—Where Can Heat Come From?

Unit 4 Review 149

Now I Get the Big Idea!

Science Notebook

Before you begin each lesson, be sure to write your thoughts about the Essential Question.

Essential Question

What Are Some Forms of Energy?

Engage Your Brain!

Find the answer to the following question in this lesson and record it here.

What makes this toy pop up?

_____

_____

_____

_____

_____

Active Reading

Lesson Vocabulary

List the terms. As you learn about each one, make notes in the Interactive Glossary.

_____ _____

_____ _____

_____

Main Idea

The main idea of a section is the most important idea. The main idea may be stated in the first sentence, or it may be stated elsewhere. Active readers look for main ideas by asking themselves, What is this section mostly about?

What's Energy?

"You have lots of energy!" People say that when you run around a lot. So what is energy?

Active Reading

As you read this page, draw circles around each paragraph's main idea.

Energy is the ability to make something move or change. If you want to put a book on a shelf, it takes energy to move it up there. What about melting snow? It takes energy to change snow to liquid water.

There are many forms of energy. **Potential energy** is stored energy. **Kinetic energy** is the energy of motion. An object can have potential energy, kinetic energy, or both. An object's **mechanical energy** [muh•KAN•ih•kuhl] is the total of its potential energy and kinetic energy.

150

Potential

The spring gained potential energy when it was pushed down. The ball gained potential energy when it was lifted up onto the table.

Kinetic

As the spring and the ball move, their potential energy changes to kinetic energy. The mechanical energy of each stays the same. It just changes form.

▶ Explore forms of mechanical energy by writing whether each thing has potential energy or kinetic energy.

potential

Where's the Energy?

Energy is all around us every day.
It has many different forms.

Active Reading As you read these two pages,
underline the names of forms of energy.

Explore Forms of Energy

How do you use energy in your home?
Write an example for each caption.

Sound Energy

Sound comes from the speakers as music.

_____

_____

Electrical Energy

Electrical energy, or electricity [ee•lek•TRIS•ih•tee], is
energy that moves through wires. It makes equipment work.

_____

_____

Heat Energy

Heat from the lights makes the musicians sweat.

_____

_____

Light Energy

Light from the spotlights helps the crowd see the band play.

_____

_____

Why It Matters

You use sound energy every day as you talk to your friends and classmates. But think of all the other ways sound energy helps you.

Use Energy

Sound from a whistle gets everyone's attention.

Sound doesn't cook food, but it lets you know when the food is ready.

154

Sound in the form of music can change your mood!

Do the Math!
Understand Data Tables

Source of Sound	Sound Level
Lawn Mower	90 dB
Mosquito	10 dB
Conversation	60 dB
Hair Dryer	90 dB
Ringing Phone	80 dB
Chainsaw	110 dB

Units called decibels (dB) are used to measure the loudness of sounds. Sounds louder than 85 dB can damage your ears.

1. Which two sources are the safest for your hearing?

_____

2. Which source makes sound that is 25 dB above the safe level?

_____

3. Which two sources give off the same amount of sound?

_____

4. Which source gives off 30 less decibels than the chainsaw?

_____

Sum It Up!

When you're done, use the answer key to check
and revise your work.

Use information in the summary to complete the graphic organizer.

Energy is the ability to move or change something. Potential energy is
stored energy. Kinetic energy is the energy of movement. An object
may have both kinetic and potential energy. The total of these is its
mechanical energy. Any form of energy can change into another form.

1 Main idea: Energy is _____

_____

2 Detail: Potential
energy is

_____

_____.

3 Detail:

_____

_____

is the energy of
movement.

4 Detail: The total of an

object's _____

and _____

_____ is

its _____

_____.

5 Pick two forms of energy. Then write
an example of one way you use each one.

_____

_____

6 _____

_____

Name _____

Word Play

1 Unscramble each word and write it in the boxes.

1. GEERNY
This lesson is about different forms of _____.

☐☐☐◯☐

2. LAPNETOTI
Stored energy

☐☐◯☐☐☐◯

3. LLEERCTIAC
A form of energy that moves through wires

☐◯☐◯☐☐◯☐◯

4. ITINECK
The energy of motion

☐◯☐◯☐◯☐

5. ATHE
A form of energy you can feel from the sun

◯☐◯☐

6. NUODS
A form of energy that might wake you up in the morning

☐☐☐◯☐

7. EVMO
Energy is the ability to make something do this.

◯☐☐☐

8. GNCAHE
Energy is also the ability to make something do this.

☐◯☐☐☐☐

Write the letters in the circles here.
Unscramble them to form two more words.

_ _ _ _ _ _ _ _ _ _ _ _ _ _ _

9. The energy that is a total of # 2 and #4

☐☐☐☐☐☐☐☐☐

10. A form of energy you can see that comes from the sun

☐☐☐☐☐

Apply Concepts

Write the form of energy each object takes in.

2

_____

3

_____

Write the form of energy each object produces.

4

_____

5

_____

_____

Take It Home!

With your family, go through your house and look for things that use or produce the following kinds of energy: light, sound, heat, and electrical. Identify two items for each kind of energy.

TEKS **3.3D** connect grade-level appropriate science concepts with the history of science, science careers, and contributions of scientists **3.6A** explore different forms of energy, including...

Learn About ...

Benjamin Franklin

Benjamin Franklin was born in January 1706. He moved from Boston to Philadelphia in 1723. Franklin worked as a printer and made newspapers. Later, he became a scientist and an inventor. He discovered that lightning is a form of electricity. In 1752, Franklin flew a kite in a rainstorm. A wire on the kite attracted electricity in the cloud. The electricity went down the string to a metal key. Scientists still study electricity today.

Fun Fact

Did you know that Franklin once used a kite to pull him while swimming?

Connect science to history! Use what you read about Benjamin Franklin to fill in each blank box in the timeline.

1750 Franklin invents the lightning rod to protect buildings from lightning.

1706 Franklin is born in Boston, Massachusetts.

Think About It!

How did Ben Franklin contribute to the scientific study of energy?

_____

_____

_____

_____

_____

Essential Question
What Is Sound?

Engage Your Brain!

Find the answer to the following question in this lesson and record it here.

Is a big drum louder than a small drum?

_____

_____

_____

Active Reading

Lesson Vocabulary

List the terms. As you learn about each, make notes in the Interactive Glossary.

_____

_____

_____

_____

Signal Words: Contrasts

Signal words show connections between ideas. Words that signal contrasts include *unlike, different from, but,* and *on the other hand.* Active readers remember what they read because they are alert to signal words that identify contrasts.

What Exactly Is Sound?

Sounds are all around us. Most of us hear sounds just about all the time. But how can you explain sound?

Active Reading As you read these two pages, draw a line under each main idea.

Let's start with a definition. **Energy** is the ability to make something move or change. An example of one form of energy is electricity. Think about ways electrical energy can make something move or change.

Sound is another form of energy. **Sound** is energy that travels in waves you can hear. In this lesson, you will learn about some properties of sound.

How can you tell that sound is energy? Maybe you've been in a thunderstorm that rattled the windows of your home. The thunder—sound energy—made the windows move.

Lightning is an example of electrical energy. It produces thunder, which is an example of sound energy. Lightning also produces heat and light— two more forms of energy.

Ordinary photographs are taken with light, which is a form of energy. But sound energy can be used to take pictures like this one of the inside of a cheetah.

This toothbrush produces sound energy—a song that lets you know how long to brush your teeth.

Energy Sources

FORMS OF ENERGY

Type of Energy	Example
Sound energy	_____
Electrical energy	_____

163

What Makes Sound?

Now you know what sound is. But how is it produced?

As you read these two pages, find and underline the definition of *vibrate*.

Sound is produced when something vibrates. **Vibrate** means "move quickly back and forth."

You can probably make your hand move quickly back and forth. Do you hear the sound it makes? Probably not. In order for something to make a sound that humans can hear, it has to move back and forth at least 20 times each second.

The jackhammer's motor vibrates, making noise. The tip of the jackhammer moves up and down very quickly. That makes more noise. Each time it moves down, it slams into the pavement, creating vibrations and much more noise.

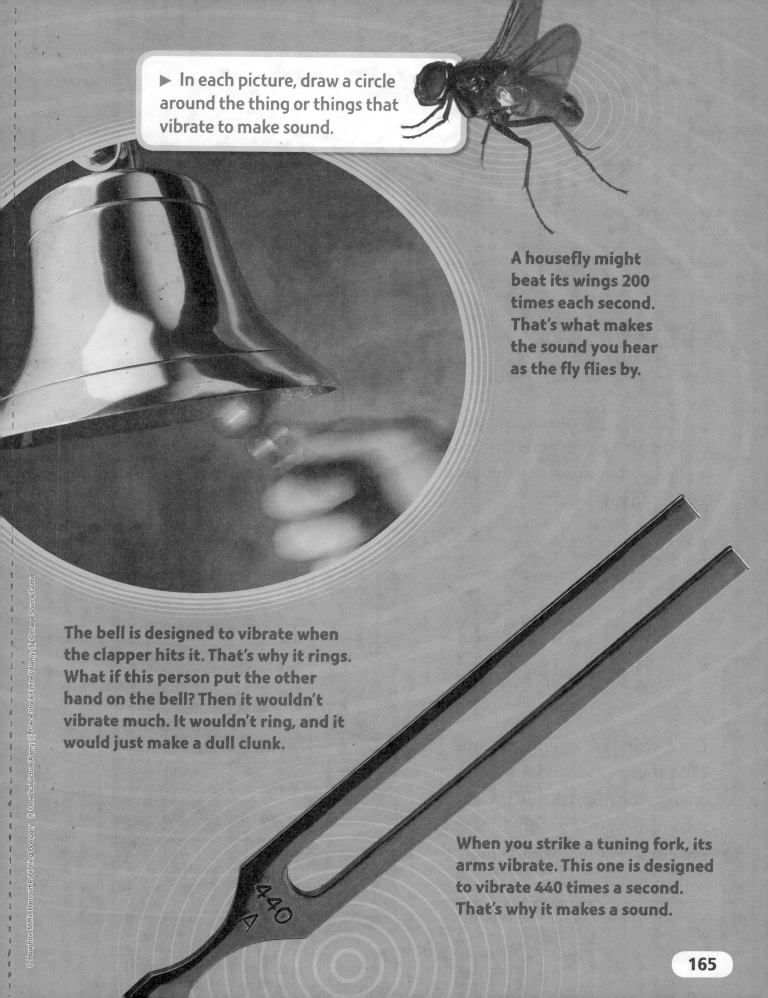

▶ In each picture, draw a circle around the thing or things that vibrate to make sound.

A housefly might beat its wings 200 times each second. That's what makes the sound you hear as the fly flies by.

The bell is designed to vibrate when the clapper hits it. That's why it rings. What if this person put the other hand on the bell? Then it wouldn't vibrate much. It wouldn't ring, and it would just make a dull clunk.

When you strike a tuning fork, its arms vibrate. This one is designed to vibrate 440 times a second. That's why it makes a sound.

Up and Down

The guitar can play high notes and low notes, loud notes and soft notes. What makes these sounds different?

Active Reading As you read these two pages, draw boxes around the two clue words or phrases that signal one thing is being contrasted with another.

Do the Math!
Subtract

The A string on a guitar vibrates 110 times per second. The G string on a guitar vibrates 196 times per second. How many more times per second does the G string vibrate?

_____

Pitch is how high or low a note or sound is. When something vibrates quickly, it makes a high-pitched sound. But when something vibrates slowly, it makes a low-pitched sound.

A housefly beats its wings 200 times each second. A mosquito beats its wings 1,000 times a second. Which one makes a higher-pitched sound when it flies?

loud noise

Volume is how loud or soft a sound is. This guitar string was plucked with a lot of force. It is producing a loud sound.

soft noise

This time, the guitar string was plucked with less force. It is moving back and forth over a smaller distance. It is producing a softer sound.

Making MUSIC Possible

What is the difference between music and sound? Music is a form of sound. But the musician controls the pitch, volume, and rhythm of the sound. If we couldn't change the pitch and volume of sound, there would be no music.

Only the part of the string below the musician's finger vibrates. The shorter the vibrating section is, the faster it vibrates. The faster it vibrates, the higher-pitched sound it makes.

The musician changes the volume by plucking the string harder or more softly.

The note is formed by air vibrating inside the tubes of the trombone. The movement of the slide controls the pitch of the note.

The musician changes volume by changing the force with which he blows into the mouthpiece.

Making Noise

Circle the parts of the instruments a musician uses to make sound.

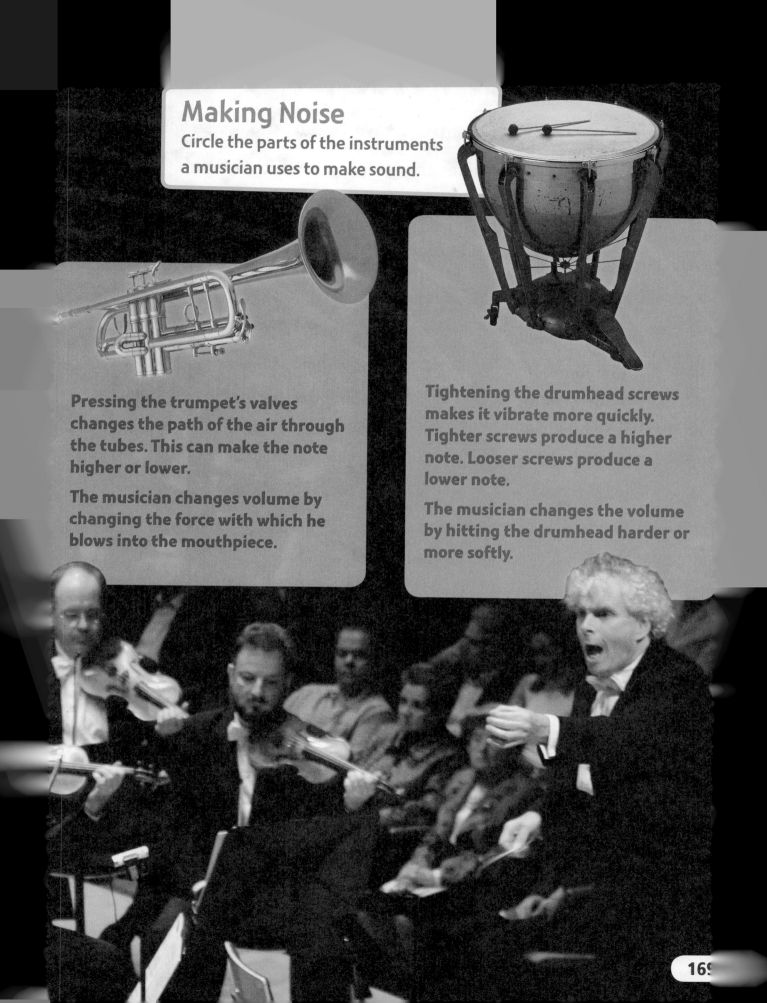

Pressing the trumpet's valves changes the path of the air through the tubes. This can make the note higher or lower.

The musician changes volume by changing the force with which he blows into the mouthpiece.

Tightening the drumhead screws makes it vibrate more quickly. Tighter screws produce a higher note. Looser screws produce a lower note.

The musician changes the volume by hitting the drumhead harder or more softly.

Sum It Up!

When you're done, use the answer key to check and revise your work.

The idea web below summarizes the lesson. Complete the web.

Energy

1 Other forms of energy include electricity, light, and _____.

2 Sound is a form of _____.

3 Sound is produced when something _____.

4 The pitch of the sound depends on the _____ of the vibration.

5 The _____ of the sound depends on the force of the vibration.

Answer Key: 1. heat; 2. energy; 3. vibrates; 4. speed; 5. volume

Name _____

Word Play

1 Use the clues below to help you write the correct word in each row. Some boxes have been filled in for you.

A. | | | I | | | | |

B. | | | I | | |

C. | | | I |

D. | | N | |

E. | | U | N | | S | S |

F. | | U | |

G. | | | |

H. | | |

A. Move quickly back and forth.

B. How high or low a note is.

C. Something vibrating quickly makes this kind of sound.

D. Sound is a form of this.

E. Another word for volume.

F. Something that vibrates produces this.

G. The force of a vibration affects this.

H. A guitar string vibrating slowly produces this kind of note.

Apply Concepts

2 Circle the one that produces the fastest vibrations. Draw a square around the one that produces the slowest vibrations.

a bumblebee

a sousaphone

a dog barking

a saxophone

a mosquito

an airplane flying high overhead

3 When a string vibrates slowly, does it have a lower or higher pitch? How about when a string vibrates quickly?

_____

_____

_____

4 How does a musician control sound to make music?

_____

_____

_____

Take It Home!

With your family, find three things in your home that make noise. Discuss the parts of each thing that vibrate to make the sound.

TEKS 3.6A explore different forms of energy, including mechanical, light, sound, and heat/thermal in everyday life

Name _____

Essential Question

How Are Sounds Changed?

Set a Purpose
What do you think you will learn from this experiment?

_____
_____
_____

State Your Hypothesis
Write your hypothesis, or testable statement.

_____
_____
_____

Think About the Procedure
Why would you press your finger against the rubber band?

_____
_____
_____

Why would you change the distance you pull the rubber band before you let it go?

_____
_____
_____
_____

Record Your Data
In the space below, make a table in which you record your observations.

Draw Conclusions

What can you conclude about how sound changes depending on how you pluck the rubber band?

_____

_____

_____

_____

Analyze and Extend

1. How did you make your observations? Explain.

_____

_____

_____

2. How did the numbers on the ruler help you make accurate comparisons?

_____

_____

_____

3. How does the sound change depending on how hard or soft you pluck the rubber band?

_____

_____

_____

_____

4. Think of other questions you would like to ask about how sounds are produced.

_____

_____

_____

_____

Call Me!

Telephone Timeline

Suppose you get some great news. You want to share it with your friend who lives many miles away. What can you do? You can send your friend a text or call him or her on the phone. Sharing news was not always this easy. Phones did not always exist. Use the timeline below to see how phones have changed over the years.

In the early 1900s, callers could dial the number they wanted or use an operator. The receiver was still connected to the phone base with a cord. Voices were clearer on these phones.

To use the first phones, callers needed an operator to connect them to the person they were calling. These phones were connected by wires. Voices were not always very clear.

Cordless phones were introduced in the 1980s. They had separate bases and could be used around the house. The receivers had buttons used for calling. Some phones had adjustable volumes to help make voices clearer.

Are the phones you use at home similar to those on this page? What are some of the differences between your phones at home and those on this page?

_____

_____

Predict an Upgrade

Today, phones can do many things. Draw in the box your idea for a phone of the future. Describe it on the lines provided. Be sure to list what new features your phone has and why.

_____

_____

_____

Build On It!

Rise to the engineering design challenge—Complete **Design It: Make a Musical Instrument** on the inquiry flipchart.

TEKS **3.2F** communicate valid conclusions supported by data in writing, by drawing pictures, and through verbal discussion **3.6A** explore different forms of energy, including mechanical, light, sound, and heat/thermal in everyday life

Essential Question

How Does Light Move?

Engage Your Brain!

Find the answer to the following question in this lesson and record it here.

What's wrong with the writing on the ambulance? It's backwards! Why?

_____

_____

_____

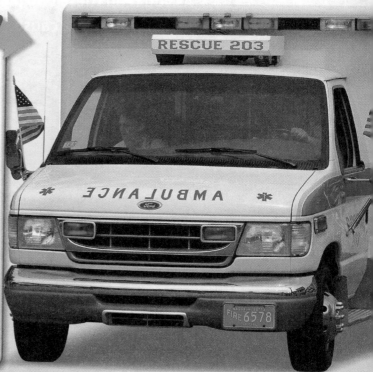

Active Reading

Lesson Vocabulary

List the terms. As you learn about each, make notes in the Interactive Glossary.

_____

_____

_____

Cause and Effect

Signal words show connections between ideas. Words signaling a cause include *because* and *if.* Words signaling an effect include *so* and *thus.* Active readers remember what they read because they are alert to signal words that identify causes and effects.

A Lighted Path

Light is all around us. Light's movement allows us to see. Let's explore how!

Active Reading As you read these two pages, draw a circle around the clue word that signals a cause.

Light moves in straight lines. In the picture at the top of this page, the flashlight beam is a straight line. The beam does not bend or curve. Look at the picture below. The top of the light beam is a straight line, and the bottom of the light beam is a straight line. The whole light beam is straight.

The light is below the boy's face. The shadow of his nose is above his nose.

What happens when light hits an object? It cannot keep going straight.

Objects can absorb light. **Absorb** means "to take in." The marshmallow and the stick block light. They either absorb or bounce back all of the light that hits them. No light goes through.

The marshmallow and stick have a shadow. A **shadow** is the dark area behind an object that has blocked light. The shadow has a shape that is similar to the object. That's because light travels in straight lines.

The light in the tent is blocked by the childrens' bodies. They absorb most of the light that hits them. You can see their shadows on the side of the tent.

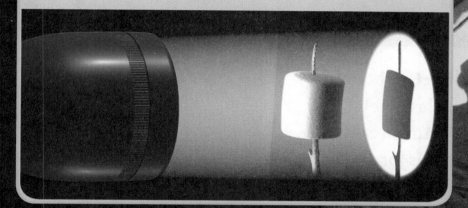

▶ One of these lights is on. It is making a shadow behind the block. Draw a circle around the light that is on.

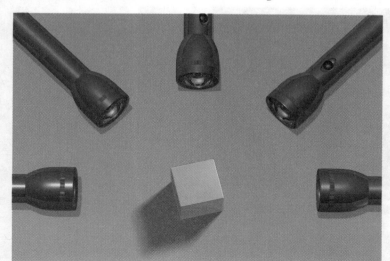

Seeing Double

Not all objects absorb light. Some objects bounce light back in the opposite direction.

Active Reading As you read these two pages, find and underline three facts about reflecting.

A surface can **reflect**, or bounce back, light. Smooth glass, metal, and water reflect well. Picture a calm lake. The image on the lake is formed by light reflecting off its surface.

The beam of the flashlight below is shining downward. It traveled in a straight line until it hit an object that reflected it. The light bounced back up when it reflected.

Did you ever notice that things look backward in a mirror? Words are hard to read if you reflect them in a mirror because they're reversed. A reflected image is always reversed.

No Fishing!

Use a hand mirror to read this sign. What does it say?

_____

▶ Gather data by looking at the reflections of other objects on the water's surface. Communicate a valid conclusion about the canoe's reflection by drawing a picture.

Bend It!

Glass and water can reflect light. They can also bend light.

Active Reading As you read these two pages, underline the definition of *refract*.

refraction

Light can **refract**, or bend, when it moves from one clear material to another. When the beam hits the water in the tank, it refracts.

▶ Fill in the cause. Then circle the place in the photo where refraction occurs.

Cause → Effect

_____

_____

An object may appear broken

refraction

It's easy to see where light is refracted. Just look for the break! What makes the duck look broken? Light reflects from the duck above water and underwater. Light from the duck's top half goes straight to your eyes. Light from its bottom half goes through water first. The light refracts as it leaves the water. This makes the duck's belly and legs look separated from the top half of its body.

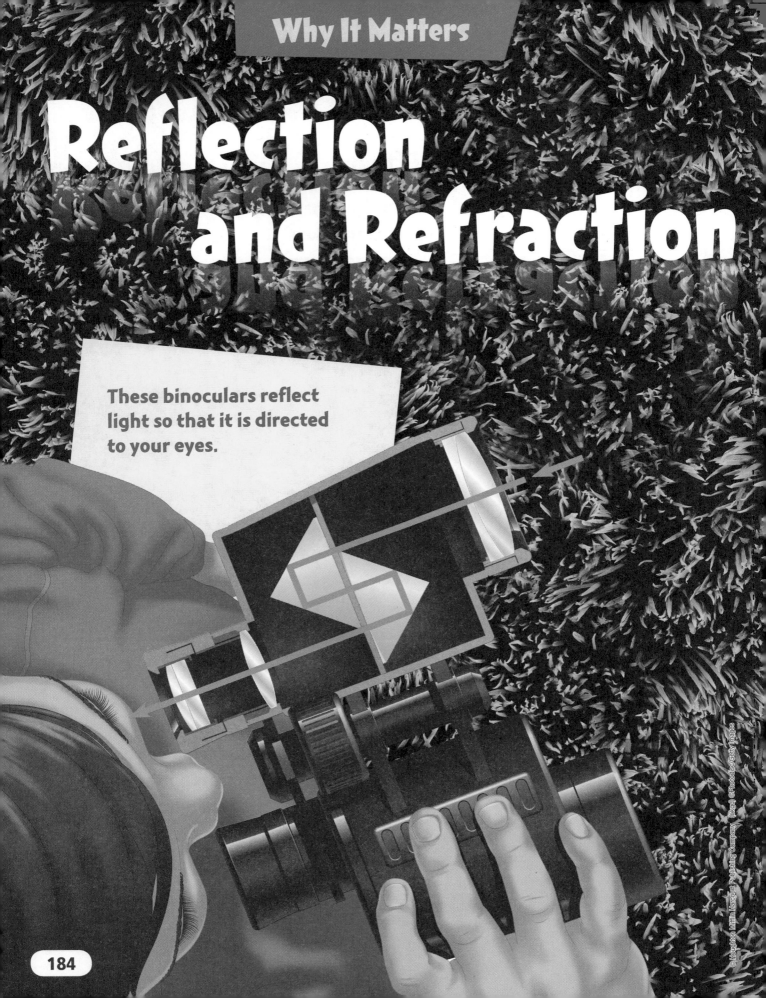

Reflection and Refraction

These binoculars reflect light so that it is directed to your eyes.

The lenses in this telescope refract light. This makes the object seem larger. Lenses in binoculars also refract light to make objects look larger.

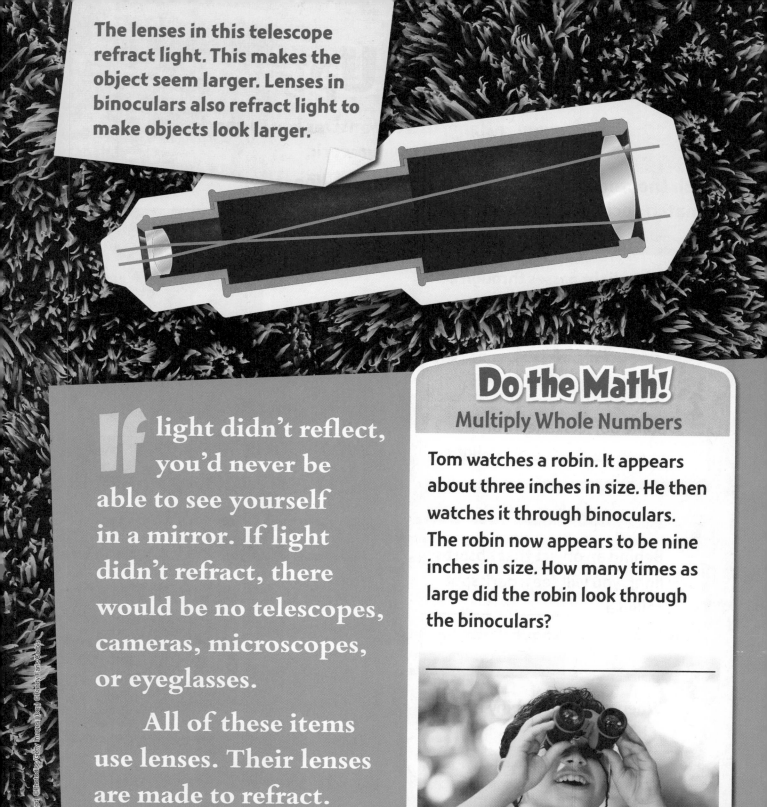

If light didn't reflect, you'd never be able to see yourself in a mirror. If light didn't refract, there would be no telescopes, cameras, microscopes, or eyeglasses.

All of these items use lenses. Their lenses are made to refract. Items such as these depend on refracting lenses to work.

Do the Math!
Multiply Whole Numbers

Tom watches a robin. It appears about three inches in size. He then watches it through binoculars. The robin now appears to be nine inches in size. How many times as large did the robin look through the binoculars?

Sum It Up!

When you're done, use the answer key to check and revise your work.

Finish the summary statements. Then draw a line to match each statement with the correct image.

1 When light passes through a clear material, it bends, or _____ .

2 Some objects take in, or _____ light.

3 Behind an object that absorbs light, you will see a dark spot called a _____ .

4 When light hits a shiny surface, it bounces back, or _____ .

5 Light travels in a _____ path.

Name _____

Word Play

1 Use the words in the box to complete the puzzle.

How does light travel?

Down

1. Its purpose is to refract light.
2. An area that light cannot reach
3. To bounce back in the opposite direction
4. Bend, as light does when it moves from air to water
5. Marshmallows reflect and _____ light when it hits them.

Across

4. Objects in mirrors look like this
6. Uses lenses to reflect and refract light
7. The kind of path light travels in

| absorb* | binoculars | lens | reflect* | refract* | reversed |
| shadow* | straight |

* Key Lesson Vocabulary

Apply Concepts

2 Draw a circle around the item that reflects light. Draw a square around the item that refracts light. Draw a triangle around the item that absorbs light.

3 Label each diagram.

_____   _____

4 In the box, draw the path the light would take from the flashlight.

Take It Home!

With your family, go through your home, looking for two things that reflect light, two things that refract light, and two things that absorb light.

TEKS **3.6A** explore different forms of energy, including mechanical, light, sound, and heat/thermal in everyday life

Lesson **5**

Essential Question

What Are Some Heat Sources?

Engage Your Brain!

Find the answer to the following question in this lesson and record it here.

The brakes on a car rub against the wheels to stop the car. But why are this car's brakes bright orange?

_____

_____

_____

Active Reading

Lesson Vocabulary

List the terms. As you learn about each one, make notes in the Interactive Glossary.

_____

_____

Main Idea

The main idea of a section is the most important idea. The main idea may be stated in the first sentence, or it may be stated elsewhere. Active readers look for main ideas by asking themselves, What is this section mostly about?

Inquiry Flipchart p. 29 — Heat Race/Where There's Light...

189

Sharing the Warmth

Here are two common words: heat and temperature. You hear them every day. Now explore what they mean!

Active Reading As you read these two pages, circle the clue word or phrase that signals a detail such as an example or an added fact.

Scientists use words very carefully. Some common words have special meanings in science. For example, when you use the word *heat*, you might mean how warm something is. In science, **heat** is energy that moves from warmer objects to cooler objects.

The temperature of the water in these hot springs is higher than the temperature of the monkeys. Heat flows from the warmer water to the monkeys. The monkeys feel warmer.

Temperature is the measure of how hot or cold something is. Temperature can be measured in degrees. Water with a temperature of 32 °C (90 °F) is hotter than water with a temperature of 12 °C (54 °F).

Remember, heat is energy. Heat always moves from an object with a higher temperature to one with a lower temperature.

Heat Can Move

In each picture, heat will flow from one object to another. Draw an arrow to show which way it will flow.

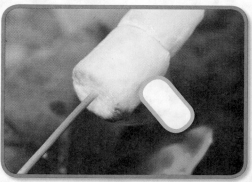

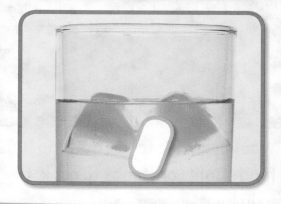

The red part of the metal horseshoe has a very high temperature. Heat moved from the fire into the red part of the horseshoe.

Turn Up the Heat

Heat moves from something warmer to something cooler. You rely on that every day. How? Here is just one way.

Would you like to eat nothing but raw food? Ugh! For things to cook, they must gain heat energy.

Heat moves from the blue flames to the pot. Then it moves from the pot to the stew. The heat cooks the stew.

1. This oven is used to bake food. Heat moves from the oven to the air inside the oven. Then it moves from the hot air to the food. The heat from the oven baked these cookies!

2. Some things slow the movement of heat. The woman in the picture is using oven mitts. The mitts slow the movement of heat, so she does not get burned.

Do the Math!
Read a Table

1. What foods are cooked at 145 °F?

_____

2. Which food needs to be cooked at a higher temperature, eggs or chicken?

_____

3. What food is cooked at 160 °F?

_____

Safe Food Cooking Temperatures

Type of Food	Cooking Temperature
Eggs	160 °F
Salmon	145 °F
Beef	145 °F
Chicken	165 °F

Hot Light

Old-fashioned light bulbs give off heat. Some newer kinds give off more light and less heat.

It is not unusual to see something glowing red and giving off heat. That's what the lava is doing in this picture.

Have you ever touched a light bulb that had been on for a while? The heat may have surprised you!

Active Reading As you read these two pages, draw a star next to what you consider to be the most important sentence, and be ready to explain why.

You've learned that heat is energy. But remember, light is a form of energy, too. Heat and light often occur together. Many things that give off light also often give off heat.

The light bulb is used for its light, but it also gives off heat. The coil inside a toaster gives off heat. That's how the bread gets toasted. But the coil also gives off an orange-red light. When something gives off both light and heat, we often want to use just one or the other.

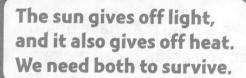

The sun gives off light, and it also gives off heat. We need both to survive.

The charcoal is giving off orange light. It also gives off the heat that cooks the meat.

Heat and Light Sources

How many things in your house give off light and heat? List some of them here.

_____

_____

_____

_____

The light from a candle's flame can let us see in a dark room. The heat from the flame melts the wax.

Burn Rubber

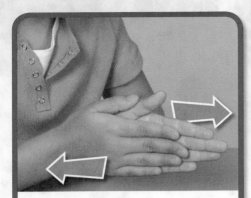

If you're ever out in the cold without gloves, rub your hands together. The heat you produce will warm your hands!

Q: Can you make a fire by rubbing two sticks together?
A: Yes, if one of them is a match!

That's an old joke, so you may have heard it before. However, you actually can make a fire by rubbing two sticks together. You have to move them quickly, and you must have something nearby to burn. But it can be done. Where do you think the heat comes from?

Active Reading As you read these two pages, draw circles around two words or phrases that are key to understanding the main idea.

The tires are rubbing against the road as they spin. They're spinning very quickly and producing a lot of heat. They're getting so hot that they're burning. That's where the smoke is coming from.

When two things rub against each other, there is *friction* [FRIK•shuhn] where they touch. Friction produces heat. The faster and harder the two things rub, the more heat is produced.

Where Is Heat Produced?

In each photo, two things are rubbing together to produce heat. Draw a circle around the point where the heat is being produced. Then write a caption for each picture.

_____

_____

_____

_____

_____

_____

Sum It Up!

When you're done, use the answer key to check
and revise your work.

Write the correct word in the blank.

1

Things that give off

_____

often give off heat as well.

2

_____

is measured in degrees.

Complete the graphic organizer.

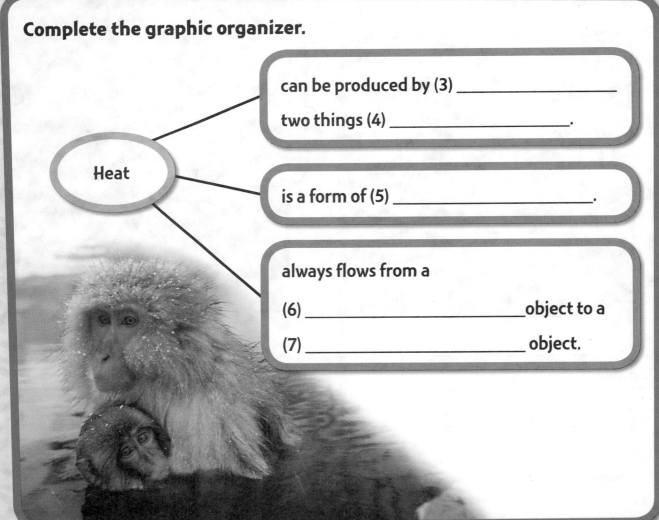

Heat

can be produced by (3) _____

two things (4) _____.

is a form of (5) _____.

always flows from a

(6) _____ object to a

(7) _____ object.

Answer Key: 1. light 2. Temperature 3. rubbing 4. together 5. energy 6. warmer 7. cooler

Word Play

1 Use the clues to help unscramble each word. Write the unscrambled word in the boxes.

Something with a higher temperature is
ETHOTR

Something that is hot may do this.
WLGO

The measure of how hot or cold something is
MTEEERPUTAR

Friction from spinning race car tires might cause this.
MKSOE

This produces heat when two things rub together.
ITRNFICO

Something with a very low temperature is this.
OCDL

Unscramble the letters in the circles to form a word that is related to this lesson.

Apply Concepts

2 Circle the object that can give off heat but not light.

sun

candle

hot chocolate

3 Name two things you sometimes do to prevent heat from being transferred.

_____

_____

_____

4 Name two things that give off both light and heat.

_____

5 Name one way that you use heat.

_____

Take It Home!

With your family, pick two rooms in your home. Go through the rooms, looking for everything that produces light. For each thing you find, discuss if that thing also produces heat.

TEKS 3.2C construct maps, graphic organizers, simple tables, charts...to organize, examine... 3.6A explore different forms of energy, including mechanical, light, sound, and heat/thermal in everyday life

Name _____

Essential Question

Where Can Heat Come From?

Set a Purpose

What do you think is the purpose of this investigation?

_____

_____

_____

_____

Think About the Procedure

Why are you using different items to rub together?

_____

_____

_____

_____

Record Your Data

Use the space below to construct a chart using tools, such as a pencil and ruler, to organize, examine, and evaluate your data.

Draw Conclusions

Compare your results with the other groups. What do you find?

_____

_____

Why might this be the case?

_____

_____

Analyze and Extend

1. If two parts of a machine rub together, what could you do to keep them from getting as hot?

_____

_____

_____

_____

2. How would you plan an investigation to find possible materials to reduce friction?

_____

_____

_____

_____

_____

3. Look at the setup below. Ramp 1 has a smooth surface. Ramp 2 has a sandpaper surface. Will the book on either ramp move? Explain.

Ramp 1

Ramp 2

_____

_____

_____

_____

_____

4. What other questions would you like to ask about how heat can be produced?

_____

_____

_____

_____

Vocabulary Review

Use the terms in the box to complete the sentences.

absorbs
electrical energy
energy
friction
kinetic energy
potential energy

TEKS 3.6A

1. Energy in a ball rolling across the floor is

   _____.

TEKS 3.6A

2. Black paper _____ most of the light that
   strikes it.

TEKS 3.6A

3. The heat produced when you rub your hands together is

   caused by _____.

TEKS 3.6A

4. Energy stored in a stretched rubber band is

   _____.

TEKS 3.6A

5. The energy that causes a light bulb to glow is

   _____.

TEKS 3.6A

6. You can move a pillow or change its shape by using

   _____.

Science Concepts

Fill in the letter of the choice that best answers the question.

TEKS 3.6A

7. Kendall feels tired after riding his bicycle. He uses a blender to make a health shake. Which types of energy does the blender use and then give off?

  Ⓐ electrical; heat and light

  Ⓑ electrical; potential and heat

  Ⓒ electrical; kinetic and sound

  Ⓓ mechanical; sound and potential

TEKS 3.6A

8. The picture below shows a ball rolling down a hill.

Which of the following describes the types of energy the ball has?

  Ⓐ only kinetic

  Ⓑ only potential energy

  Ⓒ potential and kinetic energy

  Ⓓ potential, kinetic, and mechanical energy

TEKS 3.2A, 3.6A

9. Rylee and Ming each hold an end of a bent hollow tube. They shine a light through the end, but cannot see it at the other end of the tube. Which question were Rylee and Ming trying to answer with their experiment?

  Ⓐ Does light travel in straight lines?

  Ⓑ Why is the tube bent?

  Ⓒ How fast does light travel?

  Ⓓ Will the light cast a shadow?

TEKS 3.5A, 3.6A

10. To compare temperatures from two locations, Amber placed one thermometer outside the house and another one inside the house.

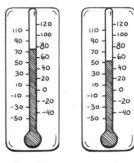

Outside   Inside

What can Amber conclude based on her experiment?

  Ⓐ It is warmer inside than outside.

  Ⓑ It is warmer outside than inside.

  Ⓒ The temperatures outside and inside are the same.

  Ⓓ One of the thermometers must be broken.

TEKS 3.6A

11. Midori's mom heats bread in an electric toaster oven. As it heats, the coils inside the oven glow. The oven beeps when the bread is done. The oven uses different types of energy. Study the chart below.

A heat	C electrical
B light	D sound

Which types of energy are present during this process?

Ⓐ A only

Ⓑ A and B only

Ⓒ A, B, and C only

Ⓓ A, B, C, and D

TEKS 3.6A

12. Which of the following would have the most mechanical energy?

Ⓐ an orange in a tree

Ⓑ a book on a bookshelf

Ⓒ a rock lying on the ground

Ⓓ a ball on the top of a building

TEKS 3.6A

13. Which object **in the home** gives off heat energy?

Ⓐ a sweater

Ⓑ a light bulb

Ⓒ a cooking pan

Ⓓ a campfire

TEKS 3.6A

14. Charlie placed a pencil in a glass of water as shown in the picture.

Why does the pencil appear broken?

Ⓐ The bottom part of the pencil refracts light.

Ⓑ The light reflects from the surface of the water.

Ⓒ The curved surface of the glass absorbs the light.

Ⓓ The light refracts as it moves from water to air.

TEKS 3.6A

15. Phil put hot water into a cup. When he picked up the cup, the handle was very hot. Which statement tells why the handle was hot?

Ⓐ Heat moved from Phil to the handle.

Ⓑ Heat moved from the water to the handle.

Ⓒ Heat moved from the handle to the air.

Ⓓ Heat moved from the air to the handle.

Apply Inquiry and Review the Big Idea

Write the answers to these questions.

TEKS 3.4A, 3.6A

16. Alana and Juan used a meter stick to mark heights of 2 m, 4 m, and 6 m above the ground. Alana dropped a ball from each height. They repeated this several times to increase the reliability of the results. Juan measured how high the balls bounced each time and recorded the information. Predict which ball bounced the highest. Explain by describing the energy of the balls.

_____

_____

TEKS 3.6A

17. Mary also dropped a ball from different heights to investigate mechanical energy. On the first drop, the ball bounced 1 m high. On the second drop, from a different height, it bounced twice as high. How high did the ball bounce the second time?

_____

TEKS 3.2A, 3.2D, 3.2F, 3.4A, 3.6A

18. Stephanie and Lucas planned an experiment to learn about sound. They used a sound recorder to record the pitch and volume of the sound made by a rubber band when it was stretched or pulled in different ways. The table below shows their results.

Length (cm)	How we plucked the rubber band	Volume	Pitch
5	gently	soft	low
5	with a lot of force	loud	low
10	gently	soft	between low and high
10	with a lot of force	loud	between low and high
15	gently	soft	high
15	with a lot of force	loud	high

Analyze the patterns in the data. Interpret the patterns to explain the results. Communicate your explanation by writing it on the lines below.

_____

_____

Forces and Work

Big Idea

Work is done by moving an object using a push or pull. Simple machines make doing work easier.

TEKS 3.2C, 3.3D, 3.6B, 3.6C

I Wonder Why

Why does a fishing pole use a reel?
Turn the page to find out.

Here's why A fishing reel is a wheel-and-axle that makes it easier to pull in a heavy fish.

In this unit, you will explore the Big Idea, the Essential Questions, and the Investigations on the Inquiry Flipchart.

Levels of Inquiry Key ■ DIRECTED ■ GUIDED ■ INDEPENDENT

Track Your Progress

Big Idea Work is done by moving an object using a push or pull. Simple machines make doing work easier.

Essential Questions

○ **Lesson 1 What Are Simple Machines?** **209**
Inquiry Flipchart p. 31—Machines and Forces/Change It!

○ **S.T.E.M. Engineering & Technology:** Reach for the Sky:
Building with Cranes. **221**
Inquiry Flipchart p. 32—Design It: Working Elevator Model

○ **Lesson 2 What Are Some Other Simple Machines?**. . . .**223**
Inquiry Flipchart p. 33—Wrap It Up/Everyday Machines

○ **Inquiry Lesson 3 How Do Simple Machines Affect Work?** . .**235**
Inquiry Flipchart p. 34—How Do Simple Machines Affect Work?

○ 👥 **People in Science:** Helen Greiner and Dean Kamen **237**

○ **Lesson 4 What Is Gravity?** **239**
Inquiry Flipchart p. 35—Measure the Force/Forces Acting on a Compass

○ **Unit 5 Review** **251**

○ **Now I Get the Big Idea!**

Science Notebook

Before you begin each lesson, be sure to write your thoughts about the Essential Question.

TEKS 3.6B demonstrate and observe how position and motion can be changed by pushing and pulling objects to show work being done such as swings, balls, pulleys, and wagons

Lesson **1**

Essential Question

What Are Simple Machines?

Engage Your Brain!

Find the answer to the following question in this lesson and record it here.

How does this boy using a rake demonstrate work being done?

_____

_____

_____

_____

Active Reading

Lesson Vocabulary
List the terms. As you learn about each one, make notes in the Interactive Glossary.

_____ _____

_____ _____

_____ _____

Cause and Effect
Some ideas in this lesson are connected by a cause-and-effect relationship. Why something happens is a cause. What happens as a result of something else is an effect. Active readers look for effects by asking themselves, What happened? They look for causes by asking, Why did it happen?

Doing Work

You've done work. You've seen other people do work. But what do scientists mean when they use the term *work*?

Active Reading As you read these two pages, find and underline the definitions.

In science, the term *work* has a special meaning. For work to be done, a person must use force. A *force* is a push or a pull.

Work is the use of a force to move an object in the same direction as the force. Work is only done if the force changes the position or motion of the object. Pushing on a tree that does not move is not work. Pulling on a locked door that does not move is not work either.

When you do work, you change the position of an object by applying a force to it. You also change the object's motion. The ball was moving toward the girl. Now it is moving away.

Push   Pull

The wagon was standing still. Then the girl applied a force to it. Now the wagon is moving. It is also in a different place.

Push   Pull

▶ In each picture, observe the work done by applying a force to an object to change its position or motion. Circle whether the force was a push or a pull.

The swing was close to the girl. It was moving toward her. She applied a force to it. Now it is far from her and moving away.

Push   Pull

Levers Help You Lift

Levers are simple machines used to lift things. How do they work?

Active Reading As you read these two pages, find and underline the definitions of *simple machine, lever,* and *fulcrum.*

Have you ever used a simple machine? A **simple machine** is a machine with few or no moving parts. You only apply one force to it. Simple machines make work easier.

A **lever** is a bar that pivots, or turns, on a fixed point. A fixed point is a point that doesn't move. The fixed point on a lever is called the **fulcrum** [FUHL•kruhm]. The load—what you are moving—is on one end of the lever. As you move the other end of the lever, the lever moves the load.

A fork is one kind of lever. The boy's thumb is the fulcrum. As he lowers his hand, the fork lifts the food—the load—to his mouth.

Lever

Fulcrum

Output

A seesaw is a lever. Its fulcrum is in the middle. The fulcrum is the object on which the seesaw sits. If your friend sits on one end of a seesaw, where would you apply force to lift her? You would sit on the other end of the seesaw.

Rakes and brooms are another type of lever. Your hands move when you rake leaves or sweep a floor, but the leaves or dirt—the load—moves farther than your hands do. This makes your job easier.

The Parts of a Lever

Draw a lever. Label the fulcrum, the load, and the applied force.

On a seesaw, you may be a load or a force. When you are coming down, your weight is the applied force. It presses down on one end of the lever, and the load on the other end goes up. Then you trade. You are the load being lifted, and your partner's weight is the force.

Using a Wheel-and-Axle

Some simple machines use circular motion to make work easier.

Active Reading As you read these two pages, underline the phrases that describe the effect of turning each wheel-and-axle.

A **wheel-and-axle** is made up of a wheel and an axle that are connected so that they turn together. A wheel-and-axle uses a circular motion to increase force. If you turn the wheel, the axle turns with greater force.

Turning the handlebar is like turning the purple wheel. The connected axle turns to steer the front bicycle wheel.

Wheel

Axle

Look at the picture of the bicycle. The handlebars are connected to a shaft. Together, these act as a wheel-and-axle. When you turn the handlebars, the shaft, or axle, turns with it. Since the axle is connected to the front wheel, the wheel also turns. In this way, you can change the position of the wheel without having to turn the wheel from side to side with your hands.

The wheels and axles at the bottom of the bicycle are not true wheel-and-axles. These wheels turn on their axles. The axles do not turn with the wheels.

Another Wheel-and-Axle

A doorknob is another example of a wheel-and-axle. When you turn the knob, the axle turns, too. As it does, it pulls back the catch, and the door opens. Which part of the doorknob is the wheel?

A pencil sharpener has a wheel-and-axle. When you turn the crank, the axle carries the movement to the sharpener. It turns to sharpen the pencil.

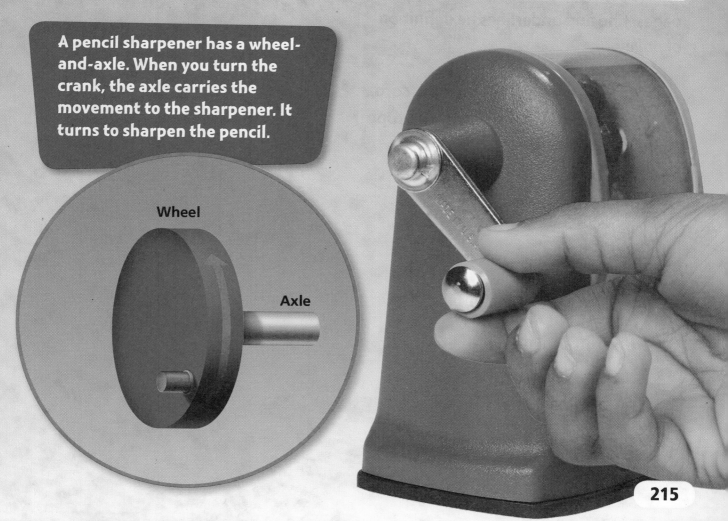

Wheel

Axle

215

Pulley Power

Going up! Coming down! You can use a simple machine, like a pulley, to lift a load straight up into the air.

Active Reading As you read these two pages, find and underline the definition of *pulley*.

A pulley is a wheel with a rope, cord, or chain around it. One end of the rope hangs on each side of the pulley. You can pull from the side, like the girls in the tree house.

The pulley is attached to the tree house. One end of the rope is in the tree house. The other end is attached to the basket. By pulling on the rope, the girls in the tree house change the position of the basket.

Single pulley

effort

output

You can also pull from below, like the girl in the sailboat. She doesn't have to climb to the top of the pole to raise the sail. Instead, she simply pulls down on the rope. In both of these examples, the pulley changes the direction of the force that is applied to the rope.

A pulley lets you stay in one place and still use your force. It lets you pull up something that is too far down to reach, like the basket on the ground. And it lets you pull up something to a point too high to reach, like the sail.

The pulley is attached to the top of the mast of the sailboat. It can be used to raise and lower the sail. Look around your school. Check the windows and the gym. Where can you find pulleys?

pulley

Do the Math!
Solve a Word Problem

Karen could lift 18 pounds with a pulley. When Marcus helped her, they could lift 32 pounds. When Antonio also helped, they could lift 19 more pounds than that.

How many more pounds could Marcus and Karen lift than Karen could lift alone?

_____

_____

How many pounds could the three children lift all together?

_____

_____

217

Sum It Up!

When you're done, use the answer key to check and revise your work.

Write the term or terms that match each picture and caption.

1
_____

These two things change when you apply a force to an object.

2

_____

This fishing rod and reel is made of two simple machines.

3
_____

The boy is applying this type of force.

4

_____

When you turn the doorknob, the latch opens.

5
_____

The lever balances on this.

Answer Key: 1. position, motion, 2. wheel-and-axle and lever 3. push 4. wheel-and-axle 5. fulcrum

Name _____

Word Play

1 In each box, use vocabulary terms to describe the simple machines from this lesson.

```
┌─────────────────┐   ┌─────────────────┐   ┌─────────────────┐
│                 │   │ _____ │   │                 │
│ _____ │   │                 │   │ _____ │
│                 │   │ _____ │   │                 │
│ _____ │   │                 │   │ _____ │
│                 │   │ _____ │   │                 │
│ _____ │   └─────────────────┘   │ _____ │
│                 │     ┌─────────────┐      │                 │
└─────────────────┘     │   simple    │      └─────────────────┘
                        │  machines   │
                        └─────────────┘
```

pulley*   work*

lever*   wheel-and-axle*

fulcrum*   *Key Lesson Vocabulary

Apply Concepts

2 Label each simple machine.

_____ _____ _____ _____

_____ _____ _____

3 Choose two of the simple machines shown above. Tell how each can be used to change the position or motion of an object. Be sure to tell the type of force you would use to change the position or motion.

_____

_____

_____

Take It Home!

Share what you have learned about simple machines with your family. With a family member, identify simple machines in your home. Discuss how they make work easier.

S.T.E.M.
Engineering & Technology

Reach for the Sky:
Building with Cranes

Cranes have levers and pulleys. The pulleys change the position of objects by pulling. Cranes lift and lower heavy loads. People use cranes for many things. Follow the timeline to see how cranes have changed.

 **2,500 Years Ago**

Cranes were first used in ancient Greece. They were used to build huge marble temples.

Cranes were made out of steel. They had gas or electric engines and could lift much heavier loads.

1800s

Steam engines were added to cranes. These cranes could move more easily and lift heavier loads.

1900s

What is the same about all the cranes?

_____

_____

Compare and Contrast

Review the cranes pictured and discussed in the timeline. Then answer the questions below.

Cranes lift beams to make the frame of a skyscraper.

2010

Today, skyscrapers are made using tower cranes. These giant cranes are made of steel. They can lift the heaviest loads. They are put together by smaller cranes, and the giant cranes can't move from place to place.

Choose any two cranes from the timeline. What is better about each newer crane? How did the design change? Give a possible reason for the change.

_____

_____

_____

Build On It!

Rise to the engineering design challenge—complete **Design It: Working Elevator Model** on the Inquiry Flipchart.

Lesson **2**

Essential Question

What Are Some Other Simple Machines?

Engage Your Brain!

Find the answer to the following question in this lesson and record it here.

The skateboarder looks like she's simply having fun, but she's also doing work. What work is being done? Which simple machine is she using?

_____

_____

_____

Active Reading

Lesson Vocabulary

List the terms. As you learn about each one, make notes in the Interactive Glossary.

_____ _____

_____

_____

Signal Words: Comparison

Signal words show connections between ideas. Words that signal comparisons, or similarities, include *like*, *same as*, *similar to*, and *resembles*. Active readers remember what they read because they are alert to signal words that identify comparisons.

Moving Up, Digging In

We use simple machines every day. A ramp? It's a simple machine. A knife? It's another kind of simple machine. How do these simple machines help us do work?

Active Reading As you read these two pages, find and underline the definitions of *inclined plane* and *wedge*.

A plane is a flat object, such as a board. An **inclined plane** is a plane that is slanted, so that one end is higher than the other. This makes it easier to lift a load. Instead of lifting the load straight up all at once, you push or pull it up the inclined plane, little by little. This spreads the work over a distance. Because of this, you are able to use less force.

It takes longer to roll a wheelchair up a ramp than to lift it. But lifting a wheelchair takes more effort. Raising the wheelchair with the ramp takes less effort because you apply a smaller force over a greater distance. You do the same amount of work, but the work is easier.

Inclined Plane

A **wedge** is two inclined planes placed back to back. One edge is sharp and pointed. The other is wide and flat. If you apply force to the flat edge, the pointed edge can split one thing into two things.

A knife is a wedge. The sharp edge of the knife opens a tiny crack. The inclined planes on either side push outward, widening the crack and separating the pieces as the wedge moves downward. The sharper the knife, the less effort is needed to get the work done.

Wedge

When you use a knife to cut, the blade splits the food into two pieces.

All Wrapped Up

A wheel-and-axle uses circular motion to do work, but so does another simple machine—the screw.

A screwdriver is a wheel-and-axle. It uses circular motion to make work easier. The tip of the screwdriver fits into the slot at the top of a screw. A **screw** is an inclined plane wrapped around a shaft or a cylinder. When you turn the screwdriver's handle, its shaft works like an axle to turn the screw. A screwdriver doesn't just turn the screw. Like other wheel-and-axles, the screwdriver takes your effort and increases that effort as it turns the screw.

As the screwdriver turns the screw, the inclined plane on the screw pulls it into the wood. The threads also make it hard to pull the screw out of the wood.

The thread around the screw is an inclined plane. This inclined plane is not straight like a ramp. It spirals around the screw.

Unlike a nail, which goes straight into the wood, a screw moves around and around as it goes in. As a result, it takes longer to insert a screw into the wood than it does a nail. But you use less force to get the screw into the wood. The closer together the threads are, the easier it is to turn the screw.

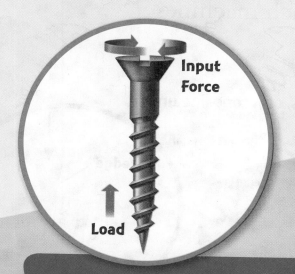

Input Force

Load

This man is using an ice auger [AW•ger]. As he turns the handle, the auger pulls the ice beneath it up to the surface. The ice is the load. As it moves up, a hole is made in the ice.

What Does a Screw Do?

Circle the screw in each picture. How does the screw help to do work?

_____

_____

_____

How Can Simple Machines Work Together?

Sometimes, two simple machines work together to get a job done. Which machines work this way?

Lever

Fulcrum

Wedge

The blades of these garden clippers are wedges, and the handles are levers.

Simple Machine	Description
Lever	Uses force at one end to move a load at the other end
Inclined Plane	Lets you lift a load using a smaller force over a greater distance
Screw	Uses an inclined plane wrapped around a post to move things up
Wedge	Lets you move two things apart or split one thing into two
Wheel-and-axle	Uses circular motion to increase force
Pulley	Uses a wheel and rope to change the size or direction of a force

A **compound machine** is a machine made up of two or more simple machines. Garden clippers are a compound machine. Bicycles are also compound machines. The handlebars are not the only wheel-and-axle on a bicycle. When you push down on the pedals, a wheel-and-axle pulls the chain. This moves the bicycle forward.

Simple and Compound Machines

Look at the photos on this page. Tell which simple machines make up each compound machine.

_____

_____

_____

Using Machines

Now that you know what to look for, you can find machines everywhere!

Simple and compound machines are all around you. Every time you use a tool, you are using a machine. Sometimes it is a simple machine. Sometimes it is a compound machine. When you use a compound machine, try to identify the simple machines it is made of.

Dustpan

_____

_____

Faucet

_____

_____

How Many Machines Can You Find?

Look at each caption. If the object named is a simple machine, place an *S* in the circle and then name the simple machine. If the object is a compound machine, place a *C* in the circle. Then tell which two simple machines make up the compound machine.

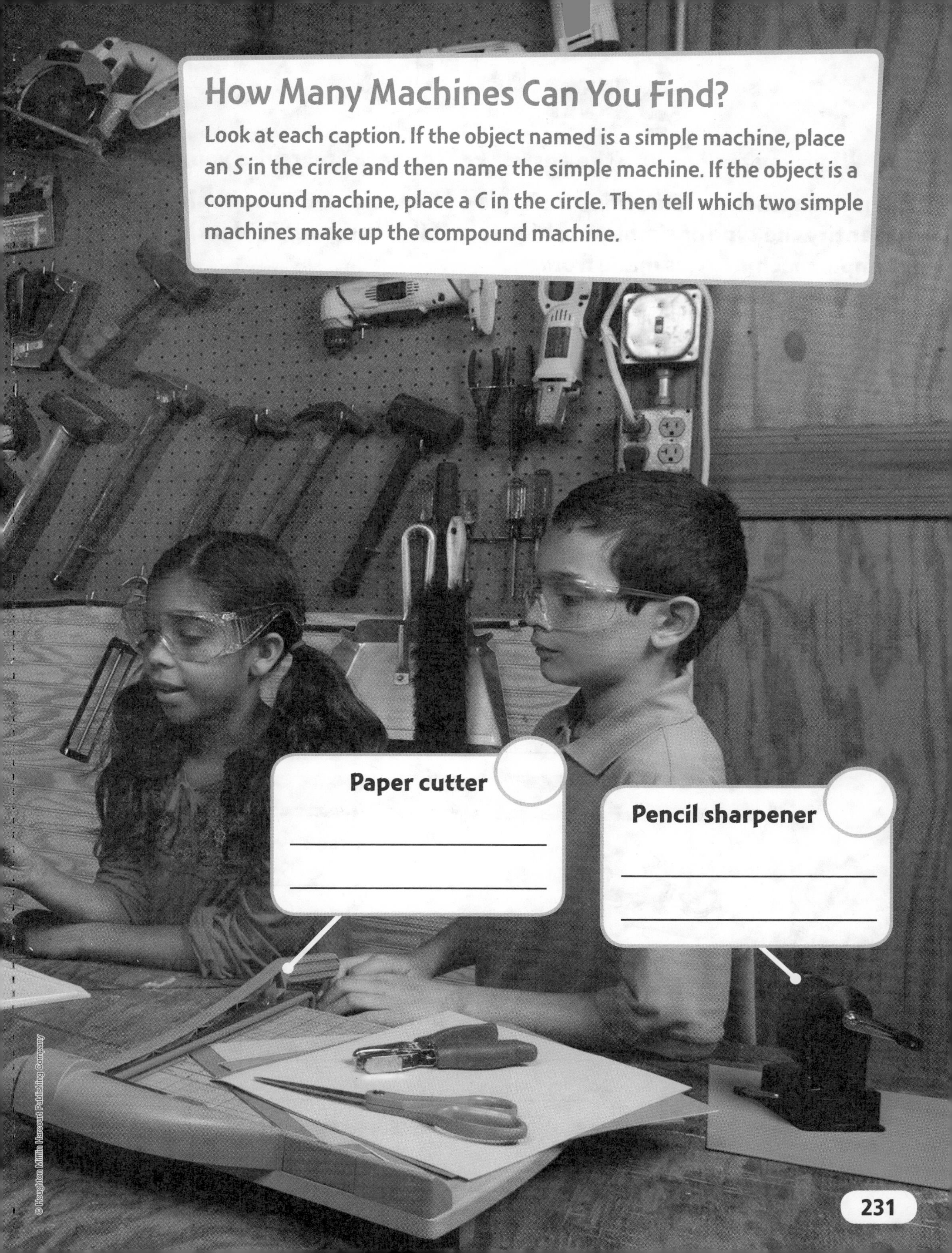

Paper cutter

_____

_____

Pencil sharpener

_____

_____

Sum It Up!

When you're done, use the answer key to check and revise your work.

Write whether each machine is simple or compound. If it is simple, identify the type of simple machine it is. If it is compound, identify the simple machines it is made from.

1 scissors

_____

_____

2 hatchet

_____

_____

3 screwdriver

_____

_____

4 faucet

_____

_____

5 pliers

_____

_____

Answer Key: 1. compound machine: two levers, two wedges 2. compound machine: wedge, lever 3. simple machine: wheel-and-axle 4. simple machine: wheel-and-axle 5. compound machine: two levers

Word Play

1 **Use the words in the box to complete the two concept webs about machines that help you do work.**

screw*	inclined plane*	paper cutter	scissors	rake
wedge*	compound machine*	screwdriver	bicycle	

* Key Lesson Vocabulary

```
            _____              _____              _____
           (         )            (         )            (         )
            _____              _____              _____

              \                       |                     /
               \                      |                    /
   _____     \        _____        /     _____
  (         )-----\------(                   )------/------(         )
   _____               Simple machine               _____
```

```
                    _____
                   (                   )
                    _____
                   /        |         \
                  /         |          \
         _____      _____      _____
        (         )    (         )    (         )
         _____      _____      _____
```

Apply Concepts

2 Identify each simple machine, and tell how it can help you do work.

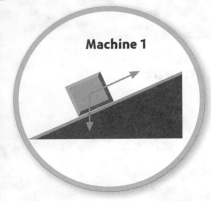

Machine 1

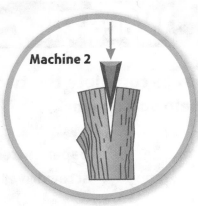

Machine 2

Machine 3

_____   _____   _____

_____   _____   _____

_____   _____   _____

_____   _____   _____

_____   _____   _____

3 Tell how your life might be different without simple machines. Include at least two ways in which it would be different.

_____

_____

_____

_____

Take It Home!

Look around your house for some simple machines. Discuss them with an adult. Share what you find with the class.

TEKS **3.2C** construct maps graphic organizers, simple tables, charts, and bar graphs using tools... to organize, examine, and evaluate measured data **3.6B** demonstrate and observe how position and motion can be changed by pushing and pulling objects to show work being done such as swings, balls, pulleys, and wagons

Name _____

Essential Question

How Do Simple Machines Affect Work?

Set a Purpose

What will you learn from this experiment?

_____

_____

_____

Think About the Procedure

How do you think the spring scale measures force?

_____

_____

Why do you think you are using ramps of different lengths?

_____

_____

_____

Record Your Data

Below, construct a simple table using tools to organize, examine, and evaluate your data. The column heads should be: *Setup* and *Measurements*

Draw Conclusions

Which moved the car a shorter distance: lifting straight up or using a ramp?

_____

_____

_____

Which was easier: lifting straight up or using a ramp?

_____

_____

On which ramp did you use the least amount of force to move the car? Why do you think this was so?

_____

_____

_____

Analyze and Extend

1. Why do you think an inclined plane makes it easier to lift objects?

_____

_____

2. Think about a hillside road that goes straight up. Why do you think many hillside roads have lots of curves?

_____

_____

_____

3. People living in ancient times built pyramids and other structures without the machines we have today. How do you think they were able to move heavy loads to the tops of the pyramids?

_____

_____

_____

4. What other questions do you have about how simple machines affect work?

_____

_____

5. **REVIEW** How did the spring scale help you to collect and analyze information?

_____

_____

_____

236

TEKS 3.3D connect grade-level appropriate science concepts with the history of science, science careers, and contributions of scientists

People in Science

Meet the Machine Engineers

Helen Greiner 1967–

Imagine a robot in every home. That's what Helen Greiner says is the future. She is a roboticist. As a young girl, she loved science and machines. Greiner started a company to build robots. Now she designs and builds robots that can be used in homes. From toys to vacuum cleaners, she creates robots that make a difference in people's everyday lives.

One of Greiner's tiny robots explored the tunnels in the Great Pyramid of Giza in Egypt.

Dean Kamen 1951–

Dean Kamen is an inventor of very useful machines. One of his famous inventions is the Segway® Human Transporter. When riding a Segway, people use their body weight to both balance and steer the machine. Kamen also started a group that holds special events to get students interested in technology.

The Segway is a two-wheeled personal transportation machine that runs on batteries.

237

Machines!

Read each clue and write the answer in the correct squares.

| Greiner | home | robot | Segway | technology |

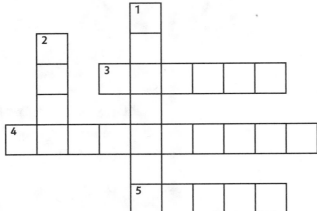

ACROSS

3. A _____ is a two-wheeled machine you can ride.

4. Kamen helps students get interested in _____.

5. A tiny _____ explored inside a pyramid.

DOWN

1. _____ is a roboticist.

2. Greiner wants every one of these to have a robot. _____

Essential Question

What Is Gravity?

Engage Your Brain!

Find the answer to the following question in this lesson and record it here.

What role does gravity play in an avalanche?

_____

_____

_____

_____

Active Reading

Lesson Vocabulary

List the terms. As you learn about each one, make notes in the Interactive Glossary.

_____

_____

_____

Cause and Effect

Some ideas in this lesson are connected by a cause-and-effect relationship. What makes something happen is a cause. What happens because of something else is an effect. Active readers look for effects by asking themselves, What happened? They look for causes by asking, Why did it happen?

Coming Down

Nothing moves on its own. An object moves because something causes it to move.

Active Reading As you read these two pages, draw one line under a cause. Draw two lines under an effect.

This player will use a push to throw the ball toward the basket, hoping it will go in. Gravity will pull the ball down.

A ball rolls along a sidewalk. Why? Because someone pushed it. A drawer opens. Why? Because someone pulled it. Any kind of push or pull is a **force**.

Gravity is a force that pulls objects toward each other. Gravity causes books to fall to the ground. It causes spilled milk to land on the floor. And if your feet slip out from under you, gravity causes you to fall. Gravity affects everything, including how much things weigh. **Weight** is a measure of the force of gravity on an object.

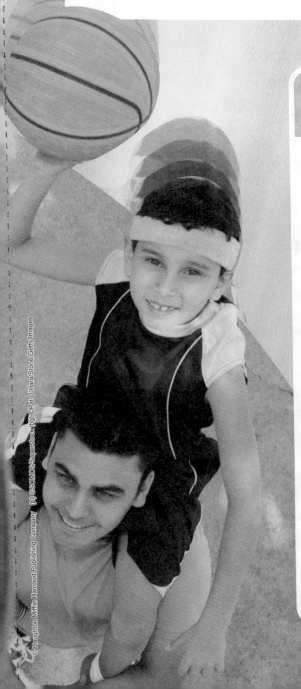

Do the Math!
Interpret a Table

A spring scale measures an object's weight in newtons. The heavier an object, the greater its weight and the more newtons measured on the spring scale.

Where would the marker on this spring scale point if each object in the table were measured? Write the letter for each object next to the correct measurement on the spring scale.

Object	Weight in Newtons
A. Baseball	2
B. Golf ball	1
C. Basketball	6
D. Football	4

Earth's Gravity

Everything that goes up must come down. Why? Gravity, of course!

As you read these pages, underline each effect of gravity you read about.

Rain falls to Earth from clouds. Why? Apples, pears, and peaches fall to Earth from trees. Why? A ball dropped from the top of a building falls to the ground. Why? The answer is gravity. Earth's gravity attracts objects and pulls them toward Earth's center.

Each autumn, you can observe the force of gravity acting on colorful leaves.

Earth's gravity affects everything on or near Earth's surface. Gravity is the reason water flows downhill, not uphill. Gravity is the reason snow slides down a mountain in an avalanche, not up the mountain. It is the reason land may suddenly sink to form a large sinkhole. It is also why objects and people don't float off into space. Imagine Earth without gravity. What would it be like?

Water can weaken some types of rock under the ground. When the rock is weakened enough, gravity pulls down the soil the rock was holding up. This forms a sinkhole.

These children are enjoying the effect of gravity, which causes the water to spill over the cliff and into the river below.

Gravity and You

Describe one way that you observe gravity affecting you every day.

_____

_____

_____

_____

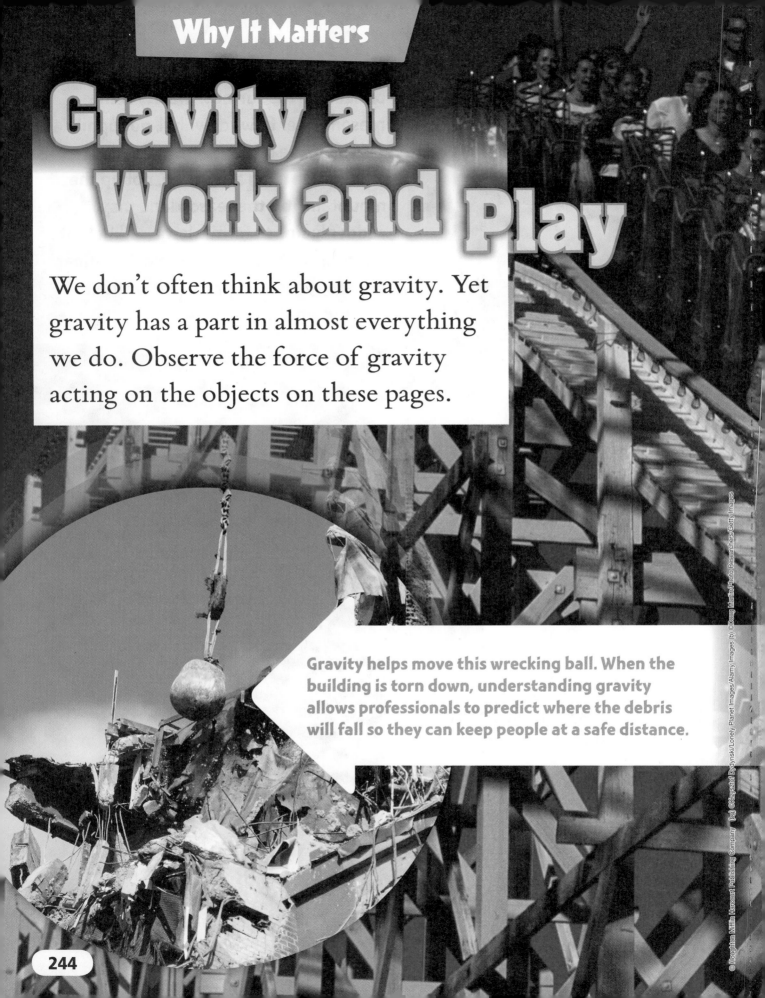

Gravity at Work and Play

We don't often think about gravity. Yet gravity has a part in almost everything we do. Observe the force of gravity acting on the objects on these pages.

Gravity helps move this wrecking ball. When the building is torn down, understanding gravity allows professionals to predict where the debris will fall so they can keep people at a safe distance.

Gravity pulls the rescue worker toward Earth. Knowing this, the helicopter pilot hovers above the person needing help so the rescue worker can do his or her job.

Gravity pulls people on slides, snow skis, snowboards, and sleds downward.

One-two-three-jump! Not everyone agrees that skydiving is fun, but without gravity pulling skydivers down to Earth, who knows where they would end up?!

▶ Gravity helps people do work and have fun, but gravity is not always fun. On the lines below, tell how gravity makes each activity more difficult.

Sledding:

_____

_____

Helicopter rescue:

_____

_____

_____

Motion in Space

Earth's gravity doesn't only affect objects on or near its surface. Earth's gravity even affects objects in space!

Active Reading As you read these pages, underline the effect that Earth's gravity has on the moon.

Gravity exists everywhere. The sun has gravity. So do the moon, the other planets, and everything else in space. Gravity is the main force that affects the motion of objects in space, including Earth and the moon.

The more mass an object has, the stronger its gravity. The sun has a very large mass, so its gravity is extremely strong. Even though the sun is very far from Earth, its gravity is strong enough to affect Earth and the moon.

Distances not to scale.

The pull of gravity between Earth and the moon is part of what causes the moon to move around Earth. The sun's gravity also has an effect on the moon's movement.

The sun's gravity is about 28 times stronger than Earth's gravity. The pull of gravity between Earth and the sun is one of the factors that causes Earth to move around the sun.

▶ Explain how the force of gravity affects Earth, the moon, and the sun.

_____

_____

_____

_____

_____

_____

_____

_____

Sum It Up!

When you're done, use the answer key to check and revise your work.

Write a summary. Answer the questions in complete sentences.

A What is gravity? **1** _____
_____
_____
_____
_____

B How does gravity affect things on Earth? **2** _____
_____
_____
_____
_____

C How does gravity affect the sun, Earth, and the moon? **3** _____
_____
_____
_____

Brain Check

Name _____

Word Play

1 Follow the directions to find the hidden word. Write the word on the line. Then draw a line from the word to its meaning.

Cross out each l, m, a, f, s, and r.

a l f w r f e s i m s g l h a s m t a

_____

A force that pulls objects toward each other

Cross out each b, u, p, x, m, and c.

u n b p x e c w p m t u o c b n x c b

_____

The unit that measures the pull of gravity on an object

Cross out each z, s, e, n, h, and d.

s n g z e r a h d e v z h i z e t h y

_____

A measure of the force of gravity on an object

Cross out each b, a, g, w, l, and q.

g w l f g a o q q w r b c l q a e w l

_____

The force of gravity that causes objects to move toward each other

Cross out each k, n, o, a, r, and w.

p k o a w u r w k l a n k r w o l k o

_____

Any kind of push or pull

| force* | gravity* | newton | pull | weight* |

* Key Lesson Vocabulary

Apply Concepts

2 Observe this skater. How will gravity affect him? Why?

_____

_____

_____

_____

_____

_____

3 What would happen to the baseball if there were no gravity?

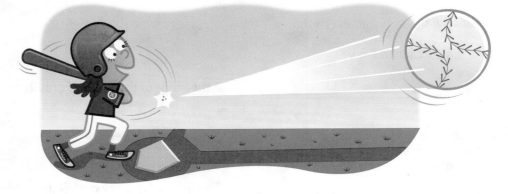

_____

_____

Take It Home! With your family, take a short walk outdoors. Identify two objects that are affected by gravity. For each thing, discuss how gravity affects both that object and you.

Vocabulary Review

Use the terms in the box to complete the sentences.

> compound machine
> fulcrum
> inclined plane
> wedge
> work

TEKS 3.6B

1. When you change the position of a heavy box by pushing it up a ramp, you are using a(n) _____.

TEKS 3.6B

2. An object made up of two or more simple machines combined is a(n) _____.

TEKS 3.6B

3. The object that supports a lever is a(n) _____.

TEKS 3.6B

4. When you use force to move an object, you are doing _____.

TEKS 3.6B

5. Two inclined planes placed together that make an edge form a(n) _____.

Science Concepts

Fill in the letter of the choice that best answers the question.

TEKS 3.6B

6. Jorge wants to demonstrate how pulling an object can change its position. Which could he do?

    (A) Use a pulley to lift a sail.

    (B) Use a wedge to cut wood.

    (C) Use a lever to lift a package.

    (D) Use an inclined plane to move a box.

TEKS 3.6B

7. Your friend wants to change the motion of a basket from stationary to moving straight up by pulling. Which one of the following simple machines would you observe him using to do this?

    (A) lever   (C) wedge

    (B) pulley   (D) inclined plane

TEKS 3.6B

8. Heather dribbles a basketball in a school basketball tournament. If you were there, what would you observe?

Ⓐ Heather is doing work by pulling the basketball, changing the position and motion of the ball.

Ⓑ Heather is doing work by pushing the basketball, changing the position and motion of the ball.

Ⓒ Heather is pulling the basketball, but no work is being done on the ball in the scientific sense.

Ⓓ Heather is pushing the basketball, but no work is being done on the ball in the scientific sense.

TEKS 3.6C

9. The picture shows a compass.

If you place a magnet at the spot marked with the star, where will the compass needle point?

Ⓐ at the N

Ⓑ at the E

Ⓒ between the N and the E

Ⓓ between the S and the W

TEKS 3.6B

10. Restaurant employees are pushing wheeled boxes of groceries. They change the motion and position of each box from stationary on the sidewalk to moving up a ramp. There are two ramps. One ramp is 3 m long. The other one is 5 m long. Both ramps have one end on the sidewalk and one end on the top step of the restaurant. Which statement accurately compares the ramps?

Ⓐ It takes less effort to wheel boxes up the 5 m ramp, but the distance is greater.

Ⓑ It takes less effort to wheel boxes up the 3 m ramp, but the distance is shorter.

Ⓒ It takes more effort to wheel boxes up the 5 m ramp, but the distance is shorter.

Ⓓ It takes more effort to wheel boxes up the 3 m ramp, but the distance is greater.

TEKS 3.6B

11. The picture shows one way a simple machine can be used.

What provides the pulling force that changes the position of the nail?

Ⓐ the hammer's head

Ⓑ the hammer's handle

Ⓒ the board's flat surface

Ⓓ the person's arm and hand

TEKS 3.6B

12. Taran will demonstrate how to change the position of an object by applying a force. The pictures show three possible ways he could use a simple machine to do this.

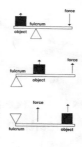

Which picture or pictures show how Taran can use a simple machine to reduce the amount of force needed to change the object's position?

Ⓐ the top picture

Ⓑ the middle picture

Ⓒ the bottom picture

Ⓓ the top and middle pictures

TEKS 3.6B

13. The picture shows a common simple machine.

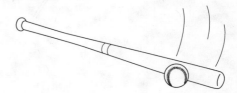

Tina uses the bat to demonstrate how motion can be changed. How does she do this?

Ⓐ Tina uses the bat to pull the ball toward her.

Ⓑ Tina uses the ball to pull the bat toward her.

Ⓒ Tina uses the bat to push the ball away from her.

Ⓓ Tina uses the ball to push the bat away from her.

TEKS 3.6B

14. Kel raises the flag in front of the school. He pulls on a rope to change the position and motion of the flag. How is Kel using a simple machine?

Ⓐ He is using a pulley to change the amount of force he needs to apply.

Ⓑ He is using a pulley to change the direction of the force he applies.

Ⓒ He is using a wheel and axle to change the amount of force he needs to apply.

Ⓓ He is using a wheel and axle to change the direction of the force he applies.

Apply Inquiry and Review the Big Idea

Write the answers to these questions.

TEKS 3.6B

15. The tool shown in the picture is a compound machine.

Identify the simple machines that make up this compound machine. Then describe whether you push or pull each machine to change its position and motion.

_____

_____

_____

TEKS 3.6B

16. Jacob did an experiment. He set up two ramps, as shown below.

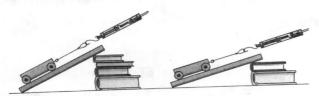

Predict what Jacob will find when he measures the force needed to pull each toy from its position on the bottom of the ramp to a new position at the top of the ramp.

_____

_____

TEKS 3.6B

17. Jessica wants to put a box on a shelf that is 120 cm off the ground. She can lift the box by grabbing it and pulling up. She can also build a ramp and push the box up the ramp. The ramp lets her use less force than she would use by lifting it straight up. Yet the distance she has to move the box is four times longer. How far does she push the box?

_____

© Houghton Mifflin Harcourt Publishing Company   (border) ©NDisk/Age Fotostock

UNIT 6
Earth's Surface

Big Idea

Processes on Earth can change Earth's landforms. Some of these changes happen slowly, while others happen quickly.

TEKS 3.2A, 3.2B, 3.3D, 3.7A, 3.7B, 3.7C

I Wonder Why

The edge of Niagara Falls moves back about 30 centimeters every year. Why does this happen? *Turn the page to find out.*

Here's why The force of the flowing water, freezing and thawing, and gravity are causing weathering and erosion at the edge of the falls.

In this unit, you will explore the Big Idea, the Essential Questions, and the Investigations on the Inquiry Flipchart.

Levels of Inquiry Key ■ DIRECTED ■ GUIDED ■ INDEPENDENT

Track Your Progress

Big Idea Processes on Earth can change Earth's landforms. Some of these changes happen slowly, while others happen quickly.

Essential Questions

Lesson 1 What Are Some Landforms?..................257
Inquiry Flipchart p. 36—Folding Up Mountains/Making Other Landforms

Lesson 2 How Does Earth's Surface Change Slowly?....270
Inquiry Flipchart p. 37—The Power of Water/Find Some Erosion!

S.T.E.M. Engineering & Technology: Sand and Surf: Erosion Technology 279
Inquiry Flipchart p. 38—Improvise It: Reducing Erosion

Inquiry Lesson 3 How Can We Model Erosion?...........281
Inquiry Flipchart p. 39—How Can We Model Erosion?

Lesson 4 How Does Earth's Surface Change Quickly?....283
Inquiry Flipchart p. 40—A Model Volcano/Simulate an Earthquake

People in Science: Hugo Delgado Granados and Waverly Person 295

Unit 6 Review 297

Now I Get the Big Idea!

Science Notebook

Before you begin each lesson, be sure to write your thoughts about the Essential Question.

Essential Question

What Are Some Landforms?

🧠 Engage Your Brain!

Find the answer to the following question in this lesson and record it here.

What landform does this river flow through, and how did it form?

_____

_____

_____

Active Reading

Lesson Vocabulary
List the terms. As you learn about each one, make notes in the Interactive Glossary.

_____ _____

_____ _____

_____ _____

Signal Words: Contrasts
Signal words show connections between ideas. Words that signal contrasts include *unlike, different from, but,* and *on the other hand.* Active readers remember what they read because they are alert to signal words that identify contrasts.

Above and Below

Look out the window at the land around you. You might see flat fields, high mountains, a hilly city, or a forest by a lake.

Active Reading As you read this page, circle the definitions of *crust, mantle, outer core,* and *inner core.*

You can see Earth's surface, but imagine what's under the ground. Earth has several layers.

Crust—The crust is Earth's outer layer. It is made of solid rock.

Mantle—The mantle is the layer below Earth's crust. It is made of soft, hot rock.

Outer Core—Earth's outer core is a layer of liquid metals at Earth's center.

Inner Core—Earth's inner core is a ball of solid metals at Earth's center.

Everything you can see—oceans and land—sits on the crust. The crust is not smooth and flat. If you travel across Earth's surface, you might climb over rolling hills or tall mountains. You might pass through canyons. Each of these is a different landform. A **landform** is a part of Earth's surface that has a certain shape and is formed naturally.

A city may be built on a flat area or on hills or mountains. What landforms are near your home?

Along the coastline, you might find flat areas, hills, or cliffs. What landforms would you travel to see?

True or False

Read each sentence. Circle *True* or *False*.

Earth's center is made of hot, liquid rock.	True	False
There is no crust under the ocean.	True	False
Every landform is part of Earth's crust.	True	False
Mountains and canyons are both landforms.	True	False

Down in the Low Places

There are many different types of landforms. You can identify and compare them based on their characteristics!

A **valley** is the low land between mountains or hills. The sides of valleys are not usually steep. Most valleys are formed by rivers. Some valleys are formed by moving ice.

A **canyon** is a valley with steep sides. Some rivers make canyons as they flow. Over time, soil and loose rock are carried away by the moving water. What is left are tall cliffs that form canyon walls on both sides of the river. The walls of some canyons are very high. The Grand Canyon is about 1,524 meters (5,000 feet) deep from top to bottom!

These people are floating on a river. The river flows between steep canyon walls.

260

© Houghton Mifflin Harcourt Publishing Company (inset) ©Blaine Harrington III/Alamy Images

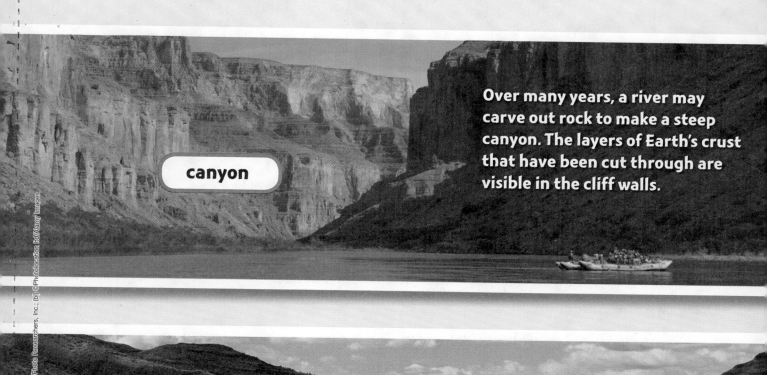

canyon

Over many years, a river may carve out rock to make a steep canyon. The layers of Earth's crust that have been cut through are visible in the cliff walls.

Other rivers flow through gentle valleys. The sides of these valleys are not as steep as the sides of canyons. Valleys are not always formed by rivers, though. Sometimes, a river appears after the valley has formed.

valley

Identify and Compare Valleys

Identify the landforms below by comparing them to the photos on these pages.

_____ _____ _____

Climbing High Above

Climbing most hills is easy, if the hill is not too high or steep. Climbing a mountain, however, is another story. The high peaks and jagged edges make it hard to climb!

Active Reading As you read, draw one line under a cause. Draw two lines under an effect.

Mountains are landforms that are much higher than the surrounding land. When two or more pieces of Earth's crust push together, a mountain or mountain range forms. Mountains can also be formed by volcanoes. Some new mountains are growing higher. They are rough and jagged. Older mountains become smaller as they are slowly worn down by wind, water, or ice. As mountains wear down, they also become more rounded. Landforms that are rounded but smaller than mountains are *hills*.

Look at the picture on this page. Identify the mountain by placing a circle on it. Identify the hill by placing an *X* on it.

Mount McKinley, Alaska
6,194 meters (20,320 feet) tall

Monte Mottarone, Italy
1,491 meters (4,890 feet) tall

Hill in Barboursville, Virginia
366 meters (1,200 feet) tall

► Compare the mountains and hill by drawing a line to the part of the scale that is closest to the height of each.

6,500 meters

6,000 meters

5,500 meters

5,000 meters

4,500 meters

4,000 meters

3,500 meters

3,000 meters

2,500 meters

2,000 meters

1,500 meters

1,000 meters

500 meters

0 meters

Do the Math!
Estimate the Difference

Estimate to find about how much higher Monte Mottarone is than the hill in Barboursville. Show your work using a number sentence.

_____

Rolling Along the Flats

Traveling across plains is much easier than climbing a mountain. The land is so flat, you can ride a bike across it. Plateaus are flat, too—but you'll have to go up to get to them!

Active Reading As you read, put brackets around clue words that signal when things are being compared or contrasted.

A **plain** is flat land that spreads out over a long distance. Plains are wide open spaces and may form where there used to be seas. Like a plain, a **plateau** is flat. However, a plateau is higher than the land around it. A plateau is typically formed when flat land is pushed high up by the movement of Earth's crust. Plateaus are sometimes found near mountains.

Identify the plateau by placing a circle on it. Identify the plain by placing an X on it.

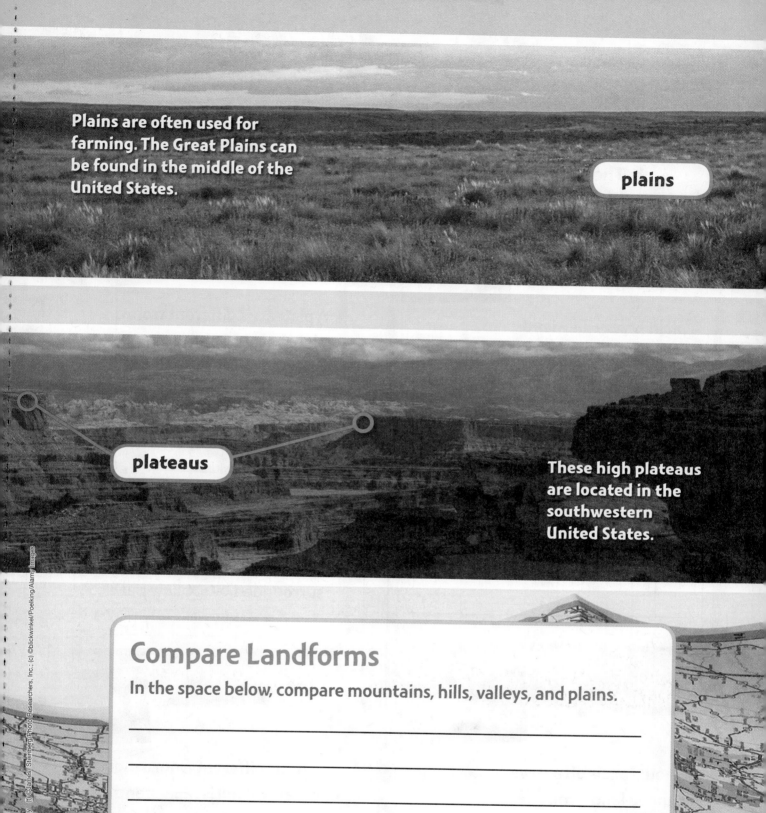

Plains are often used for farming. The Great Plains can be found in the middle of the United States.

plains

plateaus

These high plateaus are located in the southwestern United States.

Compare Landforms

In the space below, compare mountains, hills, valleys, and plains.

_____

_____

_____

_____

_____

_____

Sum It Up!

When you're done, use the answer key to check and revise your work.

The blue part of each summary statement is incorrect. Write words to replace the blue parts.

1

A plain is very hilly land.

_____

2

A plateau is different from a plain because plateaus are lower than the nearby land.

_____

3

A valley is up high between hills or mountains.

_____

4

A canyon is different from a valley because a canyon is surrounded by shallow beaches.

_____

5

A mountain is often a very short and rounded landform.

_____

6

A hill is different from a mountain because a hill is higher and more jagged.

_____

Answer Key: 1. flat 2. higher 3. down low 4. steep cliffs 5. high and jagged 6. lower and rounder

Name _____

Word Play

1 Fill in the missing letters to find each word. You will use each of the letters in the box.

A	A	A	A	A	A	A	E
E	I	I	O	O	O	U	U

1. M __ __ N T __ __ N
2. P L __ T __ __ __ __
3. C __ N Y __ N
4. V __ L L __ Y
5. P L __ __ N
6. L __ N D F __ R M S

Fill in each blank with the correct word from above.

7. A _____ may be thousands of feet high.

8. The cliffs of the _____ towered over the kayakers.

9. The town was sheltered in the deep _____.

10. The flat land was pushed up, leaving a wide _____.

11. Earth's crust is covered with different kinds of _____.

12. A _____ may have once been a sea.

2 Draw a picture of the landforms described. Identify each landform.

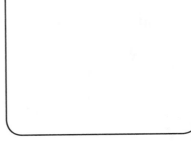

Low place between mountains

_____

Area of land with jagged peaks

_____

Large area of low, flat land

_____

3 Read the descriptions of Earth's layers. Then complete the labels. Draw lines to the correct layers.

Liquid metal layer: _____

Solid metal layer: _____

Cool, solid rock: _____

Soft, hot rock: _____

Take It Home!

Make a plan for a walking or hiking trip with your family. Think of two different landforms you can visit on your trip.

TEKS **3.7A** explore and record how soils are formed by weathering of rock and the decomposition of plant and animal remains

Essential Question

How Does Earth's Surface Change Slowly?

Engage Your Brain!

Find the answer to the following question in this lesson and record it here.

This glacier is moving slowly. How is it affecting the land around it?

_____

_____

_____

Active Reading

Lesson Vocabulary

List the terms. As you read, make notes about them in the Interactive Glossary.

_____ _____

_____

Signal Words: Main Idea

Words that signal a main idea include *most important* and *in general*. Active readers remember what they read because they are alert to signal words that identify important ideas.

What Weathering Can Do

Animals, plants, water, and temperature are just some of the things that can change Earth's surface. Explore how!

As you read these two pages, underline details about what water does to change Earth's surface.

Weathering is the breaking down of rock into smaller pieces. This can happen when tree roots push into the surface of rock. It can happen when animals burrow into the ground.

Weathering is often caused by patterns of freezing and thawing. As winter nears, the weather gets colder. Rain falls into cracks in rock and freezes. As liquid water turns to ice, it expands. This widens the cracks. When the ice melts, or thaws, the rock is weaker. Pieces crumble and fall away. Little by little, the shape of the rock changes. Smaller pieces of rock often become part of the soil as they continue to weather.

Change Takes Time

Changing seasons cause patterns of freezing and thawing. This is one way weathering happens.

Water moves into cracks and stays there.

Weathering by water has caused these rocks to become rounded. Freezing water has also caused some of the rocks to crack.

▶ Draw the next stage of weathering for this rock.

1

2

3

The water freezes. Ice forms in the cracks. The ice takes up more space than the liquid water did.

The ice widens the cracks. Pieces of rock may break off.

Erosion Motion

Water, wind, and glaciers never stop moving. They carry soil, rocks, and sand along with them. Over time, this movement changes the shape of the land.

Active Reading As you read, circle a word or a phrase that signals a main idea.

In general, **erosion** happens when soil, rocks, or sand are moved. Wind, water, and glaciers can all cause erosion. It happens everywhere. When waves at a beach wash away sand, that's erosion. When wind blows sand in a desert, that's erosion. When rainfall carries mud into a river, that's erosion.

Glaciers are another cause of erosion. A **glacier** is a large, thick sheet of moving ice. Glaciers slide along slowly. As they move, many glaciers cut paths through the ground. They pick up pieces of weathered rock, sand, and soil. Glaciers push or carry the rocks and soil as they move. Sometimes glaciers move enough soil to form a whole island!

Wind and waves cause weathering as they hit the rock. This breaks the rock into smaller pieces.

Wind and water move sand. This erosion causes one part of the beach to become smaller. Another part of the beach becomes larger when the eroded sand is left there.

Over time, erosion can cause big changes. It has caused this beach to become much smaller than it once was.

When this lighthouse was built, it was far from the cliff's edge. But wind and waves have weathered and eroded the cliff. Now, the lighthouse must be moved to a safer spot.

Sand, soil, and small rocks erode away. The eroded material moves into the water and away from the land.

Do the Math!
Solve a Word Problem

A lighthouse is 60 meters from the edge of a cliff. The cliff erodes by 3 meters each year. How long will it take for the edge of the cliff to reach the lighthouse? Show your work.

_____

Soil Moves Around

Erosion can ruin fields and forests by taking away soil the plants need. But soil that is washed away from one place can help plants in another place.

Active Reading As you read, underline the harmful and helpful effects of erosion.

As a river flows between its banks, soil and rocks are swept along. The water carries them downstream. Now, there is less soil on the riverbanks. Tree roots may be uncovered. Plants that need the soil may be affected. Without the support of their roots anchored in deep soil, the trees may fall.

But soil that is washed away from a riverbank ends up somewhere else. As a river nears the ocean, the water moves more slowly. The rocks and soil in the river are dropped. This process makes a landform called a *delta*. A river delta is full of rich soil.

Water has eroded soil from this riverbank. These trees may soon fall.

The river's motion carries soil downstream. This leaves less soil for the plants that are growing here.

As a river nears the ocean, the water slows. Soil and rocks in the river are left behind.

Over time, the rocks and soil form a delta. The rich soil of a river delta is a great place for plants to grow.

Cause and Effect

Fill in the blanks to tell the causes and effects of erosion.

1. Moving water carries rocks and _____ downstream.

2. Growing _____ along the riverbanks may become loose.

3. Tree _____ may be uncovered, causing the trees to fall.

4. The rocks and soil may be deposited, forming a _____.

Sum It Up!

When you're done, use the answer key to check and revise your work.

Fill in the missing words in the summary. Then complete the cause-and-effect graphic organizer.

Summarize

Weathering and erosion are two processes that (1) _____ the shape of Earth's surface. When large pieces of rock are broken down into smaller pieces, it is called (2) _____. Erosion is when (3) _____, wind, or glaciers carry these smaller rocks to new places. Erosion can change beaches and riverbanks by taking sand and (4) _____ away. But it can also make new landforms, such as river (5) _____.

Cause		Effect
Waves crash against a cliff.	→	6. _____ _____ _____ _____
7. _____ _____ _____ _____	→	A lighthouse needs to be moved.

1. change 2. weathering 3. water 4. soil 5. deltas 6. The waves weather and erode the cliff. 7. The land gets smaller every year.

Word Play

1 Use the words in the box at the bottom of the page to complete the puzzle.

Name _____

Across

2. A river carries soil here
4. To melt after freezing
5. This part of a plant can cause weathering.
8. When wind and water move rocks, sand, or soil
9. A large, moving sheet of ice
10. When a solid turns to a liquid

Down

1. Breaking of rock into smaller pieces
3. Another word for stones
6. Change from a liquid to a solid
7. When this is washed away, plants cannot grow.

rocks	delta
thaw	weathering*
glacier*	root
melt	erosion*
soil	freeze

* Key Lesson Vocabulary

Apply Concepts

2 For each picture, draw how the object in the picture would change.

 + time + waves =

 + time + rain =

 + time + rushing river =

3 Record how the weathering of rock helps form soil.

_____

_____

_____

Take It Home!

With your family, talk about weathering and erosion. Identify something in your neighborhood that has changed over time because of these processes.

TEKS **3.2A** plan and implement descriptive investigations, including asking and answering questions, making inferences, and selecting and using equipment or technology needed, to solve a specific problem in the natural world

Sand and Surf:
Erosion Technology

There is often more than one solution to an engineering problem. To choose the best solution, people make trade-offs. A trade-off is giving up one feature to make another feature better. Read about the trade-offs of two beach erosion solutions.

People can control beach erosion by building a jetty. A jetty begins on a beach and runs into the water. It is at a right angle to the shore.

Jetty Pluses	Jetty Minuses
Easier to build above water	Erodes beach on other side of jetty
Can be built quickly	Changes the natural look of the beach

People can control beach erosion by building a reef. A reef is under water. It runs in the same direction as the shore.

Reef Pluses	Reef Minuses
Does not erode nearby beaches	Harder to build under water
Lowers wave energy before it reaches beach	Takes time for the reef to form

Analyze Trade-offs

Below are two solutions for soil erosion. Fill in the charts to show the trade-offs. Then tell which you would choose and why.

Hay bales are made of packed dry grass. They are large and heavy. They are put on top of the ground.

Hay Bales Pluses	Hay Bales Minuses

A silt fence is made of lightweight plastic. The bottom is dug into the ground.

Silt Fence Pluses	Silt Fence Minuses

Which soil erosion solution would you choose? Why?

_____

_____

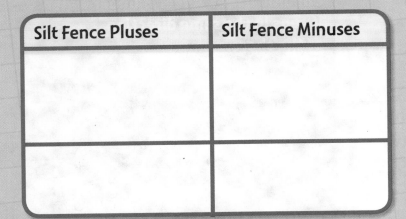

Build On It!

Rise to the engineering design challenge—complete **Improvise It: Reducing Erosion** on the Inquiry Flipchart.

Inquiry Flipchart page 39

Lesson **3**
INQUIRY

TEKS **3.2B** collect data by observing and measuring using the metric system and recognize differences between observed and measured data

Name _____

Essential Question

How Can We Model Erosion?

Set a Purpose
What will you learn from this modeling activity?

_____

_____

_____

Think About the Procedure
What does the sand represent? What does the ice cube represent?

_____

_____

_____

_____

Why will you push the ice over clay before you push it over the sand and clay?

_____

_____

_____

Record Your Observations
Use words or drawings to show how the ice and sand interact.

	Sight	Touch
Clay Without Sand		
Clay With Sand		

Draw Conclusions

How does a glacier affect the land it moves over?

_____

_____

_____

_____

Analyze and Extend

1. What force causes a glacier to move downhill?

_____

_____

_____

_____

2. You pushed the ice over the clay and soil to see the effects of a glacier. In nature, glaciers travel much more slowly. How could you model the way that glaciers move in nature?

_____

_____

_____

_____

3. As glaciers move down a slope to the sea, do they cause weathering, erosion, or both? Explain your answer.

_____

_____

_____

_____

_____

_____

4. What are some other questions you have about glaciers and how glaciers affect the land?

_____

_____

_____

_____

_____

_____

Essential Question

How Does Earth's Surface Change Quickly?

Engage Your Brain!

Find the answer to the following question in this lesson and record it here.

These used to be living plants, but now they are dead. The ground is covered in ash. What might have caused these changes?

_____

_____

Active Reading

Lesson Vocabulary

List the terms. As you learn about each one, make notes in the Interactive Glossary.

_____

_____

_____

Signal Words: Sequence

Signal words show connections between ideas. Words that signal sequence include *now, before, after, first, next,* and *then.* Active readers remember what they read because they are alert to signal words that identify sequence.

Earthquake! Shaken Up

The ground splits. Buildings crack, and some fall. Investigate this rapid change in Earth's surface!

Active Reading As you read this page, underline the clue word that signals a cause.

An **earthquake** is a shaking of Earth's surface that can cause land to rise and fall. Most earthquakes are too weak to be felt, but strong earthquakes can cause a big change to Earth's surface. What causes earthquakes?

Earthquakes happen because of movements in Earth's crust. They occur mostly in places where two pieces of crust meet. Pieces may push together, pull apart, or slide past each other. The map shows places where earthquakes are most likely to happen.

An earthquake can cause great damage over a small or large area.

► The legend next to the map shows an area's risk for earthquakes. Use the legend to answer the questions below the map.

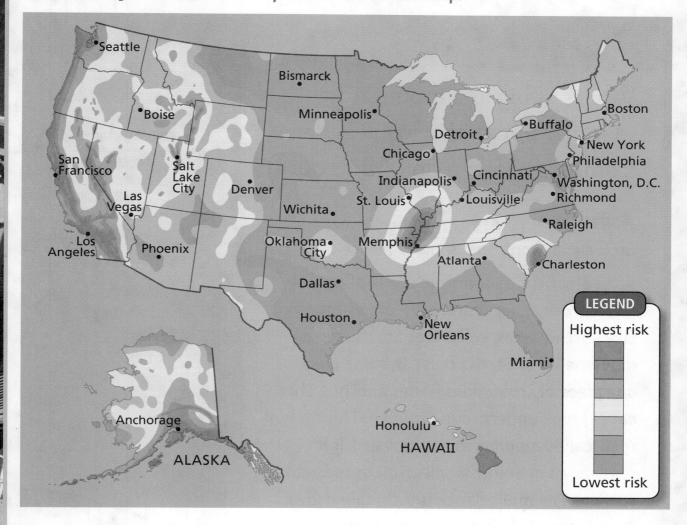

Does San Francisco or Boise have the highest earthquake risk?

_____

Find Dallas and Miami on the map. Which city has the lowest earthquake risk?

_____

Volcano!
Feel the Heat

What's as big as a mountain with so much smoke that you can see it from space? Read on to find out!

Active Reading As you read these two pages, circle signal words that show sequence.

A **volcano** is a mountain made of cooled lava, ash, or other materials from eruptions. Like earthquakes, volcanoes are caused by movements of Earth's crust. In some places, one piece of crust slides under another. This causes rock underground to melt. This melted rock, called *magma*, moves upward. If it reaches an opening, it will erupt onto Earth's surface. The melted rock is then called *lava*. As the lava cools, it gets hard. Some volcanoes grow larger with every eruption.

In some volcanoes, lava gently oozes out. Other volcanoes explode! Lava, stone, and ash are thrown from the volcano's opening with tremendous force. Exploding volcanoes can quickly change Earth's surface.

Red-hot melted rock called magma comes up from underground. When it reaches the surface, we call it lava.

In May 1980, Mount St. Helens erupted. First, there was an earthquake. Then, the volcano began to spit out lava and ash. The eruption went on for nine hours. Nearly 379 square kilometers (230 square miles) of forest was buried or blown down.

Before it erupted, Mount St. Helens, in Washington State, was 2,950 meters (9,677 feet) high. Many plants and animals lived on the mountain.

The eruption of Mount St. Helens sent more than one trillion pounds of ash across the United States. Many plants and animals that lived on the mountain died.

Years later, the mountain is more than 305 meters (1,000 feet) lower, but life has returned. The mountain again provides habitats for many different plants and animals.

What Happened Here?

Study the images above in order to investigate how Mount St. Helens has changed the land around it. Summarize the changes below.

_____

_____

_____

Big Changes
Fire, Water, Mud

A little bit of fire, water, or dirt can be very useful. But what if there is too much? Investigate how water can quickly change Earth's surface.

Active Reading As you read, underline the main idea about each big change. Circle details that tell more about each idea.

A forest fire starts small. It can be sparked by lightning, a bit of lava, or a careless person. People have to act quickly to control forest fires.

Too much rain in too short a period of time can cause a flood. A **flood** is a change that happens when streams, rivers, or lakes get too full and overflow. Entire towns can be destroyed. Many plants may die, and animals may have to find new homes. Over time, floodwater drains away, dries up, or is absorbed into the ground.

Floodwaters in
Nashville, Tennessee

Sometimes, water from rain or a flood loosens dirt on the side of a hill or mountain. The dirt slides downhill in a mudslide or landslide. It may bury part of a town.

Do the Math!

Skip Count by 5s

The Smith River overflows its banks after at least 30 centimeters of rainfall in one day. Rain is falling at 5 centimeters an hour. How long will it have to rain before the river overflows?

_____

Be Prepared
Planning Ahead

How do you prepare for a disaster? You make an emergency plan and prepare your home. You make sure any pets will be safe, too!

People do many things to prepare for disasters. Buildings are designed to withstand earthquakes. The sides of rivers are built up to prevent floods. News reports let us know about the risk of forest fires. Radio, television, and the Internet warn us about storms and other emergencies.

Emergency plans can help keep us safe. Families can talk about what to do in an emergency. A list like the one on the next page can help.

It's best to prepare for a disaster before it strikes. Keeping supplies in your car can help you be ready.

First Aid Kit

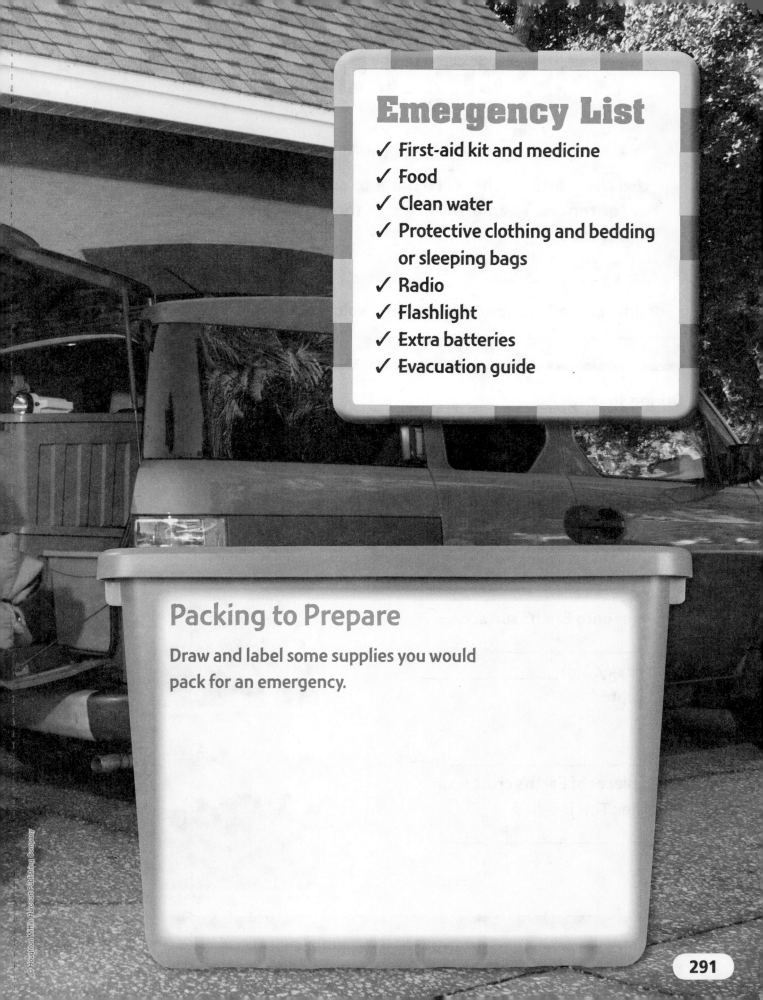

Emergency List

✓ First-aid kit and medicine
✓ Food
✓ Clean water
✓ Protective clothing and bedding or sleeping bags
✓ Radio
✓ Flashlight
✓ Extra batteries
✓ Evacuation guide

Packing to Prepare

Draw and label some supplies you would pack for an emergency.

Sum It Up!

When you're done, use the answer key
to check and revise your work.

**Use the words in the word bank to complete each group
of sentences. Then draw a line to match the sentences with
a picture.**

> drain   ground   water   lava   ash   volcano   flood   earthquake

1 During storms, _____
may overflow a river or lake. This is
called a(n) _____.
The water may _____
away or dry up later.

2 Melted rock called _____
explodes onto Earth's surface,
and _____
fills the sky. A(n) _____
has erupted.

3 The _____ shakes
when pieces of Earth's crust push
together. This is called
a(n) _____.

Brain Check

Lesson 4

Name _____

Word Play

1 Use the words in the box to complete the puzzle.

Down

1. Movements in Earth's _____ can cause earthquakes.

3. Melted rock beneath Earth's surface is called _____.

5. Too much rain can cause a _____.

7. Melted rock that flows onto Earth's surface is _____.

Across

2. Lightning can cause a _____ _____.

4. An _____ can cause buildings to fall over.

6. When a lot of wet soil moves down a hillside, it is called a _____.

8. When a _____ erupts, it can cause a lot of damage.

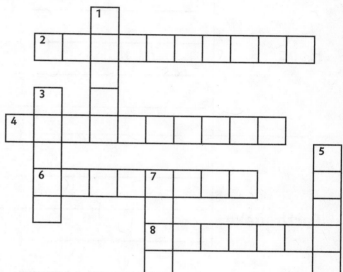

flood*	earthquake*
forest fire	**mudslide**
volcano*	**lava**
magma	**crust**

*Key Lesson Vocabulary

© Houghton Mifflin Harcourt Publishing Company

Apply Concepts

2 Suppose each environment shown went through the events listed, and you investigated the environments afterward. What might you find?

Flood		
Earthquake		
Forest fire		

Take It Home! Talk to your family about types of natural disasters that could occur in your area. Discuss some ways that you can be prepared for these events.

TEKS **3.3D** connect grade-level appropriate science concepts with the history of science, science careers, and contributions of scientists

People in Science

Meet the Earth Scientists

Waverly Person 1927–

Before he retired in 2006, Waverly Person was the director of an earthquake center. When an earthquake struck, Person calculated the size, or magnitude, of it. Then he shared the information about what had happened with news sources. He would also warn the public about any damage. Although he is retired, Person is still one of the experts that people first go to for information about earthquakes.

Hugo Delgado Granados 1957–

Hugo Delgado Granados studies the relationship between active volcanoes and Earth's moving crust. He studies the volcano Popocatépetl [poh•poh•kah•TEH•petl] in Mexico. Glaciers, or slowly moving masses of ice, cover its top. Granados uses a remote device to measure the gases coming from the volcano. Changes in the ice or gases tell Granados about the volcano's activity.

Special instruments detect earthquakes all over the world. Once detected

Glaciers cover the top of Popocatépetl. These glaciers are measured for changes caused by volcanic activity.

Be an Earth Scientist!

A scale like the one at left is used to show an earthquake's magnitude. The strength of volcanic eruptions is measured using the scale at right. Use the scales to answer the questions.

On this scale, the higher numbers mean stronger earthquakes.

Earthquake Magnitude
Scale (1–10)

10	Extraordinary
9	Outstanding
8	Far-reaching
7	High
6	Noteworthy
5	Intermediate
4	Moderate
3	Minor
2	Low
1	Insignificant

On this scale, the higher numbers mean stronger volcanic eruptions.

Volcanic Explosivity
Index (0–8)

VEI	Description
0	non-explosive
1	gentle
2	explosive
3	severe
4	cataclysmic
5	paroxysmal
6	colossal
7	super-colossal
8	mega-colossal

1. An earthquake has occurred that is a 1 on the scale. Why won't emergency crews be needed? _____

2. A far-reaching earthquake measures _____ on the scale.

3. Which volcano eruption is stronger: colossal or severe? _____

4. What does an explosive eruption measure on the volcanic scale? _____

Houghton Mifflin Harcourt Publishing Company   (bg) Comstock/Getty Images RF/Photolibrary New York

Name _____

Vocabulary Review

Use the terms in the box to complete the sentences.

> canyon
> erosion
> mountain
> volcano
> weathering

TEKS 3.7C

1. When two or more pieces of Earth's crust push together, they form a(n) _____.

TEKS 3.7C

2. When a river flows over time, it can leave a deep groove with tall sides called a(n) _____.

TEKS 3.7B

3. Lava can ooze or erupt quickly from a
   _____.

TEKS 3.7B

4. A landslide on the side of a mountain is rapid
   _____.

TEKS 3.7A

5. A rock breaks apart after freezing and thawing many times. This is an example of _____.

Science Concepts

Fill in the letter of the choice that best answers the question.

TEKS 3.7C

6. Molly describes a landform as flat land that spreads out over a long distance. Identify the landform and compare it to a mountain.

   (A) valley; A mountain is tall. A valley is a low area with sloping sides.

   (B) valley; A mountain is tall and often has jagged peaks. Valleys are shorter.

   (C) plain; A mountain is tall and has a peak. Plains are flat and are not tall.

   (D) plain; A mountain is tall with steep sides. A plain is low with steep sides.

TEKS 3.7B

7. Which of these is a sudden change in Earth's surface that can be harmful to living things?

Ⓐ erosion

Ⓑ a forest fire

Ⓒ a glacier

Ⓓ weathering

TEKS 3.7B

8. The drawing below shows the movement in two pieces of Earth's crust.

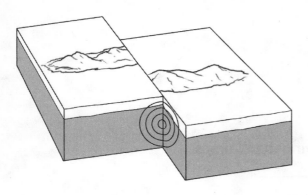

What does this drawing show?

Ⓐ an earthquake

Ⓑ a flood

Ⓒ a fire

Ⓓ a volcanic eruption

TEKS 3.7C

9. Over many years, a mountain is weathered and eroded. What landform will the mountain gradually change into?

Ⓐ a canyon

Ⓑ a hill

Ⓒ a volcano

Ⓓ a valley

TEKS 3.7A

10. Which describes how soil can be formed?

Ⓐ Rivers flow through a canyon. As they move, they deposit soil on the canyon floor.

Ⓑ Wind and water weather rocks, breaking them into smaller and smaller pieces. Tiny pieces of rock mix with organic material to form soil.

Ⓒ Glaciers are made of ice. As they move, they pick up pieces of soil and rock and move the soil and rock along with them.

Ⓓ Rain falls quickly during a storm. This causes the mud on a hill to move and large areas of dirt and rock to slide down a hill. The mud and dirt mix to form soil.

TEKS 3.7B

11. Look at the landform below.

Which choice describes how the landform in the picture was formed?

Ⓐ One piece of crust slid beneath another. Lava began to push up through the cracks.

Ⓑ Two pieces of crust pushed against each other. As they pushed, they forced part of the crust upward to create this landform.

Ⓒ Two pieces of crust pulled apart, causing vibrations and a large crack to open.

Ⓓ A river brought rocks and dirt to this point. Over time, the dirt and rocks formed layers that built up.

TEKS 3.7C

12. On which layer of Earth do you find oceans, mountains, and valleys?

Ⓐ crust

Ⓑ inner core

Ⓒ mantle

Ⓓ outer core

TEKS 3.7A

13. Keesha puts some brick pieces, sand, and water in a jar. She shakes it each day for two weeks and notices what happens to the brick pieces and water. She is modeling how soil forms from weathering in the natural world. Which is a limitation of her model?

Ⓐ size; Only large rocks weather.

Ⓑ properties; Water and sand do not cause weathering.

Ⓒ materials; Bricks do not weather in the natural world.

Ⓓ process; rocks are not shaken in a jar in the natural world.

TEKS 3.7A

14. Tran's class is visiting a delta to make observations. The students observe rich soil. What is the most likely reason for this?

Ⓐ Rocks in the delta were ground into soil.

Ⓑ The soil was carried into the delta by the wind.

Ⓒ Weathered rock was washed into the delta by a flowing river.

Ⓓ Rocks from the ocean were ground up by ocean waves.

Apply Inquiry and Review the Big Idea

Write the answers to these questions.

TEKS 3.7C

15. Tomas took a picture of the landform below. He shared it with his class.

Identify the landform. How is it like a plain? How is it different?

_____

_____

TEKS 3.7C

16. Drew went on a campout. He took this picture of the landform in which he camped.

Identify the landform that is pictured. How is it like a canyon? How is it different?

_____

_____

TEKS 3.3C

17. The Stone River is 5.2 kilometers long. In the lobby of the Stone River School there is a scale model of the river. The model is 1.3 meters long. How many times longer is the river than the model?

_____

People and Resources

Big Idea

Living things use Earth's resources to meet their needs. Some of these resources can be recycled or reused.

TEKS 3.1B, 3.2C, 3.7A, 3.7D

I Wonder Why

Why did people build a huge dam like this? What resources are they using? *Turn the page to find out.*

Here's why Dams harness the power of moving water to produce electricity from generators.

In this unit, you will explore the Big Idea, the Essential Questions, and the Investigations on the Inquiry Flipchart.

Levels of Inquiry Key ■ DIRECTED ■ GUIDED ■ INDEPENDENT

Track Your Progress

Big Idea Living things use Earth's resources to meet their needs. Some of these resources can be recycled or reused.

Essential Questions

Lesson 1 What Are Some Natural Resources?..........303
Inquiry Flipchart p. 41—Polluted Plants/Clean It Up!

Inquiry Lesson 2 How Can We Conserve Resources?....317
Inquiry Flipchart p. 42—How Can We Conserve Resources?

Lesson 3 What Is Soil?.................................319
Inquiry Flipchart p. 43—Forming Soil/Compost It!

Careers in Science: Geologist...........................333

S.T.E.M. Engineering & Technology: Technology at Work: Problems and Fixes 335
Inquiry Flipchart p. 44—Redesign It: Reduce Packaging

Unit 7 Review 337

Now I Get the Big Idea!

Science Notebook

Before you begin each lesson, be sure to write your thoughts about the Essential Question.

Lesson **1**

Essential Question

What Are Some Natural Resources?

Engage Your Brain!

Find the answer to the following question in this lesson and record it here.

How does this wind farm help people use a natural resource?

_____

_____

_____

Active Reading

Lesson Vocabulary

List the terms. As you learn about each one, make notes in the Interactive Glossary.

_____

_____

_____   _____

_____   _____

Compare and Contrast

Many ideas in this lesson are connected because they explain comparisons and contrasts—how things are alike and different. Active readers stay focused on comparisons and contrasts when they ask themselves, How are these things alike? How are they different?

Natural Resources

Most of the things you use every day come from nature. But how do we get these things? How do we use them?

Active Reading As you read, underline the definitions for *natural resource* and *renewable resource*.

A **natural resource** is something that comes from nature that people can use. The air you breathe, and the soil that crops grow in are natural resources. Other natural resources are used to make products you may use. Can you guess which natural resource is used to make paper and pencils?

Paper and pencils are made from trees. Trees are a **renewable resource**—one that can be replaced easily. We can plant more trees to make more paper and pencils.

Wood from a tree was used to make this bat. The hardness of wood makes it useful in products such as this baseball bat and most furniture.

The food we eat comes from nature. Fish that are caught in the ocean are sold to people in stores and markets.

Fish are a renewable resource. Young fish replace those that are caught. Other animals also eat fish. We have to be careful not to eat fish more quickly than they can be replaced.

Water is an important resource. We drink water and also use it for many other things. We can use falling water to produce energy. If we clean water, we can use it again.

Some natural resources are used to make reusable products. You can use this plastic water bottle over and over again.

What Resources Do You Use?

List three natural resources you see on the page. Choose a resource and describe how you use it.

_____

_____

Going, Going, Gone

Not all natural resources are renewable. Some natural resources will eventually be used up and be gone.

Active Reading As you read, underline the sentence that compares three nonrenewable resources.

Coal is a nonrenewable resource burned to make electricity. Computers, lights, and electric heaters all use electricity.

Many resources are found underground. People dig for copper at this mine. Oil, coal, and natural gas can also be found underground.

A **nonrenewable resource** is a natural resource that can be used up. Oil, coal, and natural gas are nonrenewable resources we use to produce different kinds of energy, including electricity. They are **fossil fuels**—fuels that form over many years from the remains of once-living organisms.

How can we make sure these resources don't disappear too quickly? We have to conserve them. **Conservation** is saving resources by using them wisely. What are some ways that you can use nonrenewable resources wisely? You can start by turning off lights when you don't need them.

Gemstones, like this ruby, are taken from the ground. Gemstones are a nonrenewable resource used to make jewelry.

Explore Resource Conservation

What are some ways that resources can be conserved?

_____

_____

_____

_____

_____

How Do We Use It?

Explore which characteristics make some natural resources good for products and materials.

Active Reading As you read these two pages, underline examples of products that come from natural resources.

An oil rig pumps oil, a fossil fuel, from deep within Earth.

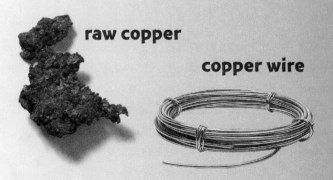

raw copper

copper wire

Have you ever wondered what is inside a computer cord? Copper! Electricity moves very well through this nonrenewable resource.

wood furniture

a wood log

Wood's hardness makes it good to use for all sorts of products. Wood is used to make paper, some tools, and furniture.

Look around the room. Everything you see comes from natural resources. Books, shelves, desks, toys—they're all made from Earth materials.

Even the materials that make up a computer come from Earth. The outside and the inside of a computer are both made from natural resources. Glass computer screens are made from sand. The plastic parts can be produced from oil. To operate, computers also need electricity from fossil fuels.

We also depend upon renewable resources. Imagine you are standing outside. You feel the sun and the wind. These are two important renewable sources of energy.

Solar cells like the ones in these solar panels turn renewable energy into energy we can use.

a cotton plant

cotton clothing

Many of the clothes we wear are made from natural materials such as cotton. Cotton is soft and light. This makes it a good material for clothing products.

Explore the Natural Resource

Think of a natural resource that is used as a product or material. What quality makes that resource useful?

_____

_____

_____

_____

_____

309

The Effects of Pollution

What's that smell? Pollution can make the air, land, and water smell awful. Some of the ways we use natural resources can be harmful.

Active Reading As you read this page, underline all the causes of pollution.

Smoke from this factory mixes with the air. This makes the air harmful to breathe.

What is pollution? **Pollution** is harmful substances in the environment. Smoke in the air is pollution. So are chemicals in water and garbage on land.

What causes pollution? Pollution often results from people using natural resources. Burning fossil fuels, such as gasoline in cars and coal for energy, can cause air pollution. Land pollution is caused when people don't put trash where it belongs. When chemicals and wastes get into water, they cause water pollution.

What's the Cause?

Write one sentence to show how people caused each type of pollution shown.

Land Pollution

_____

_____

_____

_____

Water Pollution

_____

_____

_____

_____

Air Pollution

_____

_____

_____

_____

People need natural resources to survive, but we have to use them responsibly. You can help by remembering the "3 Rs"—reduce, reuse, and recycle.

Active Reading As you read this page, underline ways to reduce, reuse, and recycle.

To *reduce* means to use less of something. There are many ways you can choose to use and conserve natural resources. You can use both sides of a piece of paper, for example. To conserve fossil fuels, you could ride a bike instead of riding in a car. And you could turn off the lights when you leave a room.

When you *reuse* something, you use it again. You can take a reusable bag to the grocery store. And you can use a refillable water bottle.

When you *recycle* something, it is made into a new product. Glass, aluminum cans, paper, plastic bottles, and yard waste can all be recycled. Even the oil from cars can be recycled!

Recycling keeps billions of pounds of material from being thrown in the trash.

WE RECYCLE

Recycle

Glass can be recycled. After glass is recycled, it can be used again.

Beyond the Book

Using a computer to collect information can help you make informed choices in ways to use and conserve natural resources. Research ways people recycle or reuse materials. List examples you can use at home or in your classroom.

The bottle is crushed then combined with more crushed glass. It is then heated to make it easy to form into new shapes.

When glass is recycled, it may not be used for the same purpose. Some of the glass in this vase came from the blue bottle.

Do the Math!
Solve a Story Problem

Akeem uses 9 sheets of paper each day. To reduce, he decides to use each sheet of paper 3 times instead of 1 time. How many sheets of paper will he use each day now? _____

Sum It Up!

When you're done, use the answer key to check and revise your work.

Change the circled part of each statement to make it correct.

1 Renewable resources are natural resources that (will run out.)

_____

2

(Gemstone fuels,) such as oil, must be conserved.

_____

3 Coal is a (renewable resource) that can be burned to produce the electricity that computers use for energy.

_____

4

Car exhaust and smoke from factories cause (land pollution.)

_____

5 By melting down aluminum cans, we can (reduce) them to make new aluminum products.

_____

314

Name _____

Word Play

1 Use the words in the box to complete the puzzle.

Across

1. When you _____ something, it is broken down and made into something new.

8. You can _____ everyday items like grocery bags to prevent them from polluting the land.

9. Things that are useful to humans and come from nature are called _____.

Down

2. The practice of saving resources by using them wisely is called _____.

3. Introducing harmful materials into the environment causes _____.

4. Energy resources that were formed from the remains of organisms that lived long ago are called _____.

5. Natural resources that cannot be reused or renewed are called _____ resources.

6. Natural resources that can be replaced easily are called _____ resources.

7. In order to help conserve fossil fuels, _____ your use of them.

natural resources*	renewable*	nonrenewable*	fossil fuels*	**reduce**
conservation*	**reuse**	pollution*	**recycle**	

* Key Lesson Vocabulary

Apply Concepts

2   Circle the renewable resources. Mark an X on the nonrenewable resources.

solar energy

vegetables

wood

wind energy

natural gas

oil

3   Identify each situation as an example of reducing, reusing, or recycling.

1. Jake uses a plastic grocery bag to pick up trash. _____

2. Aluminum soda cans are melted down to make other aluminum cans.

    _____

3. Rei walks to school instead of riding in a car. _____

4. Terry uses old gift wrap to wrap a birthday present. _____

Take It Home!

Share with your family what you have learned about resources. With a family member, find examples of resources that you have seen or that you use at home.

TEKS 3.1B make informed choices in the use and conservation of natural resources by recycling or reusing materials such as paper, aluminum cans, and plastics **3.2C** construct ...bar graphs using tools... to organize, examine, and evaluate measured data **3.7D** explore...how resrouces may be conserved

Name _____

Essential Question

How Can We Conserve Resources?

Set a Purpose
What will you learn in this activity?

_____

_____

Think About the Procedure
Why are you asked to collect all the paper you would usually throw away?

_____

_____

Why do you think you should weigh the paper for this activity?

_____

_____

_____

_____

Record Your Data
Record the weight of the paper collected each day for three weeks.

	Week 1	Week 2	Week 3
M			
T			
W			
Th			
F			
Total			

Construct a bar graph to organize the total weight of paper for each week.

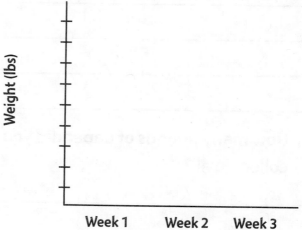

Weight (lbs)

Week 1   Week 2   Week 3

Draw Conclusions

How did the amount of paper you collected change each week? Why?

_____

_____

_____

_____

Analyze and Extend

1. How did collecting data help you learn about making choices in how to conserve paper?

_____

_____

_____

_____

2. What are some ways to reuse different types of paper so it doesn't end up in the garbage?

_____

_____

_____

_____

3. How many pounds of paper did you collect in all?

_____

4. What are some informed choices you can make in the use and conservation of natural resources? Develop a plan to reuse and recycle materials in your school. Write your plan below.

_____

_____

_____

_____

_____

5. Think of another question you would like to answer about recycling paper.

_____

_____

_____

6. **REVIEW** How did the bar graph you constructed using current technology help you examine the data?

_____

7. **REVIEW** How did the bar graph you constructed using current technology allow you to evaluate data?

_____

TEKS 3.7A explore and record how soils are formed by weathering of rock and the decomposition of plant and animal remains

Essential Question
What Is Soil?

🧠 Engage Your Brain!

Find the answer to the following question in this lesson and record it here.

Why is soil important to these peach trees and to people?

_____

_____

_____

Active Reading

Lesson Vocabulary
List the terms. As you learn about each one, make notes in the Interactive Glossary.

_____ _____

_____ _____

_____ _____

Compare and Contrast
Many ideas in this lesson are connected because they explain comparisons and contrasts—how things are alike and different. Active readers stay focused on comparisons and contrasts when they ask themselves, How are things alike? How are they different?

Soil Is Not Just Dirt

Soil is important. Why? Most plants need soil to grow. Without plants, there would be no food for animals or people.

Active Reading As you read these two pages, draw a star next to what you think is the most important sentence. Be ready to explain why you think so.

When you are in a forest or garden, or even a parking lot, what is under your feet? Below the sticks, rocks, plants, and pavement, there is soil. If you were to explore the soil in your back yard, you could find clues to how soil forms! **Soil** is a mixture of water, air, tiny pieces of rock, and humus. **Humus** is a rich mixture of the decomposed, or broken down, remains of plants and animals.

There are many kinds of soil. Soil can be black, red, brown, gray, and even white. Soil can be moist or dry. It can contain different kinds of minerals—even gold!

Explore how soil forms by drawing in the parts that make up a soil mixture.

Some kinds of soil are better for growing plants than other kinds. Soil that is very good for plants is *fertile*. It can take hundreds or even thousands of years to form. Because soil is such an important natural resource, it must be conserved.

The dead leaves on this forest floor will decompose and become part of the soil.

Farmers must take care of the soil so it will remain fertile.

Soil Is a Natural Resource

Why is soil important to people and animals?

_____

_____

_____

_____

_____

How Does Soil Form?

If you dig deep into the soil, you can explore how soil is formed.

Active Reading As you read these two pages, draw one line under a cause. Draw two lines under the effect.

The top layer of soil is called *topsoil*. It is the most fertile soil layer. Plants grow in the topsoil. Topsoil is fertile because it contains humus. Humus makes the soil darker.

The layer beneath topsoil is called *subsoil*. Subsoil does not have a lot of humus, but it does have small pieces of rock. If you dig deep enough into the soil, you will reach solid rock. This is *bedrock*.

How does soil form? It forms from bedrock. When bedrock is at Earth's surface, it breaks down by weathering. Rain, wind, and other things weather bedrock, so big pieces of rock get smaller and smaller. Eventually, bedrock is broken into small bits of rock. These mix with air, water, and humus to form soil.

Soil Layers

Bedrock is solid rock. The small pieces of rock in the upper layers of soil come from bedrock.

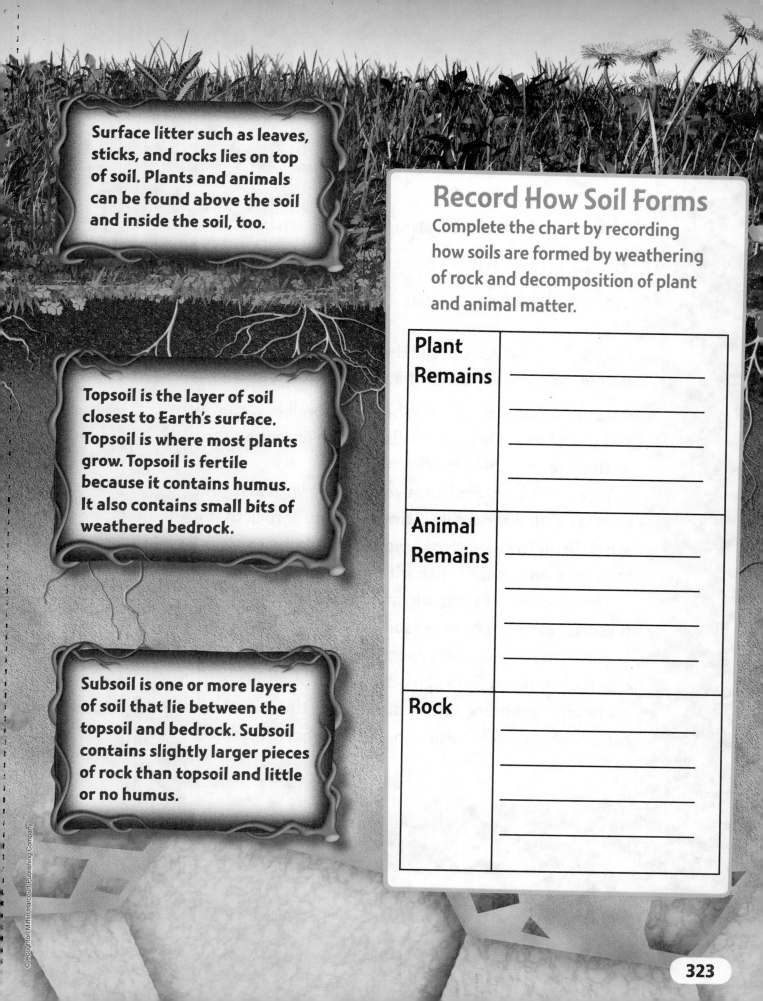

Surface litter such as leaves, sticks, and rocks lies on top of soil. Plants and animals can be found above the soil and inside the soil, too.

Topsoil is the layer of soil closest to Earth's surface. Topsoil is where most plants grow. Topsoil is fertile because it contains humus. It also contains small bits of weathered bedrock.

Subsoil is one or more layers of soil that lie between the topsoil and bedrock. Subsoil contains slightly larger pieces of rock than topsoil and little or no humus.

Record How Soil Forms

Complete the chart by recording how soils are formed by weathering of rock and decomposition of plant and animal matter.

Plant Remains	_____
	_____
	_____
	_____
Animal Remains	_____
	_____
	_____
	_____
Rock	_____
	_____
	_____
	_____

Types of Soil

There are more than 70,000 kinds of soil in the United States alone! What makes them different from one another?

Active Reading As you read these two pages, draw boxes around the names of things that are being contrasted.

As you know, soil contains humus as well as water, air, and bits of rock. One way to distinguish among soils is by the sizes of their particles.

Tiny particles of rock that you can see with just your eyes are called **sand**. **Silt** is tiny particles of rock that are difficult to see with only your eyes. Particles of rock that are even smaller than silt are called **clay**.

The amounts of sand, silt, and clay in soil give it texture. Texture is how the soil feels in your hands. Soil with more sand feels rough, while soil with more clay feels smooth. Soils can be made up of different minerals, depending on the area where the soils formed. A soil's color also depends on where it formed.

Most soils contain all three kinds of soil particles.

© Houghton Mifflin Harcourt Publishing Company (bg) ©Photodisc/Getty Images

Soils that contain a lot of clay particles are fertile but heavy and sticky. They hold moisture well. They get very cold in winter, but dry out and get hard in the summer.

Sandy soils let water pass through easily. They dry out quickly. Sandy soils are usually light and easy to dig.

Soils that are mostly silt feel slippery when they are wet. They hold moisture for a long time. They also hold nutrients very well.

▶ Why does water pass through sandy soils more quickly than through soils that contain mostly clay or silt?

_____

_____

Plants Need Soil

What do plants get from soil? They get nutrients, water, and a place to live.

Active Reading As you read these two pages, find and underline the definition of *nutrients*.

Plants need water and light to grow. They also need nutrients. **Nutrients** are substances that plants take in from the soil through their roots to help them live and grow.

The best kind of soil for most plants is called *loam*. Loam has a balance of silt, sand, and clay. It is rich in nutrients and humus, it stays moist, and it is easy to dig. Some plants, though, grow better in other types of soil.

Plants take in nutrients and water from the soil through their roots.

326

Cabbage grows well in clay soils.

Sea grapes and sea oats grow on sandy beaches.

Which Soil Matches the Plant?

Look at the images above. What can you conclude about the soil requirements of these plants?

_____

_____

_____

In which of these soils do most types of cactus grow? What does this tell you about cactuses?

_____

_____

Composting

Don't throw away that banana peel! You can use fruit peels and other kitchen scraps to help plants grow.

Active Reading As you read these two pages, find and underline two facts about compost.

Compost is humus that you make yourself. Pile plant parts, such as dried leaves and grass, into a big container. Then add scraps of fruits and vegetables. Tiny organisms too small to see will decompose the scraps to make humus. Spread compost on your plants so they will grow quickly and stay healthy.

Compost does more than help plants in your garden. Making compost means that you don't throw away as much garbage. When people throw away less garbage, that's good for everyone!

Add things like eggshells, peelings, and fruits and vegetables to compost. You can even add newspaper. Don't add animal products such as meat and cheese.

Do the Math!
Use Subtraction

It can take 850 years for 2 cm of soil to form. It can take 6 months to make 2 cm of compost for your garden. How much longer does it take soil to form than it does to make compost?

_____

_____

Sum It Up!

When you're done, use the answer key to check and revise your work.

The blue words in each summary statement are incorrect. Write words to replace the blue parts.

1 Compost is material that helps plants grow because it is contains a lot of clay.

_____

2 Soil is made quickly in nature.

_____

3 Plants need soil for support and light.

_____

4 Weathering causes humus below the soil to break into smaller pieces.

_____

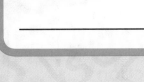

5 Silty soil contains the largest particles of rock.

_____

6 Topsoil is so important to plant growth around the world that people do not need to conserve it.

_____

Answer Key: 1. humus 2. slowly 3. nutrients 4. bedrock 5. Sandy 6. must

Brain Check

Name _____

Word Play

1 Use the words in the box to complete the puzzle.

soil*	humus*	sand*	silt*	clay*	nutrients*
bedrock	loam	compost	plants		*Key Lesson Vocabulary

Across

1. The type of soil that drains water most quickly _____

3. Living things that need soil for support _____

5. The type of soil that holds water for the longest time _____

6. The type of soil that has tiny particles of rock bigger than clay but smaller than sand _____

7. This is weathered by wind and water to make soil. _____

8. Something found in soil that is made of dead plants and animals _____

Down

1. This provides plants with the water and nutrients they need to survive. _____

2. This is the best kind of soil for plants. It is made of the three soil types. _____

4. Substances in soil that plants need to grow _____

5. Can be made using kitchen scraps and dead plants _____

331

Apply Concepts

2 Answer the questions about the picture.

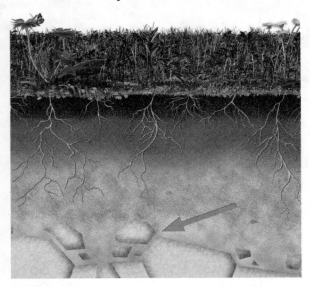

Explain why you can see darker soil toward the top of the soil layers.

_____

_____

_____

_____

What is happening where the red arrow is pointing?

_____

_____

3 Fill in the blanks to make the statements true.

When bedrock breaks down for a long time and mixes with air, water, and the decomposed remains of _____ , soil is formed. Soil is a resource because plants need it to _____ , and we depend on plants for our _____ . Soil supports plants and gives them the _____ they need to grow.

Take It Home!

With an adult, look at the soil in your yard or at a park. Which type of soil is it? Is it a mixture? Write down your observations and share them with the class.

Careers in Science

Ask a Geologist

A geologist might use a Geiger counter in exploring for minerals such as uranium.

Q. What is a geologist?

A. A geologist is a scientist who studies the solid earth and the matter it is made from.

Q. Can geologists specialize in a particular area?

A. Yes. Many geologists specialize in finding and studying natural resources such as oil, metals, water, rocks, minerals, and soil. Others work to understand processes connected to earthquakes, landslides, and floods.

Q. How do geologists study soil?

A. Geologists study soil properties. They may test the soil in an area to see if it contains the minerals and nutrients needed to support plant growth.

Q. How could a geologist be of help to farmers?

A. A geologist could help farmers decide which crops would grow best on their land and which fertilizer to use.

333

Now You Be the Geologist

Imagine you are a geologist who works with soil. Use the information you just read to answer the questions.

▶ Why do you study soil?

_____

_____

_____

▶ How does your work help farmers?

_____

_____

_____

▶ What do other geologists do?

_____

_____

_____

▶ Why would builders work with a geologist before they began construction of a large building?

_____

_____

TEKS 3.1B make informed choices in the use and conservation of natural resources by recycling or reusing materials such as paper, aluminum cans, and plastics

S.T.E.M.
Engineering & Technology

Technology at Work:
Problems and Fixes

In the past, many soft drinks came in glass bottles. Today, most soft drinks come in aluminum cans. Aluminum cans are lighter than glass and do not break. But aluminum is a nonrenewable resource. Recycling technology helps solve this problem.

From a recycling bin, used cans go to recycling centers.

Machines crush the cans. The flat cans form blocks of aluminum.

The blocks are melted and rolled into thin sheets. Then the aluminum is made into new cans and other items. Aluminum can be recycled over and over.

How does recycling help solve problems caused by using aluminum cans?

_____

_____

_____

Solve a Problem

Technology can solve problems. It can also cause problems. Today, millions of products are made from plastic, including water bottles, pens, toys, and bags. But plastic is made from fossil fuels, which are nonrenewable resources. Also, plastic does not break down easily.

Cars help people get around. But they cause air pollution.

Think of a product you use that is made from plastic. Draw your product below.

What problem does your product cause? How can technology help solve this problem?

_____

_____

_____

Build On It!

 Rise to the engineering design challenge — complete **Redesign It: Reduce Packaging** on the Inquiry Flipchart.

Vocabulary Review

Use the terms in the box to complete the sentences.

conservation
humus
nutrients
pollution
soil

TEKS 3.7A

1. A part of soil with a rich mixture of decomposing plants and animals is _____.

TEKS 3.7D

2. Turning off lights and recycling are examples of _____.

TEKS 3.7A

3. A mixture of minerals, air, water, and humus is _____.

TEKS 3.9C

4. Garbage on the land and chemicals in the air are types of _____ that can make organisms perish or move to new locations.

TEKS 3.7A

5. The _____ that plants need to grow often come from weathered rock in soil.

Science Concepts

Fill in the letter of the choice that best answers the question.

TEKS 3.7D

6. Using renewable resources is one way to conserve resources. Which source of energy is a renewable resource?

   Ⓐ coal   Ⓒ oil

   Ⓑ natural gas   Ⓓ wind

TEKS 3.7A

7. Hector wants to put some soil in a pot that will drain water quickly. Which should he use?

   Ⓐ clay   Ⓒ sand

   Ⓑ humus   Ⓓ silt

TEKS 3.1B, 3.7D

8. Aklil wants to make informed choices in the use of natural resources by reducing the resources she uses. How can she conserve resources?

   (A) place her empty cereal box in the recycling bin

   (B) place her lunch in a reusable box instead of a paper bag

   (C) plant a tree to replace the tree used for firewood

   (D) take old leaves to the dump

TEKS 3.2D, 3.7D

9. The graph below shows the percentage of aluminum cans that are recycled.

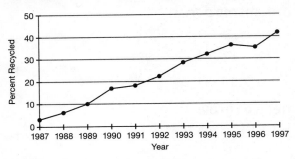

   Which **best** explains the data in the line graph?

   (A) The number of recycling bins is increasing.

   (B) The number of cans being used is increasing.

   (C) The percentage of cans recycled is increasing.

   (D) The number of people recycling cans is increasing.

TEKS 3.7A

10. Tyrone wants to make sure his soil mostly consists of clay particles. What should he look for?

   (A) The soil will dry out quickly.

   (B) The soil will be heavy and sticky.

   (C) The soil will feel grainy and rough.

   (D) The soil will have small particles that he can see.

TEKS 3.1B

11. Which is an example of reusing?

   (A) carpooling to soccer practice

   (B) turning off lights when not in use

   (C) taking cloth bags to the grocery store to carry groceries back home

   (D) putting a plastic bottle in the recycling bin

TEKS 3.1B, 3.7D

12. Abbey and her family collected newspapers in the bin below.

   Which word **best** describes what they are doing?

   (A) nutrients

   (B) pollution

   (C) recycling

   (D) renewing

TEKS 3.7D

13. Which characteristic of cotton makes it a useful natural resource for clothing material?

(A) It is hard and light.

(B) It is soft and light.

(C) It is soft and heavy.

(D) It is hard and heavy.

TEKS 3.7A

14. Giorgio is exploring how soils are formed from weathered rock. He recorded his findings and made the soil model below.

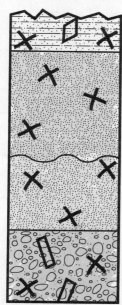

Which layer is made mainly of rock that has not been weathered?

(A) the top layer

(B) the second layer

(C) the third layer

(D) the bottom layer

TEKS 3.7D

15. An electrical cord is a product that you can buy. Which natural resource is found inside an electrical cord because of its useful characteristics?

(A) plastic because it will not melt when heated

(B) wood because it helps the computer cord keep its shape

(C) copper because electricity moves very well through this resource

(D) glass because it is a renewable resource that does not cause pollution

TEKS 3.1B

16. Look at the picture below.

Landfills often have aluminum cans and paper in them. What informed choice in the use of natural resources could someone make to reduce the amount of garbage in landfills?

(A) Shred paper before throwing it away.

(B) Recycle aluminum cans and paper.

(C) Crush aluminum cans to make them smaller.

(D) Place paper and aluminum cans in a larger garbage can.

Apply Inquiry and Review the Big Idea

Write the answers to these questions.

TEKS 3.7A, 3.2F

17. Look at the drawing below.

What process is shown in this drawing? How can soil form from this process?

_____

_____

_____

TEKS 3.7A

18. Two students investigate how dead plants and animals affect the soil. They record the results of their investigation. What do they record?

_____

_____

_____

TEKS 3.1B, 3.2D

19. Ami's family puts about 4 pounds of material in the trash each day. The family wants to recycle and reuse 1/2 of the materials they now throw away. How much less trash would they throw away each week?

_____

_____

Water and Weather

© Houghton Mifflin Harcourt Publishing Company

© Emanuele Taroni/Getty Images; (inset) © Nordicphotos/Alamy Images; (corda) © NDisc/Age Fotostock

Big Idea

Water is important to all living things in many different ways. The sun is the source of energy for the water cycle and weather.

 3.2A, 3.2B, 3.2C, 3.2F, 3.3D, 3.4A, 3.8A, 3.8B

I Wonder Why

Why does a frozen waterfall start to flow once the sun comes out? *Turn the page to find out.*

Here's why The frozen waterfall will flow when the sun comes out. This is because the sun's energy adds heat to the ice. The ice changes its state from a solid to a liquid. Liquid water will flow.

In this unit, you will explore the Big Idea, the Essential Questions, and the Investigations on the Inquiry Flipchart.

Levels of Inquiry Key ■ DIRECTED ■ GUIDED ■ INDEPENDENT

Big Idea Water is important to all living things in many different ways. The sun is the source of energy for the water cycle and weather.

Essential Questions

Lesson 1 What Is the Water Cycle? 343
Inquiry Flipchart p. 45—Weather in a Box/A Salty Change!

Careers in Science: Hydrologist 355

Lesson 2 What Is Weather? 357
Inquiry Flipchart p. 46—Measuring Wind Speed/Check the Weather

Inquiry Lesson 3 How Can We Measure Weather? 369
Inquiry Flipchart p. 47—How Can We Measure Weather?

S.T.E.M. Engineering & Technology: Keeping Dry:
Raincoat vs. Poncho 371
Inquiry Flipchart p. 48—Design It: Build a Wind Streamer

Unit 8 Review 373

Now I Get the Big Idea!

Science Notebook

Before you begin each lesson, be sure to write your thoughts about the Essential Question.

States of Water

Water vapor

Air is a mixture of gases. One of these gases is water vapor. You can't see water vapor. The space between the clouds has water vapor in it.

Liquid water

Liquid water fills the ocean, lakes, and streams. Clouds are made of small droplets of liquid water. Fog, mist, and falling rain are also liquid water.

Ice

This glacier is an example of ice, Earth's solid water. Glaciers cover land that is close to the North Pole and the South Pole. They also cover some mountains.

Where Is the Water?

1. Where can you find water vapor in nature?

   _____

2. Where can you find liquid water in nature?

   _____

   _____

3. Where can you find solid water in nature?

   _____

Changing States

Water changes state. For example, liquid water can change to ice and to water vapor. What causes water to change state?

Find sentences that contrast two things. Draw a line under each sentence.

Water changes state when it is heated or cooled. When enough heat is added to ice, it becomes liquid water. This change of state is called *melting*. The reverse of melting is *freezing*.

When liquid water gains enough heat, it evaporates to become water vapor. **Evaporation** is the change of state from a liquid to a gas.

When water vapor loses enough heat, it changes back to liquid water. The change of state from a gas to a liquid is called **condensation**. Condensation and evaporation are opposite processes.

For water vapor to condense, it needs something to condense on. Even the drops of water in clouds have condensed on tiny pieces of dust.

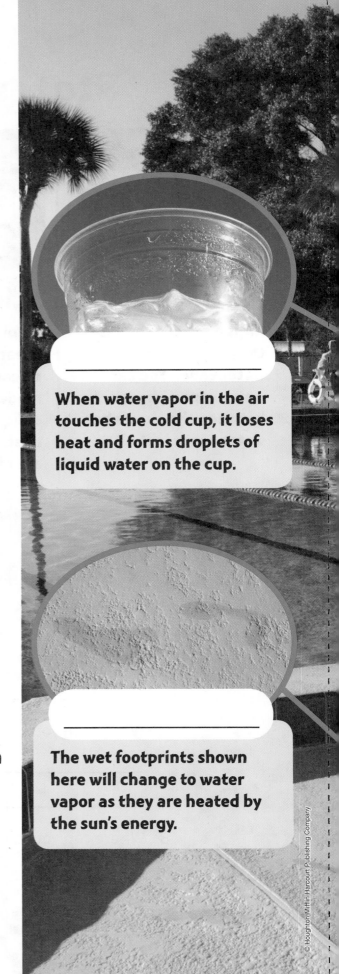

When water vapor in the air touches the cold cup, it loses heat and forms droplets of liquid water on the cup.

The wet footprints shown here will change to water vapor as they are heated by the sun's energy.

Finding Evaporation and Condensation

Look at the photos on these pages. Label the photos as either condensation or evaporation.

_____

After a cool night, you may wake up to find water droplets called dew covering the grass. This happens when water vapor in the air that is directly above the cool ground forms water droplets on the grass.

The Water Cycle

Water is always moving. In fact, water moves continuously from Earth's surface to the atmosphere and back to Earth.

Active Reading A cause tells why something happens. Draw one line under each cause.

The sun heats the ocean. This causes water to evaporate and become water vapor. The water vapor mixes with other gases and moves high up in the air.

As the water vapor rises, it cools. If it loses enough heat energy, it condenses to form water droplets in clouds. This water can fall back to Earth as **precipitation**. Precipitation can be rain, sleet, snow, or hail. The type of precipitation that falls depends on the temperature of the air around it.

After water falls, it moves across land. Some water flows underground. This is *groundwater*. Groundwater and surface water flow back to the ocean. More water in the ocean is heated and evaporates again. This never-ending movement of water between Earth's surface and the air is called the **water cycle**.

The sun's energy warms the surface of the ocean or other bodies of water. Some of the water evaporates and enters the air as water vapor.

As water vapor rises and cools, it condenses to form clouds. The tiny water droplets in the clouds bump into each other to make larger droplets.

When the droplets become too heavy to stay up in the air, they fall to Earth as precipitation.

Some precipitation soaks into the ground. Precipitation can also run over the ground and flow into streams, rivers, lakes, and eventually the ocean.

The Sun and the Water Cycle

What role does the sun play in the water cycle?

_____

_____

_____

_____

Sum It Up!

Complete the graphic organizer using details from the summary below.

Water is matter. It can exist as a solid, a liquid, or a gas. When water is a solid, it is called ice. When water is a liquid, it is called water. When water is a gas, it is called water vapor.

Water changes state when it warms or cools. For example, when heat is added to ice, ice changes state to become liquid water. If even more heat is added, liquid water becomes water vapor.

Main Idea
Water can exist in three states: solid, liquid, and gas.

1 Detail: _____

_____

_____

2 Detail: _____

_____

_____

3 Detail: _____

_____

_____

_____

Word Play

1 Unscramble each word and write it in the boxes.

1. TASL TAWRE
   Clue: Earth is mostly covered with this

   ☐☐☐☐ ☐☐◯☐◯☐

2. NOCENDASNOIT
   Clue: When water vapor becomes liquid

   ☐◯☐☐☐☐◯☐◯☐☐

3. ARTEW AVOPR
   Clue: What evaporating water becomes

   ☐☐☐◯☐ ☐☐☐◯☐

4. TEARW EYCCL
   Clue: The movement of water from ocean to land and back

   ☐◯☐☐☐ ☐☐☐◯◯

5. CIPERPNOITITA
   Clue: Water that falls from the sky

   ◯☐☐◯☐☐☐☐☐☐◯☐☐

6. EHSFR REAWT
   Clue: Found in rivers and lakes

   ☐◯☐☐☐ ☐☐◯☐☐

7. TERWADNGROU
   Clue: What flows underground

   ◯☐◯☐☐☐☐☐☐☐☐

Write the letters in the circles on the lines below. Unscramble them to form two more words.

_____

_____

8. Clue: One form of frozen water at the South Pole

   ☐☐☐☐☐☐

9. Clue: When liquid water becomes water vapor

   ☐☐☐☐☐☐☐☐☐☐

Apply Concepts

2 Look at the picture of the water cycle. Add labels to show three processes that are part of the water cycle. Label the salt water and the fresh water.

2. _____

1. _____

3. _____

5. _____

4. _____

3 What gives water the energy it needs to move around the world in the water cycle?

_____

Take It Home!

Share what you have learned about the water cycle with your family. With a family member, look around for places where processes from the water cycle are taking place.

TEKS **3.3D** connect grade-level appropriate science concepts with the history of science, science careers, and contributions of scientists

Careers in Science

6 Things You Should Know About Hydrologists

1 Hydrologists study the quality and movement of water on Earth.

2 They care about and protect the water in rivers, streams, and oceans.

3 Hydrologists test water to make sure it is safe to drink or swim in.

4 They help cities and farms get the amount of water they need.

5 They also help prevent problems from floods and droughts.

6 Hydrologists help design dams to make electricity and sewers to drain water.

Be a Hydrologist!

Answer these five questions about hydrologists.

1 What do hydrologists study?

_____

_____

_____

_____

2 Why do hydrologists test our drinking water?

_____

_____

_____

_____

3 How do hydrologists help farmers?

_____

_____

_____

4 How do hydrologists help cities?

_____

_____

_____

_____

5 Write and answer your own question about hydrologists.

_____

_____

_____

_____

TEKS 3.2B collect data by observing and measuring using the metric system... 3.2F communicate valid conclusions supported by data...by drawing pictures... 3.4A collect, record, and analyze information... 3.8A observe, measure, record, and compare day-to-day weather changes in different locations at the same time that include air temperature, wind direction...

Essential Question

What Is Weather?

Engage Your Brain!

Find the answer to the following question in this lesson and record it here.

How could the weather in this city be measured?

_____

_____

_____

_____

_____

Active Reading

Lesson Vocabulary

List the terms. As you learn about each one, make notes in the Interactive Glossary.

_____ _____

_____ _____

Using Headings

Active readers preview headings and use them to pose questions that establish purposes for reading. Reading with a purpose helps active readers focus on understanding and recalling what they read in order to fulfill the purpose.

A World of Weather

The sun's energy causes the water cycle. It also affects the weather. As the sun heats Earth, temperatures change. Changing temperatures mean changing weather!

Active Reading As you read these two pages, underline lesson vocabulary each time it is used.

Earth is surrounded by a layer of gases. This layer of gases is Earth's **atmosphere**. **Oxygen** is one of the gases in Earth's atmosphere. Most living things need oxygen to survive. Water vapor is another type of gas in Earth's atmosphere.

Conditions in the atmosphere can change. **Weather** is the condition of the atmosphere at any one place and time. If the atmosphere over your school is warm and dry in the morning, your weather is warm and dry. But the atmosphere, and your weather, could change. The weather could be cool and rainy by the afternoon.

This cloud is a *cumulonimbus* [kyoo•myuh•loh•NIM•buhs] cloud. These clouds are often tall and have a flat top. They sometimes look like mushrooms and often produce thunderstorms.

Types of Clouds

There are many types of clouds. Each type of cloud has a different shape. The type of clouds in the sky can tell you what kind of weather may be coming.

Cirrus [SIR•uhs] clouds are thin and feathery. Cirrus clouds form high up in the atmosphere, where temperatures are cold. They are often a sign that the weather is about to change.

Cumulus [KYOO•myuh•luhs] clouds have flat bottoms and are puffy on top. They look like piles of cotton. Cumulus clouds usually mean fair weather, but they can develop into cumulonimbus clouds.

Stratus clouds look like thin blankets. Often, they hang low in the atmosphere. Stratus clouds can mean that light rain or snow is coming.

▶ Suppose the weather is fair. Use that data to tell which kinds of clouds might be in the sky. Draw a picture and label it to communicate your conclusion.

Measuring Weather

It's okay to say, "It's cold and rainy outside." But when we need to know exactly what the weather is, we must measure it.

Active Reading As you read this page, turn the heading into a question in your mind and circle sentences that answer the question.

Temperature is a measure of how hot or cold something is. The tool we use to measure temperature is a *thermometer*. Air temperature is measured in degrees Celsius (°C) or degrees Fahrenheit (°F).

The temperature of the atmosphere affects the kind of precipitation that falls. Above 0 °C, rain is likely. Below 0 °C, the air is so cold that rain, sleet, or snow may fall.

Sometimes it rains so much that it's hard to see anything. A *rain gauge* is a tool that collects rain and shows how much has fallen.

If the wind is blowing, we can tell the direction it's coming from with a *wind vane*. A *wind meter* tells how fast the wind is blowing.

Thermometer

A thermometer is a tube filled with a liquid. When the air gets hotter, the liquid moves up the tube. When the air gets cooler, the liquid moves down the tube. To find the temperature, read the number next to the top of the liquid.

_____

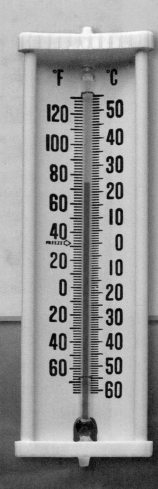

Rain gauge

A rain gauge measures rainfall. How do you read a rain gauge? Look at the water in the gauge. Read the number where the water lines up with the scale. Rain can be measured in centimeters or inches. A rain gauge is emptied after each use to measure more rainfall.

Wind vane

A wind vane shows the way the wind is blowing. The bird below looks in the direction the wind is coming from. The wind can come from the east, west, north, south, or somewhere in between.

Wind meter

A wind meter measures how fast the wind blows.

▶ Use the tools to collect information by measuring and observing. Record the weather data on the lines provided.

Do the Math!

Solve a Word Problem

At 9:00 a.m., the air temperature was 18 °C. By 4:00 p.m., it had risen to 32 °C. How much warmer was it at 4:00 p.m. than at 9:00 a.m.?

Being Ready For Weather

Weather affects us in many ways. We have to consider weather when we choose what to wear, what items to use, and where to go.

To stay safe and comfortable, we wear clothing that's right for the weather. When it's raining, we stay dry with a raincoat, boots, and umbrella.

The weather also affects the activities we can do. We can swim when it's warm. We can ski only when it's cold enough for snow.

To help us, scientists try to predict the weather. When we know what kind of weather is coming, we can make plans to dress right, and we can choose the right kinds of activities.

This child is wearing the right clothes and using an umbrella to stay safe and comfortable in the rain.

This child is using the right items to stay safe and comfortable during a hot, sunny day at the beach.

What to Wear

Look at each item. In what type of weather do you need each of these? How does each item protect you from the weather?

winter hat

sunglasses

Watch Out For Weather!

    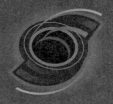

Weather can be severe and even dangerous. Hurricanes, thunderstorms, tornadoes, and blizzards are examples of severe weather.

Active Reading As you read this page, find and underline examples of severe weather.

A *hurricane* is a tropical storm with winds of 119 kilometers (74 miles) per hour or more. Hurricanes form over warm ocean water. They become slow, large storms soon after they reach land. Hurricanes can blow trees over and cause large areas of flooding.

Thunderstorms are strong storms that have thunder and lightning. Often there is heavy rain and strong wind, too.

Tornadoes are small, spinning columns of very strong wind.

A *blizzard* is a snowstorm with strong wind and a very low temperature.

To be safe in severe weather, follow directions from a teacher, parent, or other adult who knows what to do.

Tornado

Tornadoes are most common in states, such as Texas and Kansas, where there are large plains. Tornado winds are so strong that they can rip a tree out of the ground and move a car through the air.

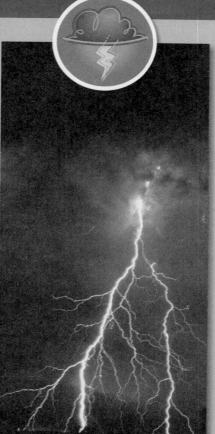

Blizzard

During blizzards, the snow blows so fast it is hard to see through. Being out in a blizzard is cold and dangerous!

Thunderstorm

Lightning is a flash of electricity that happens during a thunderstorm. Lightning can kill people. Always stay indoors during a thunderstorm.

Hurricane

Since hurricanes form over warm ocean waters, they lose power quickly when they move over land. But hurricanes can still do a lot of damage when they reach land.

Staying Safe In Severe Weather

Sara thinks that thunderstorms are exciting. She wants to go outside during one. Sara asks her mother to go with her. What should Sara's mother tell her?

_____

_____

_____

Sum It Up!

When you're done, use the answer key to check and revise your work.

Write the vocabulary term that matches each photo and caption.

1 This tool is used to measure how much rain has fallen.

_____

2 This tool is used to measure the direction of wind.

_____

3 This tool is used to measure the temperature of the air.

_____

Summarize

Fill in the missing words to tell about weather.

You can recognize clouds by their (4) _____. (5) _____ clouds

are thin and wispy. Clouds that look like thin blankets are

(6) _____ clouds. The clouds that look like piles of cotton are

(7) _____ clouds. Each different type of cloud means a different type

of weather is coming. Stratus clouds usually mean that light (8) _____

or snow is coming. If you see a cumulus cloud, you know that (9) _____

weather is coming. Some weather can be severe. (10) _____ form over

ocean water. Strong winds and lots of snow occur during a (11) _____.

Brain Check

Name _____

Word Play

1

Read the clues. Unscramble the words to complete the sentence.

1. You use a thermometer to measure air ___ ___ ___ ___ ___ ___ ___ ___ ___ ___ ___ .	etmrepatuer
2. The gases that surround Earth make up the ___ ___ ___ ___ ___ ___ ___ ___ ___ ___ .	hperesmoat
3. One type of gas in the atmosphere is ___ ___ ___ ___ ___ ___ .	negoyx
4. The condition of the atmosphere at one place and time is the ___ ___ ___ ___ ___ ___ .	rwehate
5. Fast wind that moves in a spiral is a ___ ___ ___ ___ ___ ___ ___ .	troanod
6. You measure wind direction with a ___ ___ ___ ___ ___ ___ ___ ___ ___ .	diwn vean

Apply Concepts

2 Draw yourself measuring the weather. Show the tool or tools that you use. Describe how to use each measuring tool that you draw.

_____

_____

_____

_____

_____

_____

_____

3 Label the pictures of severe weather. Draw a line from each label to the correct description of the severe weather.

_____ _____ _____

| Starts over the ocean; strong wind and rain | Thunder, lightning, and usually rain | Lots of snow and wind; very cold |

Take It Home!

Watch the weather forecast for the next week with an adult. Measure the week's weather. Discuss whether or not the forecast was correct.

TEKS **3.2C** construct...charts, and bar graphs using tools and current technology to organize, examine, and evaluate measured data **3.2D** ...interpret patterns in data to construct reasonable explanations based on evidence from investigations... **3.8A** observe, measure, record, and compare day-to-day weather changes in different locations at the same time that include air temperature, wind direction, and precipitation

Name _____

Essential Question

How Can We Measure Weather?

Set a Purpose
What will you learn during this investigation?

_____

_____

_____

_____

What might cause you to get an incorrect measurement?

_____

_____

_____

_____

_____

Think About the Procedure
Which tools measure air temperature, wind direction, and rainfall? What is a weather condition that is not measured by these instruments?

_____

_____

_____

_____

_____

_____

Record Your Data
Use the chart to record weather data for the first week. Construct a similar chart using current technology to organize, examine and evaluate your data for the remaining weeks.

	Temperature	Wind Direction	Amount of Rain
Monday			
Tuesday			
Wednesday			
Thursday			
Friday			

Draw Conclusions

Compare how the temperature, wind direction, and precipitation changed from day-to-day over the first week.

_____

_____

_____

_____

_____

Analyze and Extend

1. Compare your data to the data of another group of students. Are your data the same? If not, how do you account for the differences?

_____

_____

_____

_____

2. **REVIEW** Did you observe any patterns in your data? Interpret these patterns to make a weather prediction for the next two days.

_____

_____

_____

_____

3. How did analyzing all of your collected data help you make your weather prediction?

_____

_____

_____

_____

_____

4. How might you use a measurement of temperature, wind direction, or amount of rainfall?

_____

_____

_____

5. Think of other questions you would like to ask about measuring weather and making weather predictions.

_____

_____

_____

_____

S.T.E.M.

Engineering & Technology

Keeping Dry:
Raincoat vs. Poncho

Often, more than one design can meet the same need. Each design may have different features. Compare the features of the raincoat and poncho below.

A raincoat with snaps or buttons fits more closely around the body. It does not blow around in the wind.

The poncho is cut large. It fits easily over any clothes.

The material is lightweight. It folds into a small package. It is easy to carry around.

Buttons tighten the ends of sleeves. This keeps water from getting in.

Pockets help keep objects dry in the rain.

When is the raincoat a better choice? When is the poncho a better choice? Explain.

_____

_____

_____

Design a Better Product

Can you design a better way to stay dry? Answer the question by creating a design using parts of both the poncho and raincoat. Draw your design below.

Rain boots are other tools that help us stay dry.

Why is your product better than the raincoat or the poncho?

_____

_____

_____

Build On It!

Rise to the engineering design challenge—complete **Design It: Build a Wind Streamer** on the Inquiry Flipchart.

Vocabulary Review

Use the terms in the box to complete the sentences.

atmosphere
condensation
temperature
water cycle
weather

TEKS 3.8A

1. Cold, rainy, and windy are examples of different types of _____.

TEKS 3.8B

2. Water continually moves from Earth's surface to the air and back in a process called the _____.

TEKS 3.8A

3. When weather forecasters record the day-to-day temperature of the air around Earth, they are recording data about Earth's _____.

TEKS 3.5A

4. On a hot summer day, you can use a thermometer to measure the _____.

TEKS 3.8B

5. Water vapor changes into liquid water in the process of _____.

Science Concepts

Fill in the letter of the choice that best answers the question.

TEKS 3.8A

6. George and Bella live in different locations. They look out the window at the same time. George doesn't think it will rain. Bella thinks there will be a thunderstorm. Compare the kinds of clouds they see at their different locations.

Ⓐ George sees stratus clouds. Bella sees cirrus clouds.

Ⓑ George sees cumulus clouds. Bella sees stratus clouds.

Ⓒ George sees cirrus clouds. Bella sees cumulonimbus clouds.

Ⓓ George sees cumulonimbus clouds. Bella sees stratus clouds.

TEKS 3.8A

7. Jahi calls Rebecca and asks her what the weather is like. She says it is raining where she lives. He tells her it is snowing at his house. They both observed and recorded the temperature. Which temperatures could they have recorded?

Ⓐ 24 °C, 12 °C Ⓒ 18 °C, 10 °C

Ⓑ 28 °C, –9 °C Ⓓ 4 °C, 21 °C

TEKS 3.3D

8. Ms. Grady is a meteorologist. Which warning is she likely to give people to help them prepare for a thunderstorm?

Ⓐ stay inside a building, in a safe room away from windows

Ⓑ make sure indoor heating works

Ⓒ make sure their snowblowers work

Ⓓ use sheets to cover plants that might freeze

TEKS 3.4A

9. Antwan is analyzing the data he collected with a rain gauge over a one week period. Which is most likely to be his analysis?

Ⓐ The storm on Tuesday was moving from the east to the west.

Ⓑ The rain on Sunday lasted 23 minutes.

Ⓒ It rained more in the front yard than it did in the backyard on Sunday.

Ⓓ It rained 3 cm more on Tuesday than on Thursday.

TEKS 3.4A, 3.8A, 3.8B

10. It rained in the morning, leaving puddles in Camilla's driveway. An hour later, she noticed that the puddles in a sunny part of the driveway had dried up. The puddles in a shady part of the driveway were still there. The thermometers below show the temperatures in the two areas.

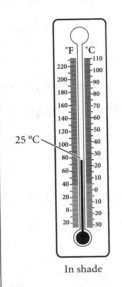 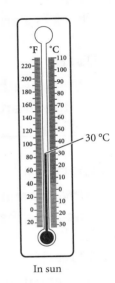

25 °C   30 °C

In shade   In sun

Compare the temperatures. Which conclusion can Camilla draw from her observations?

Ⓐ Puddles make temperatures fall.

Ⓑ Evaporation makes temperatures rise.

Ⓒ Heat from the sun makes water condense more quickly.

Ⓓ Heat from the sun makes water evaporate more quickly.

TEKS 3.8A

11. You and a friend observe, measure, and record the precipitation your cities get over three days in the table below.

Amount of Precipitation (cm)			
	Day 1	Day 2	Day 3
Dallas, TX	0	8	4
Denver, CO	3	2	6

Compare how much precipitation each city received.

Ⓐ Dallas received 1 cm more of total precipitation.

Ⓑ Dallas received 2 cm more of total precipitation.

Ⓒ Denver received 1 cm more of total precipitation.

Ⓓ Both cities received the same total amount of precipitation.

TEKS 3.8B

12. Mr. Rose's class is reviewing the sun's role in the water cycle.

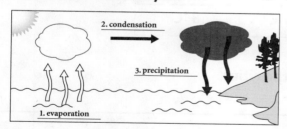

How would you describe the role of the sun in the picture above?

Ⓐ It heats the cool water.

Ⓑ It makes rain fall to the ground.

Ⓒ It cools water vapor in the air.

Ⓓ It makes water vapor form clouds.

TEKS 3.8A

13. Winds from the south usually mean warmer temperatures. Winds from the north usually mean cooler temperatures. You observe, measure, and record the data in the chart below.

Wind Direction				
	Day 1	Day 2	Day 3	Day 4
Casper, WY	From the north	From the north	No wind	From the south
Amarillo, TX	From the north	No wind	From the south	From the south

Compare the wind direction for both cities. On which day did the temperatures of both cities most likely increase?

Ⓐ Day 1   Ⓒ Day 3

Ⓑ Day 2   Ⓓ Day 4

TEKS 3.8A

14. It is an afternoon in November. At two different locations in the same town, the thermometer reads 2 °C. The wind meter measures wind speed at 35 km per hour. The rain gauge shows 2 cm of precipitation. Compare the weather outside at both locations.

Ⓐ cold with high winds and sunny

Ⓑ cold with little wind and sunny

Ⓒ cold with little wind and snowy

Ⓓ cold with high winds and rainy

Apply Inquiry and Review the Big Idea

Write the answers to these questions.

TEKS 3.8A

15. Below is the beginning of a five-day forecast for your home and your school.

Our Weather				
Monday	Tuesday	Wednesday	Thursday	Friday
we think	we think			

You know that cold weather is coming after Tuesday. Record the forecast for Wednesday. Explain why you predicted the weather that you did.

_____

_____

_____

TEKS 3.5A, 3.8A

The table shows day-to-day air temperatures for two Texas cities for three days. Use the table to answer questions 16 and 17.

Temperatures in Celsius			
	Monday	Tuesday	Wednesday
Corpus Christi	13 °C	11 °C	12 °C
Lubbock	5 °C	5 °C	8 °C

TEKS 3.5A, 3.8A

16. Find the average day-to-day temperatures for the cities.

_____

TEKS 3.5A, 3.8A

17. Compare the average day-to-day temperatures for the cities.

_____

Space

Big Idea

The position and motion of the sun, Earth, and the moon cause patterns that can be seen in nature as repeating cycles.

TEKS 3.3C, 3.3D, 3.8B, 3.8D

I Wonder Why

Why is it night on one side of Earth while it's day on the other? *Turn the page to find out.*

Here's why The Earth is always spinning around. As it turns, one part of Earth is in the sun's light while the other part of Earth is in a dark shadow.

In this unit, you will explore the Big Idea, the Essential Questions, and the Investigations on the Inquiry Flipchart.

Levels of Inquiry Key ■ DIRECTED   ■ GUIDED   ■ INDEPENDENT

Track Your Progress

Big Idea The position and motion of the sun, Earth, and the moon cause patterns that can be seen in nature as repeating cycles.

Essential Questions

Lesson 1 How Do Earth and the Moon Move? 379
Inquiry Flipchart p. 49—Tilted Earth/Darkness Falls

People in Science: Katherine Johnson and Amanda Nahm........393

Inquiry Lesson 2 How Can We Model the Moon's Phases?....................395
Inquiry Flipchart p. 50—How Can We Model the Moon's Phases?

Lesson 3 What Are the Sun and Stars?...............397
Inquiry Flipchart p. 51—Starry Lights/Let's Cook!

Lesson 4 What Are the Planets in Our Solar System?.........................409
Inquiry Flipchart p. 52—How Can We Model the Orbit of Comets and Planets?/Planet Map

Inquiry Lesson 5 How Can We Model the Sun and Planets?.......................423
Inquiry Flipchart p. 53—How Can We Model the Sun and Planets?

S.T.E.M. **Engineering & Technology: How It Works: Keck Observatory** 425
Inquiry Flipchart p. 54—Owner's Manual: Using a Telescope

Unit 9 Review 427

Now I Get the Big Idea!

Science Notebook

Before you begin each lesson, be sure to write your thoughts about the Essential Question.

TEKS **3.8C** construct models that demonstrate the relationship of the Sun, Earth, and Moon, including orbits and positions

Lesson **1**

Essential Question

How Do Earth and the Moon Move?

Engage Your Brain!

Find the answer to the following question in this lesson and record it here.

The ocean is reflecting light from the full moon. How is the moon acting on the ocean?

_____

Active Reading

Lesson Vocabulary

List the terms. As you learn about each one, make notes in the Interactive Glossary.

_____ _____

_____ _____

Sequence

Many ideas in this lesson are connected by a sequence, or order, that describes the steps in a process. Active readers stay focused on sequence when they mark the transition from one stage of an idea or step in a process to another.

Turning Through the Day

Look at your desk. Is it moving? It may not look like it, but everything in your classroom is moving—including you!

Looking at Earth from above the North Pole, we see that Earth turns in the opposite direction to a clock. As Earth turns, half of it gets light from the **Sun** sun, and half of it is in darkness. It is day on the lit half of Earth. It is night on the dark half of Earth. Day changes to night as Earth turns.

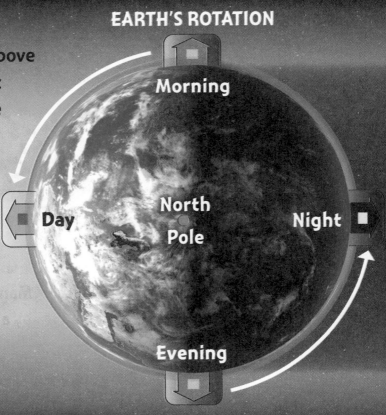

EARTH'S ROTATION

Morning

North Pole

Day

Night

Evening

Picture a line going through Earth from the North Pole to the South Pole. This imaginary line is Earth's **axis**.

Like a wheel on a bike, Earth rotates, or turns, on its axis. Earth's **rotation** [ro•TAY•shuhn] causes the cycle of day and night. One full rotation takes 24 hours, or one full day.

From one sunrise to the next, we spin through the parts of a day—morning, daytime, evening, and night. The day-night cycle happens over and over again. Think about the things you do in each part of this cycle. When do you wake up? Eat? Sleep? People follow a cycle, too!

What Time Is It?

Label each picture to show all four parts of the day-night cycle. Number the parts to show the correct sequence.

(1) morning

___ _____

___ _____

___ _____

Reasons for Seasons

Winter, spring, summer, fall. Like day and night, the seasons make a cycle.

spring

Active Reading As you read these two pages, find and underline the definition of *revolution*.

As Earth turns on its axis, it also moves around the sun. Each complete trip of Earth around the sun is one **revolution** [reh•vuh•Loo•shuhn]. Each revolution takes about 365 days, or one year.

The seasons change as Earth moves around the sun. The diagram shows that Earth is tilted on its axis. The part of Earth that points toward the sun gets more direct sunlight. The part that points away from the sun gets less. As Earth moves around the sun, the part that gets more direct sunlight changes. The part with the most direct sunlight has summer. The part with the least direct sunlight has winter. During fall and spring, neither the top nor the bottom half of Earth is tilted toward or away from the sun.

summer

Look at the image labeled *summer*. When the North Pole is pointing toward the sun, people who live north of the equator—in the Northern Hemisphere—have summer. Those in the Southern Hemisphere have winter.

summer

fall

winter

What Season Is It?
Label the images with the correct season.

Winter Days!

What is winter like for kids in the United States? That depends on where you live!

In Phoenix, Arizona, winter temperatures are usually in the 60s or 70s. In Portland, Oregon, they are usually in the 40s or 50s. But someone in Madison, Wisconsin, would be used to temperatures in the 20s or 30s!

In the Northeast, a big snowstorm can bring everything to a stop!

In the South, winter is usually sunny and warm. But even there, it may get cold at times!

In the Midwest, heavy snow, ice, sleet, and freezing rain are possible. Freezing rain can cause a lot of damage.

Do the Math!
Use a Data Table

Use the table to answer the questions below.

High Temperature In January			
Detroit	San Diego	Seattle	Washington, D.C.
31 °F	66 °F	47 °F	42 °F

How much warmer is San Diego than Detroit in January? _____

Which city has the coldest temperature in January? _____

Phases of the Moon

On some nights you see a round moon.
On other nights you see a sliver of moon.
Sometimes you see no moon at all. Why?

Active Reading As you study the diagram on the next page, number the moon phases to show their sequence. Begin with the new moon. Write your answers in the caption boxes.

Does moonlight really come from the moon? No! The moon doesn't produce its own light. It reflects light from the sun. This reflected light is what we see from Earth. At any time, half of the moon is lit by the sun.

As the moon revolves around Earth, different amounts of its lit side can be seen. This is what causes the different shapes, or phases, of the moon. Eight moon phases make up one cycle. A full cycle happens in about one month. Then the cycle repeats.

The Big Four Phases

The four main moon phases are new moon, full moon, and both quarter moons. Label the missing phase below. Then fill in the dark part of the moon. Use the diagram at right to help you.

full moon   _____   new moon   first-quarter moon

The moon's phases make up a cycle that repeats each month.

Moon Phases

The lit side of a new moon faces away from Earth. We see no moon at all.

We see crescent moons just before and just after a new moon.

During a crescent moon, just the edge of the lit side can be seen.

A third-quarter moon looks like a half-circle, but it is lit on the left side.

A first-quarter moon looks like a half-circle and is lit on the right side.

As we see less of the moon's lit side, we say that the moon is *waning*.

As we see more of the moon's lit side, we say that the moon is *waxing*.

We see all of the moon's lit side during a full moon.

Daily Highs and Lows

Both pictures show the same beach.
Why is the water so low in one picture and
so high in the other? It's because of tides.

Active Reading As you read these two pages, draw boxes around the
names of the two things that are being compared.

These people enjoy walking along
the beach near this structure
during low tide.

Tides are changes in the height of ocean water. The pull
of the moon's gravity causes ocean tides. When the moon is
above an ocean, it causes high tide on that part of Earth and
on the opposite side, too.

In the parts of the ocean between the two areas of high tide,
the water level is lower. At those places, a low tide occurs.

Where have all the people gone? They didn't want to get wet! They left before it was high tide.

At most beaches, there are high tides and low tides every day. The tides make a cycle. How do you know it is high tide here now? Before, we saw people walking on the beach. Now, the beach is covered with water!

Pattern of Tides

On the lines below, tell where the moon might have been when the picture on this page was taken.

_____

_____

_____

_____

_____

In the space below, draw a picture to communicate what the image on this page will look like next as it continues its cycle.

Sum It Up!

When you're done, use the answer key to check
and revise your work.

**Finish each statement. Then draw a line from
the statement to the picture that matches it.**

1 Each month the moon cycles
through eight _____.

2 Earth's _____ causes the
cycle of day and night.

3 When the North Pole tilts away
from the sun, it is this _____
in Earth's northern half.

4 At low _____ , you can find
seashells on the beach.

5 Earth makes one _____ in
about one year.

6 The Earth is tilted to one side on
its _____.

A

B

C

D

E

F

Answer Key: 1. F, phases 2. A, rotation 3. D, season 4. C, tide 5. B, revolution 6. E, axis

Name _____

Word Play

1 Unscramble each word to complete the sentence. Write it in the boxes.

1. h e s a p

We see different shapes of light in each _____ of the moon.

⬡☐☐☐☐

2. d i s e t

The pull of the moon on Earth's oceans results in _____.

☐⬡☐☐☐

3. i n o t r v e u l o

It takes Earth a year to make one complete _____.

⬡☐☐☐☐☐☐☐☐

4. o a n o t t r i

Earth's _____ causes the cycle of day and night.

☐☐☐☐☐☐☐⬡

5. x a s i

Earth's _____ passes through the North and South Poles.

☐☐☐⬡

6. p i n n s i g n

Earth's _____, or rotating, causes day and night.

☐☐☐☐☐☐☐⬡

Write the circled letters here. Unscramble them to form a word that answers the riddle.

___ ___ ___ ___ ___ ___

7. In this season, plants begin to grow.

☐☐☐☐☐☐

Apply Concepts

2 Put a circle around the image of Earth that shows winter in the Northern Hemisphere. Put an X on the image that shows summer in the Southern Hemisphere. Put squares around the images that show spring and fall.

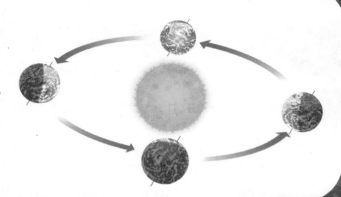

3 Explain how Earth is moving. Tell what cycle this motion causes.

_____

_____

_____

_____

4 Draw and label pictures to show the four main phases of the moon in order.

_____ _____ _____ _____

Take It Home!

Go outside with your family on a clear night. Tell your family what phase the moon is in now. Tell them what phase it will enter next. Explain how you know.

People in Science

Meet the Space Scientists

Katherine Johnson

Katherine Johnson was a "human computer" at NASA. With her knowledge of math, she helped astronauts travel into space. Johnson computed the path the spacecrafts would take. In 1961, she figured out the flight path for the first American in space, Alan Shepard. By 1962, NASA was using real computers for John Glenn's orbits around Earth. But they still called on Johnson to check the computers' numbers.

In 1969, Johnson worked to help the *Apollo 11* spacecraft travel into space. During this trip, Neil Armstrong became the first human to walk on the moon.

Amanda Nahm

Amanda Nahm is a planetary scientist. She studies the surfaces of planets and the moon. When a meteoroid hits the surface of a planet or moon, it forms a crater, or hole. The craters on the moon have been there for billions of years. Larger craters often have cracks, or faults, that form around them. By studying these craters and faults, Nahm can learn about the history of the moon's formation.

Nahm studies the Orientale Basin—the youngest impact crater on the moon. An arrow points to the young crater.

393

Moon Mission

Connect science concepts to the contributions
Amanda Nahm and Katherine Johnson have made.
Write the correct name below each statement.

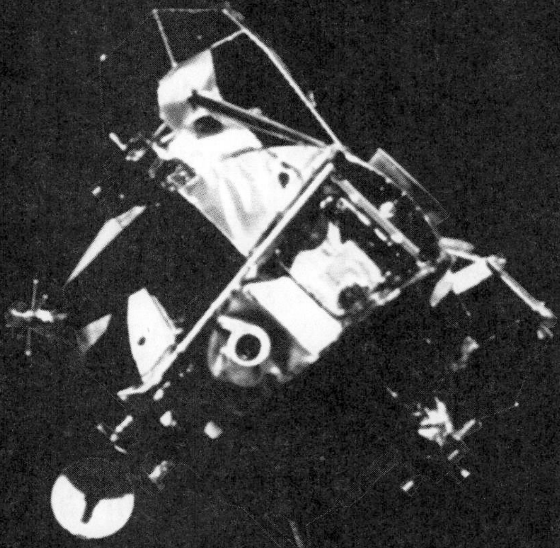

1 I study impact craters on the surface of the moon.

_____

2 I computed the flight path to the moon.

_____

3 I worked for NASA for many years.

_____

4 I want to learn about the history of the moon's formation.

_____

Lesson 2

INQUIRY

TEKS **3.4A** ...analyze information using tools, including...Sun, Earth, and Moon system models... **3.8C** construct models that demonstrate the relationship of the Sun, Earth, and Moon, including orbits and positions

Name _____

Essential Question

How Can We Model the Moon's Phases?

Set a Purpose

What will you learn from this modeling activity?

_____

_____

_____

Think About the Procedure

Why does only one person move?

_____

_____

_____

Why is the student in the center position drawing the moon?

_____

_____

_____

Record Your Observations

Add shading to the circles to show the part of the moon's surface that is dark. Label each moon phase.

Position 1

_____

Position 2

_____

Position 3

_____

Position 4

_____

Draw Conclusions

How did the model help you understand why the moon's phases occur?

_____

_____

_____

_____

Analyze and Extend

1. Why does the moon appear to change when viewed from Earth?

_____

_____

_____

_____

2. During a full moon, is the whole moon lit? Explain.

_____

_____

_____

_____

3. If you were on the sun, would the moon look the same as it does from Earth? Explain.

_____

_____

_____

_____

4. Analyze the information you collected using the sun-Earth-moon system model. Where would the student holding the ball stand to model a crescent moon? How do you know?

_____

_____

_____

_____

5. What other questions do you have about the phases of the moon?

_____

_____

_____

_____

Lesson 3

Essential Question

What Are the Sun and Stars?

Find the answer to the following question in this lesson and record it here.

How can a star affect Earth?

_____

_____

_____

Active Reading

Lesson Vocabulary
List the terms. As you learn about each one, make notes in the Interactive Glossary.

_____

_____

_____

Using Headings
Active readers preview headings and use them to pose questions about the material they will read. Reading to find an answer helps active readers focus on understanding and remembering what they read.

Stars
Up Close!

On a clear night you can see many stars in the sky. By day, you see the sun shining. How are the sun and other stars alike and different?

Active Reading As you read these two pages, underline the definition of *sun*.

The Sun

Our **sun** is a medium-size star. The sun appears much larger than other stars. It also appears much brighter. That is because the sun is much closer to Earth than other stars are.

From Earth, our sun looks like a giant ball of light. The sun, like other stars, gives off light and heat.

The sun is close enough to Earth to provide heat energy for the water cycle.

Stars

A **star** is a ball of hot, glowing gases. From Earth most stars look like small points of light. This is because they are far away. The sun and other stars are both present in the daytime. You cannot see the other stars because the sun makes the sky so bright.

The surface of other stars may look very much like the surface of our sun.

▶ **Compare and contrast** the sun with another star by describing them. Tell two ways they are alike and two ways they are different.

Sun	Both Stars	Other Star

Great Balls of Fire

From far away, stars look very similar. Up close, stars have many different characteristics. How are stars alike? How are they different?

Active Reading Draw circles around the headings. What are you going to read about stars? Read to see if you were correct.

▶ Use the space below to draw your own star. Describe your star based upon its color, size, and brightness.

Stars are born in giant clouds of gas and dust like this one.

Brightness

Brightness tells how much light a star gives off. A very bright star gives off a lot of light. Some stars are much brighter than our sun. Others are dimmer.

Size

Supergiant stars are the largest stars. Hundreds or thousands of our sun could fit inside one supergiant star! The smallest stars are called white dwarfs. Space is filled with many different kinds of beautiful stars!

Color

Stars have different colors. Our sun is a yellow star. Blue, white, and red are other colors of stars. Blue stars are the hottest. Red stars are the coolest.

Full of Energy

Earth would be a cold, dark, and empty planet without the sun. Life could not survive. Read on to find out why.

The Sun Lights Earth

Radiant [RAY•dee•uhnt] energy is energy that can travel through space! Stars give off radiant energy. The sun is our closest star. Some of its radiant energy travels to Earth as light. This light energy helps people and animals see.

Plants use light energy to make their own food. Without light energy from the sun, there could be no plants on Earth. So without the sun, there would be no plants or animals on Earth.

The sun's light makes day brighter than night.

The Sun Heats Earth

Other radiant energy from the sun warms Earth's land, air, and water. The sun provides heat energy for the water cycle. During the night, some heat leaves Earth. That is why it is cooler at night than during the day.

You cannot see the sun's energy heating Earth, but you can feel it. When you walk on a beach heated by the sun, the sand feels hot. Without the sun's radiant energy, Earth would be too cold for people to live.

Plants need light to survive.

The sun's energy warms Earth's water.

▶ Illustrate the sun to show the two forms of energy it provides, and to show how the sun's energy affects the water cycle. Describe the sun below your image.

Stargazing

Away from city lights, you can see thousands of stars in the night sky. You can see many more stars if you use a telescope.

Active Reading As you read this page, underline the sentences that tell what a telescope does.

A **telescope** is a tool that makes faraway objects seem larger. It makes faraway objects seem closer, too. With a telescope, you can see many more stars than you can with your eyes. Stars that are bright look even brighter. Stars that are dim look brighter, too.

Even with a telescope, most stars look like points of light in the sky. That's because they are so far away. Only the sun looks different. The sun is much closer to Earth than the other stars. Because the sun is so close to Earth, you should never look directly at it.

A telescope is a long tube with lenses at both ends. The lenses make objects appear larger and closer.

With a telescope, stars look brighter and clearer.

You can see many stars with just your eyes.

Do the Math!
Solve a Word Problem

Max looks at a part of the sky through a hollow tube. He counts 8 stars. Then he looks at the sky with a telescope. He sees 5 times as many stars. How many stars does Max see now?

_____

Sum It Up!

When you're done, use the answer key to check and revise your work.

Read the summary statements below. Each one is incorrect. Change the circled part of the summary to make it correct.

1 The sun is a star that gives off light and (electric energy).
_____

2
Stars look like (flashes) of light in the night sky.
_____

3 You can see (fewer) stars with a telescope than with just your eyes.
_____

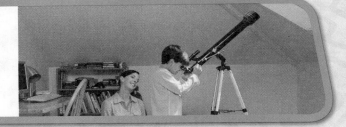

4
The sun is a ball of hot, glowing (clouds).
_____

5 Stars are grouped by their color, brightness, and (shape).
_____

Brain Check

Name _____

Word Play

1 Read each definition below. Write the word. Then find and circle the word in the Word Search.

A ball of hot, glowing gases _____

The kind of energy from the sun that helps people see _____

An instrument that makes stars look brighter and closer _____

The star that is closest to Earth _____

The kind of energy that can move through space _____

Features of stars are brightness, size, and _____

b	v	t	e	r	d	s	a	p	i	u	l	w	m	o	q	j
a	b	t	h	y	j	d	f	w	e	x	s	o	l	k	m	g
r	y	c	t	e	l	e	s	c	o	p	e	u	a	h	s	d
v	c	b	n	r	t	i	a	e	k	i	l	o	s	e	d	b
p	o	e	w	g	t	x	g	p	o	s	t	y	p	a	h	k
x	l	e	r	i	d	t	a	h	u	b	g	s	s	t	a	r
w	o	a	g	t	d	r	a	p	t	h	m	u	a	d	o	n
i	r	a	d	i	a	n	t	p	q	y	d	n	d	f	w	b
y	d	r	l	o	g	a	r	m	b	r	t	d	a	c	z	y

Apply Concepts

2 Draw stars you might see with your eyes. Then draw stars you might see with a telescope.

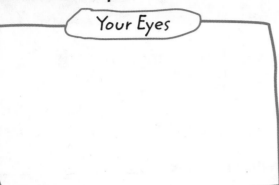

Your Eyes

A Telescope

3 Illustrate the sun and how it affects the water cycle. Describe your picture

_____

_____

4 The sun shines on the town in the picture. Tell some of the ways that the sun affects this town.

_____

_____

_____

Take It Home!

Share what you have learned about the sun with your family. With a family member, identify three ways the sun affects your everyday life.

Essential Question

What Are the Planets in Our Solar System?

🧠 Engage Your Brain!

Find the answer to the following question in this lesson and record it here.

Which planets are between Jupiter and the sun?

_____

_____

_____

_____

_____

Active Reading

Lesson Vocabulary
List the terms. As you learn about each one, make notes in the Interactive Glossary.

_____

_____

Compare and Contrast
Many ideas in this lesson are connected because they describe comparisons and contrasts. Terms that signal comparisons include *similar to*. Terms that signal contrasts include *on the other hand*. Active readers focus on comparisons and contrasts when they ask, How are these things alike and different?

In Our Corner of Space

You are familiar with Earth, the sun, and the moon. What are some other objects that are a part of the solar system?

Active Reading As you read this page, circle the name of a smaller object in the solar system.

Earth and millions of other objects make up our solar system. A **solar system** is made up of a star and the planets and other bodies that revolve around it. The sun is the star at the center of our solar system.

Our solar system has eight planets. In distance from the sun, they are Mercury, Venus, Earth, Mars, Jupiter, Saturn, Uranus, and Neptune. A **planet** is a large round body that revolves around a star in a clear orbit.

The solar system has smaller objects, too. A *comet* is a ball of rock and frozen gases. Astronomers think that trillions of comets orbit the sun in areas at the edge of the solar system.

As a comet approaches the sun, the sun's heat turns the comet's frozen parts into gas. This gas may look like a fiery tail streaming away from the sun. The tail of a comet can be much longer than the comet itself.

Mars

Earth

Venus

Mercury

Images not to scale

The *inner planets* are those closest to the sun—Mercury, Venus, Earth, and Mars. Earth is the largest and densest of the inner planets.

Neptune

Uranus

Saturn

Jupiter

The *outer planets* are those farthest from the sun—Jupiter, Saturn, Uranus, and Neptune. These planets are the largest in our solar system. In fact, Jupiter is larger than all of the other planets combined.

Identify the Planets and Their Positions

Draw the sun and planets. Be sure the planets are in their correct positions in relation to the sun. Identify each planet with labels.

Planets Near and Far

The solar system's planets are divided into two groups. How are the planets in each group different?

Active Reading As you read these pages, underline phrases or sentences that compare inner and outer planets.

The inner planets are the smallest and warmest planets in our solar system. They have hard surfaces made of rock. The inner planets revolve around the sun more quickly than the outer planets.

The outer planets are giant balls of cold gases. These planets are larger and do not have a hard surface like the inner planets. They rotate quickly, which makes for a short day.

Mars

Earth

Venus

Mercury

Inner Planets

The inner planets revolve around the sun more quickly than the outer planets. The inner planets are the only planets where probes from Earth have landed.

Neptune

Uranus

Saturn

Jupiter

Outer Planets

It takes the outer planets a long time to revolve once around the sun. Unlike the inner planets, the outer planets have rings.

Do the Math!
Calculate Distance

Mercury is the closest inner planet to the sun. Jupiter is the closest outer planet to the sun.
If Mercury is 58 million km from the sun and Jupiter is 778 million km from the sun, how much farther from the sun is Jupiter than Mercury?

_____

_____

_____

fflin Harcourt Publishing Company

The Inside Track

The inner planets are Earth's closest neighbors. How are the inner planets alike and different?

As you read these pages, draw a star next to words or phrases that identify characteristics shared by all of the inner planets.

The inner planets are alike in some ways. They are all small and rocky. They have few moons—or none at all. Still, each planet is unique. Mercury has a thin atmosphere of carbon dioxide with a surface like our moon. Venus has a thick carbon dioxide atmosphere, which makes it boiling hot. Drops of acid fall from Venus's clouds. Mars is dry and freezing cold. Huge dust storms blow across Mars's surface. Only Earth has water, soil, and air to support life.

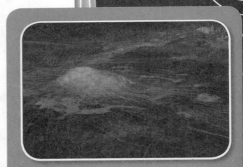

Images taken by the *Venus Express* probe show one of the more than 1,600 volcanoes on Venus's surface. For a long time, it was hard to study Venus's surface because of the thick clouds hiding it. These same clouds trap heat on Venus, making it the hottest planet.

Venus

Mercury

Mercury is the smallest planet in our solar system. Images taken by the *Messenger* space probe show the deep craters on Mercury's surface. Rocky objects slammed into Mercury, leaving deep scars.

The Mars *Spirit* rover has sent images of Mars's surface back to Earth. Mars's surface has mountains, wide plains, canyons, and volcanoes. Its surface looks red because of the iron oxide in its soil.

Mars

Earth

Satellite images of Earth show large green areas. Earth is the only planet with visible life, a large supply of liquid water, and an atmosphere mostly made of nitrogen, oxygen, and carbon dioxide.

Survivor—Mars!

Suppose you have the chance to go to Mars. Think about what Mars is like. Make a list of things you would need to survive on Mars, and explain your choices.

_____

_____

_____

The Outside Track

The outer planets are so far away that even the fastest space probes take many years to reach them.

Active Reading As you read these pages, underline the sentence that contains the main idea.

Astronauts and probes will never land on Jupiter, Saturn, Uranus, or Neptune—the outer planets. The outer planets are very different from the inner planets. These huge planets do not have solid surfaces. They are *gas giants*, made up mostly of gases.

All the outer planets have many moons and are surrounded by rings made of dust, ice, or rock. Jupiter and Saturn are the largest planets in our solar system. Uranus and Neptune are smaller and are the coldest planets.

Jupiter has at least 63 moons. Astronomers think that Europa, one of Jupiter's moons, has an icy surface that covers a cold, slushy ocean. Jupiter's atmosphere is in constant motion. Its Great Red Spot is a swirling storm that has raged for more than 300 years.

Jupiter

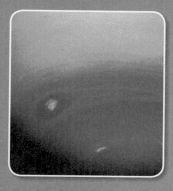

Neptune is the planet farthest from the sun. From space, its atmosphere looks blue; sometimes, high white clouds of methane ice crystals blow across Neptune. Physical changes inside Neptune are thought to slightly increase its temperature. Neptune has 13 known moons. Triton is Neptune's largest moon.

Neptune

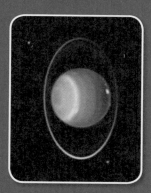

Uranus tilts so far on its axis that it looks as if it's revolving around the sun on its side. Methane gas in its atmosphere gives Uranus its blue color. Uranus is very cold—its temperature is about –215 °C (–355 °F).

Uranus

▶ Circle a feature on each planet that may help you identify it.

Saturn

Saturn has thousands of rings. Scientists think that these rings are leftover pieces of comets, asteroids, or moons that broke up long ago. Saturn's atmosphere has winds that can blow at speeds of 1,800 km/hr (1,118.5 mi/hr), which is many times faster than Earth's strongest hurricane wind.

The Right Spot

Living things like those found on Earth do not exist elsewhere in the solar system, which makes Earth a unique place.

Out of the eight planets in our solar system, only Earth has life as we know it. Why? Scientists think it is because Earth is the only planet within the solar system's life zone. The *life zone* is the region of space where the temperature range allows life to thrive.

Venus and Earth are sometimes called sister planets, but Earth supports life and Venus does not. It's all because of Earth's position within the solar system's *life zone*.

Our solar system's life zone begins just outside Venus's orbit and ends before the orbit of Mars. If Earth were outside this zone, it would be either too hot or too cold for life to exist on our planet. Earth sits near the center of the life zone.

Our moon is also within the life zone, yet it has no life. Why? The moon doesn't have an atmosphere or liquid water. Earth's atmosphere does many things to support life. It traps solar energy to keep Earth's temperature comfortable. It contains the gases that most living things need. It also protects living things from harmful solar radiation.

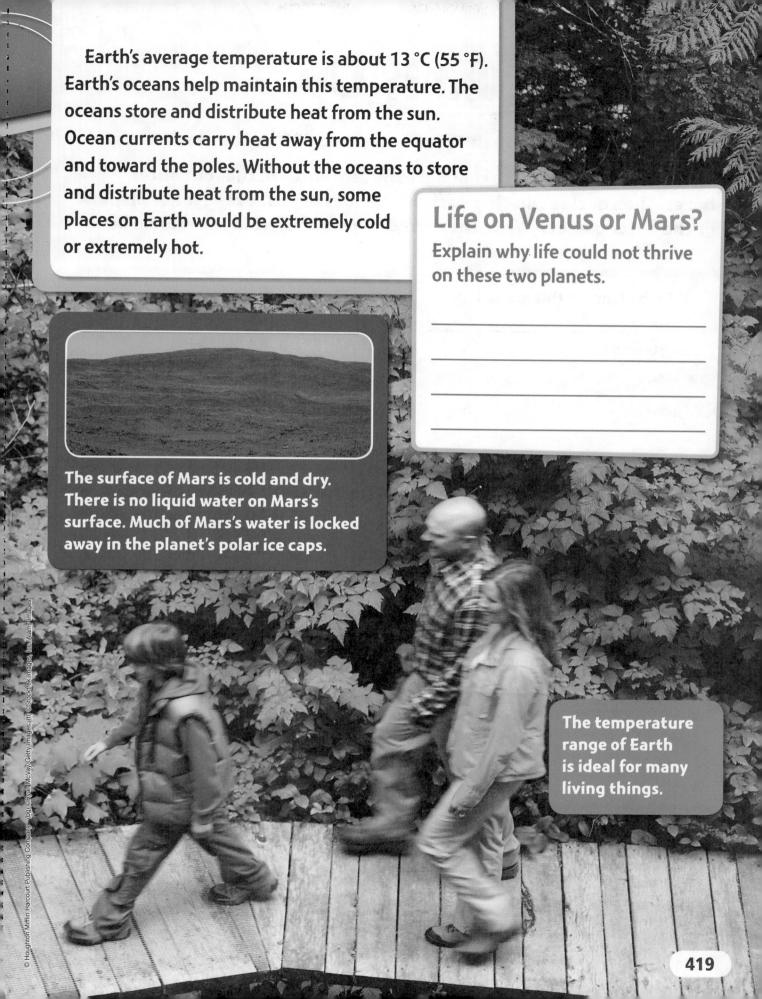

Earth's average temperature is about 13 °C (55 °F). Earth's oceans help maintain this temperature. The oceans store and distribute heat from the sun. Ocean currents carry heat away from the equator and toward the poles. Without the oceans to store and distribute heat from the sun, some places on Earth would be extremely cold or extremely hot.

The surface of Mars is cold and dry. There is no liquid water on Mars's surface. Much of Mars's water is locked away in the planet's polar ice caps.

Life on Venus or Mars?

Explain why life could not thrive on these two planets.

_____

_____

_____

_____

The temperature range of Earth is ideal for many living things.

Sum It Up!

When you're done, use the answer key to check and revise your work.

Write the correct word to complete the sentences in the four outer boxes. Then decide whether each set of clues describes the inner planets or the outer planets. Write the correct type of planet in the middle box.

1. Each planet in this group has many _____ orbiting it.

2. These distant planets are sometimes called _____ .

5. _____

3. Only the planets in this group have _____ around them.

4. Because of their distances from the sun, these planets have lower _____ .

6. Probes have landed on these planets because their surfaces are _____ .

7. Some planets in this group have one or two _____ . Others have none.

10. _____

8. None of the planets in this group has _____ around it.

9. These planets' _____ are smaller than those of the planets in the other group.

Answer Key: 1. moons 2. gas giants 3. rings 4. temperatures 5. Outer Planets 6. hard 7. moons 8. rings 9. diameters 10. Inner Planets

© Houghton Mifflin Harcourt Publishing Company

Name _____

Word Play

1 Unscramble the names of each planet and write them on the lines. Then draw a line between each planet's name and the clue that describes it.

_____

_____

_____

_____

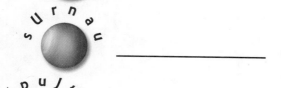
_____

_____

_____

_____

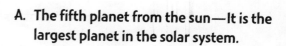

A. The fifth planet from the sun—It is the largest planet in the solar system.

B. The seventh planet from the sun—Its tilt is so great that it seems to revolve on its side.

C. The first planet from the sun—It is the smallest planet in the solar system.

D. The sixth planet from the sun—Its rings are the largest and easiest to see.

E. The fourth planet from the sun—It looks red because of the iron oxide in its soil.

F. The third planet from the sun—Liquid water covers most of its surface.

G. The second planet from the sun—Thick clouds of carbon dioxide make it the hottest planet in the solar system.

H. The eighth planet from the sun—It is the coldest and windiest planet in the solar system.

Apply Concepts

2 Circle the planet that does not belong with the group. Then explain your choice on the lines below.

_____

_____

3 Draw a picture of our solar system. Label the planets in your image to identify them and their order from the sun.

Take It Home!

With a family member, explore NASA's website to learn more about efforts to detect water on the surface of the moon and Mars. Make a poster or write a report to share your findings with your class.

Inquiry Flipchart page 53

TEKS 3.3C represent the natural world using models such as volcanoes, or Sun, Earth, and Moon system and identify their limitations, including size, properties, and materials **3.8D** identify the planets in Earth's solar system and their position in relation to the Sun

Name _____

Essential Question

How Can We Model the Sun and Planets?

Set a Purpose
What do you think you will learn from this activity?

_____

_____

Think About the Procedure
Why did you trace models of the planets instead of drawing your own models?

_____

_____

Record Your Data

In the box below, use numbers to identify and order the planets according to distance from the sun. Start with the planet closest to the sun. After that, identify and order the planets according to size. Start with the smallest planet.

Planet	Distance from the sun	Order of planet from the sun	Order of planet from smallest to largest
Earth	150 million km		
Jupiter	778 million km		
Mars	228 million km		
Mercury	58 million km		
Neptune	4,498 million km		
Saturn	1,427 million km		
Uranus	2,871 million km		
Venus	108 million km		

Draw Conclusions

Identify the planet that is farthest from the sun. Identify the planet that is closest to the sun.

_____

_____

Analyze and Extend

1. Why would scientists want to model the sun and planets?

   _____

   _____

   _____

   _____

2. Your model had limitations. How did size, materials, and properties limit your model?

   _____

   _____

   _____

   _____

   _____

   _____

3. What pattern did you observe about the distances of inner planets and outer planets from the sun?

   _____

   _____

4. Think about how you could use your constructed model to show how planets orbit the sun. Draw a picture below to show your model.

5. What other questions would you like to ask about objects in the solar system?

   _____

   _____

   _____

TEKS 3.3D connect grade-level appropriate science concepts with the history of science, science careers, and contributions of scientists

How It Works:
Keck Observatory

An observatory is a kind of system. It has many parts that work together. Scientists use observatories to study space. Read about the parts of the Keck Observatory in Hawaii.

The Keck Observatory has two telescopes. Both are as tall as eight-story buildings!

The dome protects the telescope's mirrors from rain and sunlight.

An opening in the dome turns to show different areas of the sky.

The 10-meter main mirror is a powerful magnifier. It is made up of smaller mirrors.

This planet was photographed by the Keck Observatory.

Can You Fix It?

Each part of a system plays a role. If one part breaks, the system may not work. The picture below shows the telescope's main mirror.

Trace the path of the light through the telescope by following the red arrows in the image below.

What would happen if one part of the mirror broke? How could you fix the telescope if this happened?

_____

_____

_____

Build On It!

Rise to the engineering design challenge—complete **Owner's Manual: Using a Telescope** on the Inquiry Flipchart.

Name _____

Vocabulary Review

Use the terms in the box to complete the sentences.

| axis |
| planets |
| revolution |
| rotation |
| solar system |
| star |
| sun |
| telescope |

TEKS 3.3C

1. A model of Earth can be used to show that Earth takes 24 hours to complete one full _____.

TEKS 3.8D

2. Earth, Venus, and Jupiter are examples of _____.

TEKS 3.3D

3. Sir Isaac Newton was a scientist who built a _____ to better see faraway objects in the night sky.

TEKS 3.8C

4. The closest star to Earth is the _____.

TEKS 3.8C

5. Earth changes from season to season as it moves around the sun. This movement is called a _____.

TEKS 3.8B

6. Carly drew a picture of an object in the night sky that gives off heat and light. Her picture showed a _____.

TEKS 3.8C

7. Earth and all the other objects in our _____ orbit around the sun.

TEKS 3.3C

8. In a model of Earth, you would show that Earth spins around a tilted _____.

© Houghton Mifflin Harcourt Publishing Company (border) ©NDisk/Age Fotostock

Science Concepts

Fill in the letter of the choice that best answers the question.

TEKS 3.8D

9. Which feature would you find only on or near an outer planet?

- Ⓐ atmosphere
- Ⓑ moons
- Ⓒ rings
- Ⓓ rocks

TEKS 3.8B

10. The sun's radiant energy travels through space to Earth. Which is **not** an effect of radiant energy on Earth?

- Ⓐ It heats up Earth's land.
- Ⓑ It heats up Earth's oceans.
- Ⓒ It lights up the daytime sky.
- Ⓓ It causes objects to fall to Earth.

TEKS 3.3C, 3.4A

11. Liam wants to make a model of the moon. First, he needs to observe and analyze the moon's surface. Select the equipment or technology he needs to make the best observations.

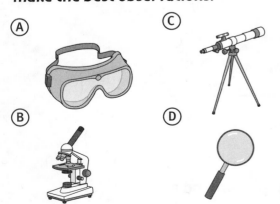

Ⓐ   Ⓒ

Ⓑ   Ⓓ

TEKS 3.3C, 3.4A

12. Mrs. Perez's students made a sun, Earth, and moon system model. It shows the sequence of some of the moon's phases over a two-week period. Collect and analyze information using the model to answer the question.

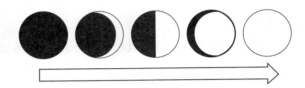

Which statement **best** describes these changes in the moon's phases?

- Ⓐ The moon is waning from a new moon to a full moon.
- Ⓑ The moon is waxing from a new moon to a full moon.
- Ⓒ The moon is waxing from a full moon to a new moon.
- Ⓓ The moon is waning from a full moon to a new moon.

TEKS 3.3C, 3.8C

13. Jim wants to make a model that shows Earth's day-night cycle. Which would make the **best** model?

- Ⓐ a model showing the sun revolving around Earth every 24 hours
- Ⓑ a model showing Earth revolving around the sun every 24 hours
- Ⓒ a model showing the sun shining on Earth for 12 hours each day
- Ⓓ a model showing different parts of Earth in sunlight as Earth rotates

---

TEKS 3.8D

14. You want to sort the planets into groups. Which planets would you group together and why?

Ⓐ Earth, Mercury, Venus, and Titan are closest to the sun

Ⓑ Mercury, Venus, Earth, and Mars are closest to the sun

Ⓒ Jupiter, Saturn, Europa, and Neptune are farthest from the sun

Ⓓ Mars, Neptune, Jupiter, and Venus are farthest from the sun

TEKS 3.4A, 3.8C

15. The diagram below is a model. It shows Earth's rotation around its axis. It also shows Earth's revolution around the sun. Collect and analyze information from this sun, Earth, and moon system model to answer the question.

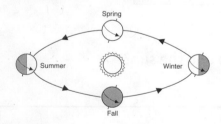

What changes are shown in this diagram during Earth's motions?

Ⓐ The sun begins to revolve around Earth.

Ⓑ The part of Earth tilted toward the sun changes.

Ⓒ Earth changes the direction of its rotation around its axis.

Ⓓ Earth changes the direction of its revolution around the sun.

TEKS 3.2C, 3.8D

16. The table shows the positions of the first four planets in the order of distance from the sun.

Planets in Order of Distance from the Sun
1. Mercury
2. Venus
3. Earth
4. Mars

What is the correct order of the other planets that would complete the table?

Ⓐ Jupiter, Saturn, Uranus, Neptune

Ⓑ Neptune, Uranus, Jupiter, Saturn

Ⓒ Saturn, Neptune, Uranus, Jupiter

Ⓓ Uranus, Jupiter, Saturn, Neptune

TEKS 3.3C

17. Marisa uses a black box with pinholes to model stars in the night sky. She shines a flashlight into the box. Points of light project onto a wall in a dark room. Which of the following is NOT a limitation of her model?

Ⓐ It cannot show that stars are different sizes.

Ⓑ It cannot show that stars are made of gases.

Ⓒ It cannot show the true sizes of the stars.

Ⓓ It cannot show that stars are different colors.

Apply Inquiry and Review the Big Idea

Write the answers to these questions.

TEKS 3.8B

18. The picture shows the water cycle. The water cycle shows how water moves from Earth's surface to the atmosphere and back again.

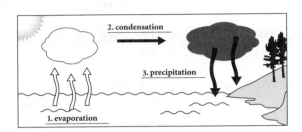

Describe the sun and its role in the water cycle.

_____

The following chart lists the dates on which some phases of the moon occur over a four-month period. Use this chart to answer questions 19–21.

Moon Phases—Summer 2005				
Month	New moon	First quarter	Full moon	Third quarter
June	6	15	22	28
July	6	14	21	28
August	5	13	19	26
September	3	11	18	25

TEKS 3.2D, 3.8C

19. On which dates is the moon's position between Earth and the sun?

_____

TEKS 3.2D

20. Use the chart to estimate the dates for each moon phase for October and November.

October _____

November _____

TEKS 3.2D

21. How many days were there between the third-quarter moon in June and the third-quarter moon in September?

_____

Ecosystems and Interactions

© Houghton Mifflin Harcourt Publishing Company (border) ©NDec/Age Fotostock; (b) ©Carol Farneti Foster/Photolibrary New York; (inset) ©Nicholas Smythe/Photo Researchers, Inc.

Big Idea

Living, once-living, and nonliving things all interact in an ecosystem. All living things need energy to survive and grow.

TEKS 3.2A, 3.2C, 3.3D, 3.9A, 3.9B, 3.9C

I Wonder Why

Why does this acacia ant live in a bull-horn acacia tree? *Turn the page to find out.*

Here's Why Acacia ants get food from the tree. In return, the ants protect the tree against animals and plants that are harmful to the tree.

In this unit, you will explore the Big Idea, the Essential Questions, and the Investigations on the Inquiry Flipchart.

Levels of Inquiry Key ■ DIRECTED ■ **GUIDED** ■ INDEPENDENT

Track Your Progress

Big Idea Living, once-living, and nonliving things all interact in an ecosystem. All living things need energy to survive and grow.

Essential Questions

Lesson 1 What Are Ecosystems? 433
Inquiry Flipchart p. 55—Take a Closer Look/Study an Ecosystem

Inquiry Lesson 2 What's in an Ecosystem? 445
Inquiry Flipchart p. 56—What's in an Ecosystem?

👥 **People in Science:** Dení Ramírez and Cassandra Nichols 447

Lesson 3 What Is a Food Chain? 449
Inquiry Flipchart p. 57—Break It Down/Make a Food Chain

Inquiry Lesson 4 What Are Some Food Chains? 461
Inquiry Flipchart p. 58—What Are Some Food Chains?

Lesson 5 How Do Environmental Changes Affect Living Things? 463
Inquiry Flipchart p.59—Too Much Water!/Not Enough Water!

S.T.E.M. Engineering & Technology: Firefighting Tools: Controlling Forest Fires 477
Inquiry Flipchart p. 60—Design It: Draw a Safari Backpack

Unit 10 Review 479

Now I Get the Big Idea!

Science Notebook

Before you begin each lesson, be sure to write your thoughts about the Essential Question.

TEKS **3.9A** observe and describe the physical characteristics of environments and how they support populations and communities within an ecosystem

Lesson **1**

Essential Question

What Are Ecosystems?

Engage Your Brain!

Find the answer to the following question in this lesson and record it here.

This woodpecker stores acorns in this tree. How does this tree support the woodpecker?

_____

_____

_____

Active Reading

Lesson Vocabulary

List the terms. As you learn about each one, make notes in the Interactive Glossary.

_____ _____

_____ _____

_____

Main Idea and Details

Detail sentences give information about a topic. The information may be examples, features, characteristics, or facts. Active readers stay focused on the topic when they ask, What fact or information does this sentence add to the topic?

Animals and Plants at Home

What do sand, salt water, crabs, and seaweed all have in common? You can find them at the beach, of course!

Active Reading As you read these two pages, draw two lines under each main idea.

When you go to the beach, you find lots of living things. Nonliving things, like sand and salt water, are also part of the beach. Everything that surrounds a living thing is its **environment**. This includes living and nonliving things. Your desk, teacher, books, and air are all part of your classroom environment.

An **ecosystem** is all of the living and nonliving things in a place. In an ecosystem, living things interact with each other and with the physical characteristics of their environment. Think of bees that use an old log to build their hive. They gather nectar from flowers to make honey. A bear eats the honey. These interactions make up a part of an ecosystem.

Living things in the same ecosystem share resources. Many of them also share a habitat. A **habitat** is the space where a plant or animal lives. A frog's habitat is a pond. A frog's environment is everything around the frog.

This crab's habitat is on the sand. The crab and sand are both part of an ecosystem.

An ocean ecosystem includes salt water, seaweed, fish, and other animals. Each depends upon the other to survive.

Sea anemones, sea stars, and mussels live in tide pools. The physical characteristics of their environment support their survival in the ecosystem.

What Makes Up an Ecosystem?

Choose an ecosystem from the photographs. Observe and describe the physical characteristics of the environment from that ecosystem.

_____

_____

Communities of Populations

You live in a community. You are also part of a population. Animals and plants are part of populations in communities, too.

Active Reading As you read these two pages, find and underline an example of a population.

Wolves, bears, snakes, birds, and many other plants and animals all live in Yellowstone National Park. A **population** is all of one kind of organism living in the same area. All of the wolves in Yellowstone National Park make up a wolf population.

Animal and plant populations in an area may be a part of the same community. A **community** is all of the populations that live and interact in an ecosystem. An ecosystem can have many different populations.

Grassland Ecosystem

Yellowstone National Park has a large population of bison. The bison are part of a community that includes the grasses that bison eat and this population of antelope.

This bull snake is also part of the Yellowstone National Park community along with the wolves and bison.

This wolf is a part of the wolf population that lives in the same area. To survive, wolves eat other animals in their community.

Do the Math!
Make a Bar Graph

Use the measured data in the table to construct a bar graph. Organize, examine, and evaluate populations of animals in a community within Yellowstone National Park.

Animal	Population
Bald Eagle	5
Gray Wolf	35
Elk	70
Bull Snake	15

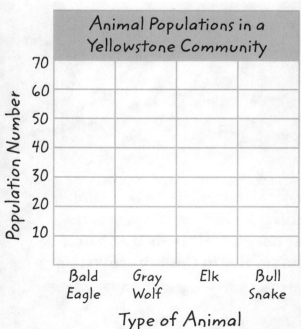

Animal Populations in a Yellowstone Community

Population Number

70
60
50
40
30
20
10

Bald Eagle | Gray Wolf | Elk | Bull Snake

Type of Animal

Living on the Land

You've seen that bison live in grassland ecosystems. What other types of land ecosystems are there?

Active Reading As you read these two pages, draw circles around the names of ecosystems that are described.

Forest ecosystems have a lot of trees. Tropical rain forests have many different kinds of trees. These forests are warm and wet all year long. Animals like jaguars, toucans, and monkeys live in tropical forests.

Some forests have warm summers and cold winters. Woodpeckers, squirrels, deer, and bears are common. The trees, such as oaks and maples, lose their leaves in the fall.

Other land ecosystems are shown on these two pages.

Desert Ecosystem

Kangaroo rats, rattlesnakes, and cactus populations live in deserts. They have adaptations that help them survive in this dry ecosystem.

Ecosystems on Mountains

Steller's jays, mountain goats, and pine trees live in different mountain ecosystems. These ecosystems are found high on the sides of mountains. They are cold for most of the year.

This Steller's jay uses materials from its environment to build a nest. It also finds food in its environment.

The elf owl eats insects that live in cactuses. The cactuses provide a place for the owl to live and help the owl survive in its environment.

Beyond the Book

Research a land ecosystem that you would like to learn more about. Observe how the physical characteristics of the environment in that ecosystem support populations and communities within it. Describe what you observe in a report.

Under the Water

Most of Earth is covered with water. There are many different living things below the surface of ponds, lakes, rivers, and oceans.

Active Reading As you read these two pages, draw a line from the picture to the sentences that describe it.

If you look at a globe, you'll notice a lot of blue! That blue represents Earth's oceans. The oceans consist of salt water. Animals like sea turtles, whales, and lobsters live in ocean ecosystems. Some ocean animals, like coral, don't look like animals at all. The ocean also has plantlike life forms such as kelp and seaweed.

Rivers, lakes, ponds, and streams are usually fresh water. Fresh water has much less salt than ocean water. Frogs, ducks, and many kinds of fish live in fresh water. Alligators are found in freshwater wetlands. Land animals like deer, foxes, and raccoons drink this fresh water.

Ocean Ecosystem

This huge underwater ecosystem is made by tiny ocean animals called corals.

Clownfish live around sea anemones in their habitat. The clownfish are immune to the anemone's stings, but animals that might eat the clownfish are not!

River Ecosystem

Rivers carry water to the ocean. This flowing water is an ecosystem made of fresh water.

River otters build their shelters next to rivers where they swim and catch fish.

Using the Environment

Describe how the animals in the two photographs use the resources in their environment.

_____

_____

Sum It Up!

When you're done, use the answer key to check
and revise your work.

**Read each statement. Draw a line to match each statement
with the picture it describes.**

1 This saltwater ecosystem covers
much of the earth's surface.

Desert

2 This ecosystem's main plant
is grass.

Ocean

3 This ecosystem has the
cactus, a plant that stores
water in its stem.

River

4 Steller's jays and mountain
goats live in this ecosystem.

Mountain

5 Fox and deer drink the fresh
water from this water
ecosystem.

Grassland

Answer Key: 1–Ocean 2–Grassland 3–Desert 4–Mountain 5–River

Name _____

Word Play

1 Use the clues to help unscramble each word. Write the unscrambled word in the boxes.

1. NOACE

   This ecosystem contains salt water.

   ⬚⬚⬚⬚⬚

2. SLSADNAGR

   Bison and antelope roam this flat ecosystem.

   ⬚⬚⬚⬚⬚⬚⬚⬚⬚

3. SMCEYOTSE

   The living and nonliving things that interact in the same area

   ⬚⬚⬚⬚⬚⬚⬚⬚⬚

4. TBHTAAI

   Where a plant or an animal lives

   ⬚⬚⬚⬚⬚⬚⬚

5. NDPO

   Cattails and water lilies live near or on this freshwater ecosystem.

   ⬚⬚⬚⬚

6. TMVEINNRONE

   The living and nonliving things that surround a living thing

   ⬚⬚⬚⬚⬚⬚⬚⬚⬚⬚⬚

7. YOMCNTUMI

   The populations that live in one place

   ⬚⬚⬚⬚⬚⬚⬚⬚⬚

8. RTSEDE

   Plants and animals that can survive with little water live in this ecosystem.

   ⬚⬚⬚⬚⬚⬚

9. OLTOPNPUAI

   All of one type of organism in the same place

   ⬚⬚⬚⬚⬚⬚⬚⬚⬚⬚

10. SATRORFENI

    Jaguars, toucans, and monkeys live in this ecosystem.

    ⬚⬚⬚⬚⬚⬚⬚⬚⬚⬚

Apply Concepts

2 In what kind of ecosystem would you find these living things? Write the name of the area underneath each one.

Clownfish

_____

Alligator

_____

Fish

_____

Zebra

_____

Cactus

_____

Toucan

_____

3 Explain the difference between a population and a community. Give an example of each.

_____

_____

_____

_____

Take It Home!

Go outside and observe the physical characteristics of the environment around you. How does it support populations and communities? Record your observations.

TEKS **3.2C** construct maps, graphic organizers, simple tables, charts, and bar graphs using tools and current technology to organize, examine, and evaluate measured data **3.9A** observe and describe the physical characteristics of environments and how they support populations and communities within an ecosystem

Name _____

Essential Question

What's in an Ecosystem?

Set a Purpose

What will you discover in this activity?

_____
_____
_____
_____

Think About the Procedure

Why do you think you will look at the environment inside the coat hanger instead of looking at a larger area?

_____
_____
_____

What living and nonliving things do you expect to find in your environment?

_____
_____

Record Your Data

In the space below, construct a chart using tools, such as a pencil, to organize the number of living and nonliving things in your ecosystem. Examine and evaluate the data.

Use current technology to construct another chart to describe the physical characteristics of the environment you observed. Include interactions between living and nonliving things. Use the chart to organize, examine, and evaluate your measured data.

Draw Conclusions

How did the wire hanger help you?

_____

_____

_____

_____

What did you learn about the larger ecosystem by studying a small part of it? Explain.

_____

_____

_____

_____

Analyze and Extend

1. What did you find out when you compared your observations with the observations of a classmate? What were some similarities? What were some differences?

_____

_____

_____

_____

_____

2. What did you observe about how the parts of the environment interacted?

_____

_____

_____

3. How have people affected the environment you observed?

_____

_____

_____

_____

4. What are some other questions you have about ecosystems around you?

_____

_____

_____

_____

Meet the Ecosystems Scientists

Dení Ramírez

Dení Ramírez is a marine biologist. She studies the world's largest fish—the whale shark. She spends most of her time in the waters of Mexico. After taking pictures of each shark, she tags them to track their movement. She records where they eat, migrate, and reproduce. Her work helps people understand and protect whale sharks and their habitat.

Each whale shark has a different pattern of spots on its back. Ramírez uses these spots to identify the whale sharks.

Cassandra Nichols

Cassandra Nichols is a scientist who studies climate change. She and a team of scientists study the rain forest in Australia. To reach the top of the rain-forest trees, Nichols uses a very tall crane. Other scientists on the team study the soil, insects, birds, and other animals in the rain forest. Nichols and her team hope to learn how changes in climate affect this ecosystem.

A special tool called a porometer is used to study the leaves of the rain forest.

Know Your Ecosystem!

Label each clue with the letter of the matching picture.

1 These animals live in an ocean ecosystem. _____

2 A rain-forest ecosystem has many nonliving things on the forest floor such as this. _____

3 This is the very top of the rain-forest ecosystem. _____

4 This type of animal is found in the rain forest. _____

5 Most of an ocean ecosystem is made up of this. _____

6 This strange-looking organism lives in the ocean. _____

A

B

C

D

F

E

TEKS **3.9B** identify and describe the flow of energy in a food chain and predict how changes in a food chain affect the ecosystem such as removal of frogs from a pond or bees from a field

Lesson **3**

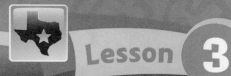

Essential Question

What Is a Food Chain?

Engage Your Brain!

Find the answer to the following question in this lesson and record it here.

What do these two animals and the grasses have in common?

_____

_____

_____

Active Reading

Lesson Vocabulary

List the terms. As you read, make notes about them in the Interactive Glossary.

_____ _____

_____ _____

_____

Sequence

Many ideas in this lesson are connected by a sequence, or order, that describes the steps in a process. Active readers stay focused on sequence when they mark the transition from one step in a process to another.

Soak Up the Sun

Plants need energy to grow and reproduce. Where do you think this energy comes from?

Active Reading As you read these pages, draw one line under the source of energy for producers. Draw two lines under the product of photosynthesis that contains energy.

You eat food, such as tomatoes, to get energy. But all green plants, like these tomato plants, must produce, or make, their own food. A **producer** is a living thing that makes its own food.

The process a plant uses to make food is called **photosynthesis** [foht•oh•SIHN•thuh•sis]. During photosynthesis, plants use the energy from sunlight to change water and carbon dioxide [dy•AHKS•yd], a gas in the air, into sugars. A plant uses the sugars as food for growth, or it stores them. During photosynthesis, plants give off oxygen, a gas that both animals and plants need.

sunlight

Photosynthesis happens in leaves. The sun's energy is used to make sugars, which the plant uses or stores.

▶ What does a plant take in for photosynthesis? What does the plant produce?

Plants Take In	Plants Produce

water

carbon dioxide

When we eat tomatoes, we get energy from the sugars that a tomato plant made and stored.

Nature's Dinnertime

Animals cannot make their own food. So where do animals get the energy they need?

Active Reading As you read, find and underline the definitions of *herbivore, carnivore,* and *omnivore.*

Animals get their energy by eating other living things. A living thing that eats other living things is called a **consumer**. When a rabbit eats grass, it gets energy from the grass. A rabbit is a *herbivore*, an animal that only eats plants. Some animals get energy by eating only other animals. These meat-eating animals are called *carnivores.* A wolf is a carnivore because it eats animals like rabbits. Some animals, such as raccoons, eat both plants and animals. They are called *omnivores.*

There are also living things that get energy from once-living things. An organism that breaks down dead organisms for food is called a **decomposer**. Earthworms, bacteria, and mushrooms are all examples of decomposers.

A giraffe's neck is long so it can reach the high leaves on trees.

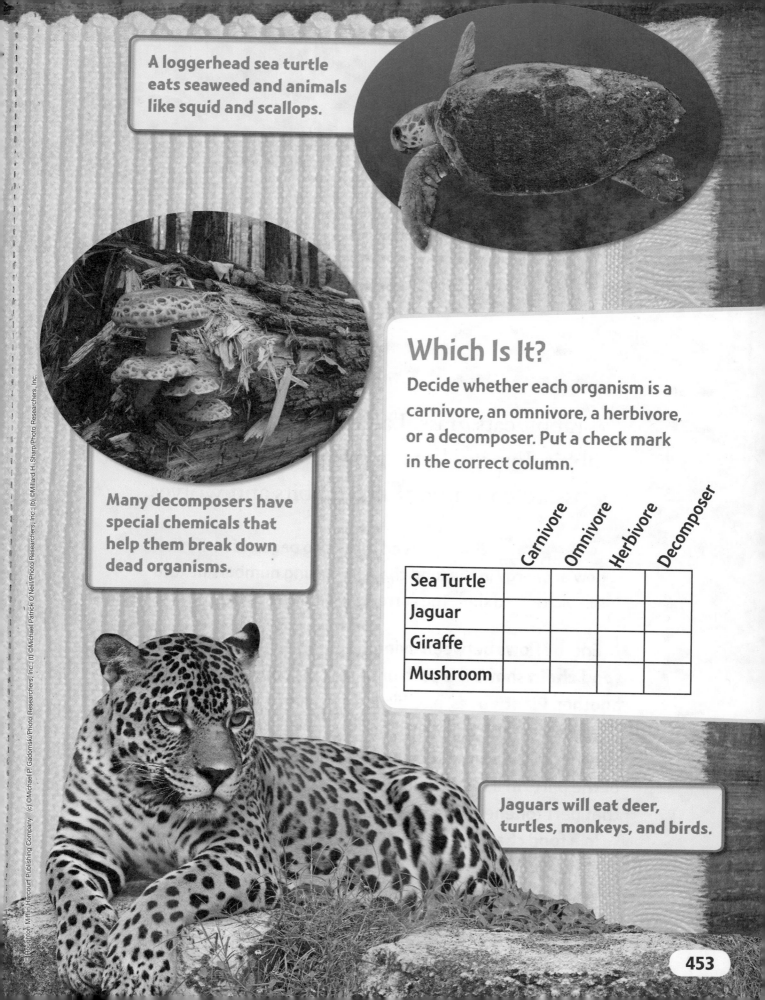

A loggerhead sea turtle eats seaweed and animals like squid and scallops.

Many decomposers have special chemicals that help them break down dead organisms.

Which Is It?

Decide whether each organism is a carnivore, an omnivore, a herbivore, or a decomposer. Put a check mark in the correct column.

	Carnivore	Omnivore	Herbivore	Decomposer
Sea Turtle				
Jaguar				
Giraffe				
Mushroom				

Jaguars will eat deer, turtles, monkeys, and birds.

Mesquite trees use energy from the sun to produce sugars. They store some of the sugars in their seeds.

Food Chains

A rabbit eats grass. Later, a wolf eats the rabbit. Energy flows from producers, like grass, to consumers, like rabbits and wolves.

Active Reading As you read these two pages, identify the flow of energy in the food chain by writing numbers next to the pictures to show the correct order of the energy flow.

Energy flows between living things in an ecosystem. A **food chain** shows the path of food from one living thing to another. Plants, bees, and birds are part of a food chain. The bees eat nectar from plants, and the birds eat the bees. Energy flows from the sun to the plants to the bees to the birds. If one of the parts in a food chain disappears, the animals that eat that part for energy have to find different food or die.

In a food chain, many animals eat other animals. An animal that hunts other animals for food is a *predator*. An animal that is hunted for food is called *prey*. A shark hunts and eats fish in a food chain. The shark is a predator. The fish are the prey.

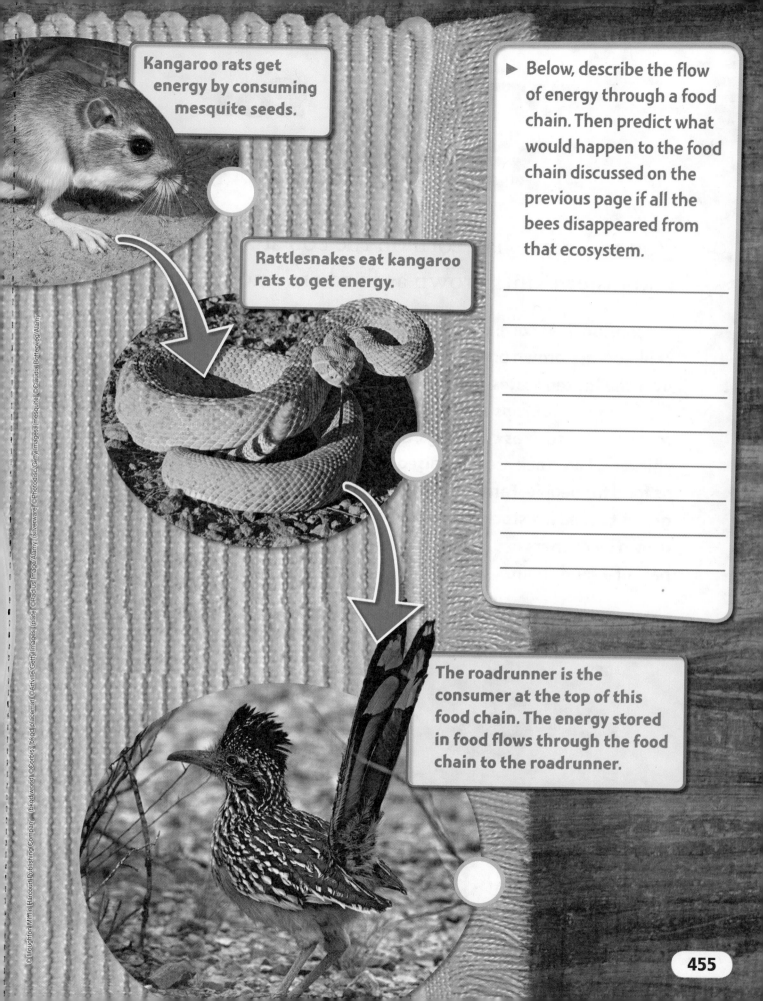

Kangaroo rats get energy by consuming mesquite seeds.

Rattlesnakes eat kangaroo rats to get energy.

The roadrunner is the consumer at the top of this food chain. The energy stored in food flows through the food chain to the roadrunner.

► Below, describe the flow of energy through a food chain. Then predict what would happen to the food chain discussed on the previous page if all the bees disappeared from that ecosystem.

_____

_____

_____

_____

_____

_____

_____

_____

What's for Dinner?

You may have had corn on the cob at a picnic. Corn and other plants grown as food are known as crops.

Crops, such as corn, carrots, and cabbage, are grown on farms all over the United States. Crops are food for people. Crops are also food for livestock, such as cows, pigs, and chickens. Livestock are also raised as food for people. Farmers grow grains to feed livestock. The crops grown by farmers are an important part of a food chain.

Corn is a producer.

Chickens are consumers. They eat corn.

Farmers must meet the needs of plants in order for crops to grow. Crops must get plenty of air, sunlight, and water. To get water to the crops, farmers may dig long ditches. Water is pumped through the ditches to the crops. Farmers also might use sprinklers to water crops.

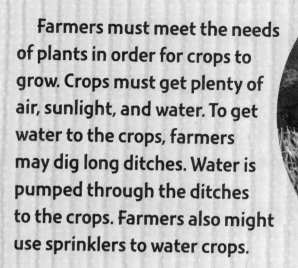

Sprinkler irrigation brings water to this crop of corn.

Do the Math!
Solve a Word Problem

It takes 8 pounds of corn to feed 40 chickens each day. How many pounds of corn does it take to feed 40 chickens in one week?

_____

_____

_____

You are a consumer who might eat corn, chicken, or both.

Sum It Up!

When you're done, use the answer key to check
and revise your work.

**Find and circle the incorrect word in each summary statement.
Write the correct word on the line.**

1 Plants need carbon dioxide from the air, water, and oxygen to make food.

_____

4 A food chain shows the path of energy from consumers to animals.

_____

2 Carnivores eat both plants and animals.

_____

5 Crops are at the beginning of an important food grain.

_____

3 Animals that are hunted by other animals are known as predators.

_____

Answer Key: 1. oxygen; sunlight 2. carnivores; omnivores 3. predators; prey
4. consumers; producers 5. grain; chain

Name _____

Word Play

1 Use the clues to complete the crossword puzzle.

Across

1. A living thing that makes its own food

2. The path of food from one living thing to another

6. A living thing that eats other living things

7. An animal that is hunted for food

8. A living thing that breaks down dead organisms for food

Down

1. The process that plants use to make food

3. An animal that eats both plants and animals

4. An animal that hunts other animals for food

5. An animal that eats only plants

6. An animal that eats only other animals

food chain*   producer*   consumer*

herbivore   carnivore   omnivore

decomposer*   predator   prey

photosynthesis*   * Key Lesson Vocabulary

Apply Concepts

2 Look at the picture of the food chain below. Label each as either producer or consumer.

_____ _____ _____

3 Label the predator and the prey in each pair of animals.

Shark

Rabbit

Snake

_____ _____ _____

Fish

Wolf

Mouse

_____ _____ _____

4 Draw a food chain in which you are the last link. Describe the flow of energy through it.

Take It Home!

What crops do you eat? Make a list. Ask members of your family to add to your list. Find out where these crops come from. Are they local, or are they from far away?

Lesson 4

INQUIRY

TEKS 3.9B identify and describe the flow of energy in a food chain and predict how changes in a food chain affect the ecosystem such as removal of frogs from a pond or bees from a field

Name _____

Essential Question

What Are Some Food Chains?

Set a Purpose
What will you discover in this activity?

_____

_____

_____

What does connecting the cards with yarn and tape show?

_____

_____

_____

Think About the Procedure
Why do you think that the index cards are numbered in the food chain?

_____

_____

_____

_____

_____

Record Your Data
On the lines below, describe the flow of energy in your food chain.

_____

_____

_____

_____

_____

Draw Conclusions

Predict what would happen if the frog was removed from this ecosystem.

_____

_____

_____

_____

How does the model you made help you to understand food chains?

_____

_____

_____

Analyze and Extend

1. Which animals in the food chain are herbivores? Which animals are carnivores?

_____

_____

_____

2. Which animal is most likely an omnivore? Explain.

_____

_____

_____

3. How do animals and plants in a food chain depend on each other?

_____

_____

_____

_____

_____

4. What do you think would happen if there was a lot of food for the frogs? How would this affect the hawks?

_____

_____

_____

_____

_____

5. What other food chains would you like to learn about?

_____

_____

_____

_____

_____

Essential Question

How Do Environmental Changes Affect Living Things?

Engage Your Brain!

Find the answer to the following question in this lesson.

What would the prairie dogs need to do if their habitat was flooded?

_____

_____

_____

Active Reading

Lesson Vocabulary

List the terms. As you read, make notes about them in the Interactive Glossary.

_____ _____

_____

Cause and Effect

Words signaling a cause include *because* and *if*. Words signaling an effect include *so* and *thus*. Active readers remain alert to cause-and-effect signal words.

© Houghton Mifflin Harcourt Publishing Company • © Pat Tielle/Alamy Images

Inquiry Flipchart p. 59 — Too Much Water!/Not Enough Water!

463

Fragile Ecosystems

In an ecosystem, plants, animals, and other living things share the same environment. But what happens when that environment changes?

Active Reading As you read these two pages, draw a circle around the clue word that signals a cause.

Strong winds have destroyed this forest ecosystem.

In an ecosystem, both living and nonliving things interact. If nonliving things cause the ecosystem to change, the living things will be affected. A powerful storm, for example, may kill plants and animals. Some animals may have to leave to survive. Other animals may stay and have to compete for resources.

Fires cause flame, heat, smoke, and ash. As a result, they can change ecosystems. Fires can be caused by a natural event, like lightning. Fires can also be caused by people. Their effects can be both positive and negative.

NEGATIVE Fires destroy trees and other plants as well as animal habitats.

NEGATIVE This coyote left the fire-burned area to look for a new habitat.

POSITIVE Fires clear space for new plant growth. Ashes from burned plants add nutrients to the soil.

POSITIVE Pinecones open to let their seeds out. Some pinecones will only open when fire heats them.

Write a Headline

Write one headline that describes a positive effect of fire and one headline that describes a negative effect of fire.

_____

_____

The Right Amount of Water

Physical characteristics of an environment support populations and communities. What happens when the environment changes?

Active Reading As you read these two pages, find and underline the definitions of *erosion*, *flood*, and *drought*.

Earth's surface is always wearing down and breaking apart. **Erosion** is when small pieces of rock are carried away by water and sometimes by wind. As the land in some locations wears away, habitats for plants, animals, and people disappear. They must find a new place to live.

Erosion is not the only way water affects the environment. Both floods and droughts affect the environment. A **flood** is a large amount of water that covers normally dry land.

Water loosens and moves sand and rock away from the beach.
Areas where grass once grew have been washed away by the water.

A **drought** occurs when it does not rain for a long time. The land can become very dry during a drought.

Some organisms can't survive in areas that are flooded or where there are droughts. They either perish or move to new locations. Some organisms, such as mold, can thrive during floods. Some insects thrive on dying plants during droughts.

Describe the Change

Describe each environmental change. Tell how some organisms thrived, perished, or moved to a new location.

_____   _____

_____   _____

_____   _____

_____   _____

_____   _____

_____   _____

_____   _____

Natural Changes

Water, wind, and other nonliving things can change the environment. But living things can also cause changes.

Active Reading As you read these two pages, draw a star next to what you consider to be the most important sentence, and be ready to explain why.

Animals and plants can make big changes to their environments. Animals can change the environment when they build shelters. Beavers can cause a new lake to form when they build a dam across a river using trees and sticks. The mounds that termites build add nutrients to the soil. The nutrients help plants grow.

Plants can change their environment, too. One kind of plant may take over all the space in an area. This makes it harder for other plants to survive. It can also make it harder for animals to live there.

Some very small living things change environments by causing disease in plants and animals. Diseases harm plants and make animals sick, and can even kill them.

Beavers change the environment when they cut down trees, make canals, and build dams.

Termites can build mounds as high as a three-story building!

Do the Math!

Interpret a Graph

Interpret the line graph. What do you think might have happened to the beech trees in 1999?

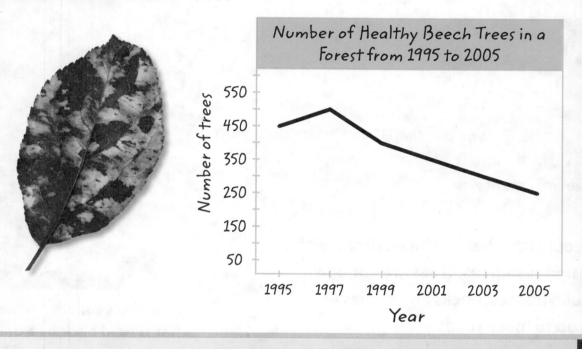

Number of Healthy Beech Trees in a Forest from 1995 to 2005

Some algae blooms release poisons. Algae blooms use up oxygen in the water when the algae die and decompose.

People and the Environment

Can you change the environment?
You can and you do! People change
the environment every day.

Active Reading As you read these two pages,
find and underline two ways that people change
the environment.

Reservoirs collect the water
that is held back by a dam.
People boat, swim, and fish in
the reservoir.

People can change the environment
by using resources. Trees are cut down
to build houses. Rocks and stones are
dug up to make roads.

People can change the environment
by causing pollution. The exhaust from
cars and trucks can pollute the air.
Trash can pollute water and land.

People sometimes cause events that
usually happen naturally. When people
are careless, they can start wildfires.
Habitats can be lost when people build
dams. In some places, new dams can
even cause floods.

People build large dams to control
the flow of water. The flow of water
is controlled so cities and towns
receive just the right amount.

Write an Effect

For each cause, write an effect.

Campers forget to put out their campfire.

_____

_____

Workers build a new road through the forest.

_____

_____

Garbage trucks collect people's trash.

_____

_____

How Can We Help?

Ecosystems change over time. Some changes are natural. Some changes are caused by people. How can people affect the environment in positive ways?

Adding plants to sand dunes can help prevent erosion.

There are many things we can do to help the environment. Turning off a dripping faucet helps conserve water. Turning off lights you are not using helps save energy. If we use less energy, we need fewer resources from the environment.

We can also clean up the environment by cleaning up pollution. We can make smart choices to reduce the amount of trash we throw away. What can you do to help?

Helpful or Not Helpful?

Circle *yes* if the activity helps the environment and *no* if it does not.

polluting the water

yes   no

cleaning up litter

yes   no

recycling

yes   no

bicycling

yes   no

polluting the air

yes   no

planting trees

yes   no

Sum It Up!

When you're done, use the answer key to check and revise your work.

The table below summarizes this lesson. Complete the table.

Environmental Changes Affect Living Things

People Affect Living Things	Natural Events Affect Living Things
1. People can cause events that also occur naturally, such as _____.	4. Fire forces animals to leave, but it also makes space for _____.
2. People can cause _____ of air, water, and land habitats.	5. Plants and animals are made sick by _____.
3. One way people can help plants and animals survive is to _____.	6. A beaver building a dam is an example of how animals affect the _____.
	7. Natural events caused by water or lack of it include _____, _____, and _____.

Name _____

Word Play

1 Fill in the missing letters in each word. You will use each of the letters in the box.

A	B	E	F	G	I	I
N	O	O	R	R	S	T

1. ___ R O ___ I O ___
2. D ___ ___ U ___ H ___
3. H A ___ ___ T ___ T
4. ___ L ___ O D
5. F ___ ___ E

Fill in the blanks with the correct word from above.

6. When rising water causes a _____, animals have to move to dry land.

7. Shorelines and beaches are worn away by _____.

8. A change in the environment can cause an animal to lose its _____.

9. One positive effect of _____ is that some pinecones only open after being heated.

10. When there is not enough rain, _____ can hurt crops.

Apply Concepts

2 Describe the missing cause or effect for each picture.

Cause: flood

Effect: _____

Cause: wildfire

Effect: _____

Cause: drought

Effect: _____

Cause: trash

Effect: _____

Cause: one plant uses too

many resources

Effect: _____

Cause: _____

Effect: land is flooded

3 Write three ways you could help protect a beach habitat.

_____

_____

Share what you have learned about environments with your family. Talk about how you can change the environment in positive ways.

© Houghton Mifflin Harcourt Publishing Company   (cr) ©blickwinkel/McPHOTO/CWY/Alamy Images; (tr) ©Gregory G. Dimijian/Photo Researchers, Inc.; (tc) ©Jeremy Walker/Photo Researchers, Inc.; (c) ©Nigel Cattlin/Alamy Images; (b) ©RF/Stock/Alamy Images; (cl) ©Robert Thompson/Photo Researchers, Inc.; (tl) ©Wayne Hutchinson/Alamy Images

TEKS 3.2A plan and implement descriptive investigations, including asking and answering questions, making inferences, and selecting and using equipment or technology needed, to solve a specific problem in the natural world

S.T.E.M.
Engineering and Technology

Firefighting Tools:
Controlling Forest Fires

Fires play an important role in many forest ecosystems. But large forest fires can damage habitats and homes. Firefighters use special tools to help control forest fires.

Tools like the Pulaski help clear trees and brush. This creates a *firebreak*. Firebreaks stop fires from moving into certain areas.

Some tools protect firefighters. This coat is made from material resistant to fire.

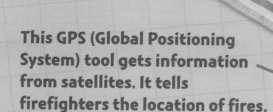

This GPS (Global Positioning System) tool gets information from satellites. It tells firefighters the location of fires.

Special aircraft dump water or chemicals that stop fires.

How can tools help firefighters protect an important habitat?

_____

_____

_____

Solve a Problem

Firefighters need tools to help them stay safe. Other people need safety tools, too. Think of a tool that can help people stay safe. Draw the tool. Tell how it works.

A shovel helps clear underbrush.

How does your tool help people stay safe?

Build On It!

Rise to the engineering design challenge—complete **Design It: Draw a Safari Backpack** on the Inquiry Flipchart.

Name _____

Vocabulary Review

Use the terms in the box to complete the sentences.

consumer
environment
food chain
habitat
producer

TEKS 3.9A

1. The place in a forest where a bear lives is called its

_____.

TEKS 3.9A

2. Everything that surrounds a living thing is its

_____.

TEKS 3.9B

3. Because an oak tree can make its own food, it is a(n)

_____.

TEKS 3.9B

4. Producers and consumers are connected in a(n)

_____.

TEKS 3.9B

5. A deer eats other living things, so it is a(n)

_____.

Science Concepts

Fill in the letter of the choice that best answers the question.

TEKS 3.9A

6. Krystina draws a sketch of a desert in her notebook. She includes lizards, cacti, spiders, owls, rocks, and soil. Which physical characteristics in the environment help support the communities within this ecosystem?

Ⓐ lizards and cacti   Ⓒ rocks and owls

Ⓑ cacti and soil   Ⓓ rocks and soil

TEKS 3.9B, 3.9C

7. Pablo is studying how environmental changes affect living things. He set up a terrarium like the one shown here.

What would most likely happen if he removed the plants from the terrarium?

Ⓐ The insects would reproduce faster.

Ⓑ The insect population would stay the same.

Ⓒ The insects would not get enough food to eat and would die.

Ⓓ The insects would grow bigger because there would be more room in the tank.

TEKS 3.9C

8. The weather report says that some parts of the country should expect heavy rainfall for the next two weeks. How might this affect the environment?

Ⓐ A drought will speed up the process of erosion.

Ⓑ A drought will cause some of the plants to die.

Ⓒ Flooding will provide shelter for more animals.

Ⓓ Flooding will cause some animals to have to move away.

TEKS 3.9B

9. Mei wants to start a vegetable garden in her yard. A neighbor who is a scientist told her to check the soil for earthworms before she starts planting. Why would the neighbor suggest this?

Ⓐ Earthworms cause disease and could harm the plants.

Ⓑ Earthworms are producers and give nutrients to the garden plants.

Ⓒ Earthworms are consumers and will eat the seeds before they can sprout.

Ⓓ Earthworms are decomposers and add nutrients to the soil by breaking down dead organisms.

TEKS 3.9A

10. Animals live in a certain habitat depending on their traits and how they live. Look at the picture below.

Which environment provides the physical characteristics that this animal needs to survive?

Ⓐ a desert

Ⓑ a grassland

Ⓒ a rain forest

Ⓓ a river

480 Unit 10

TEKS 3.9A

11. Soojinn visited a pond near her house and drew the sketch below. It includes ducks, two kinds of fish, and two kinds of plants.

Which physical characteristic in this environment supports all of the populations living in this ecosystem?

(A) air

(B) soil

(C) grass

(D) water

TEKS 3.9A

12. Ecosystems are made of different parts that are related. Which statement below best describes how plants and animals support communities in their ecosystem?

(A) Plants give off carbon dioxide that animals breathe in.

(B) Plants give off oxygen that animals breathe in.

(C) Plants decompose the dead bodies of animals.

(D) Plants take in air and give off water for animals.

TEKS 3.9B

13. Anthony wants to show the flow of energy in a food chain. Identify how energy flows among these four organisms.

(A) grass —> rabbit —> fox —> jaguar

(B) grass —> fox —> rabbit —> jaguar

(C) jaguar —> grass —> rabbit —> fox

(D) fox —> jaguar —> grass —> rabbit

TEKS 3.1B

14. Shante is starting an environmental club at her school. Which of the activities listed below is a direct way that students can make informed choices in conserving resources?

(A) drive instead of bike to school

(B) recycle cans and bottles

(C) leave lights on during the day

(D) use plastic bags instead of paper bags

TEKS 3.9B

15. A scientist studies a group of zebras that all live together in the same area. She records how the zebras interact with the living and nonliving things in their environment. Which part of an ecosystem is she studying?

(A) community

(B) environment

(C) habitat

(D) population

Apply Inquiry and Review the Big Idea

Write the answers to these questions.

TEKS 3.9A

16. David is investigating the ecosystem in his backyard. The picture below shows his house and yard.

a. Describe the living and nonliving parts of this environment.

_____

_____

_____

b. Give an example of how the physical characteristics of the environment support the communities within this ecosystem.

_____

_____

_____

TEKS 3.2F, 3.9C

17. The population of monkeys in a forest was 100. Many trees in the forest were cut down. The environment changed. Three-fourths of the monkeys had to move to new locations.

How many monkeys moved to new locations?

_____

UNIT 11
Living Things Grow and Change

Big Idea

All living things go through a cycle of growth. Living things have adaptations that allow them to survive in their environments.

TEKS 3.2E, 3.2F, 3.3A, 3.3D, 3.9B, 3.10A, 3.10B, 3.10C

I Wonder Why

Why is this mantis shrimp these colors?
Turn the page to find out.

Here's Why The colorful shell of the mantis shrimp helps it blend in with its surroundings. Blending in helps the mantis shrimp hide from predators and surprise prey.

In this unit, you will explore the Big Idea, the Essential Questions, and the Investigations on the Inquiry Flipchart.

Levels of Inquiry Key ■ DIRECTED ■ **GUIDED** ■ INDEPENDENT

Track Your Progress

Big Idea All living things go through a cycle of growth. Living things have adaptations that allow them to survive in their environments.

Essential Questions

Lesson 1 What Are Some Plant Life Cycles? 485
Inquiry Flipchart p. 61—Make It Germinate!/Flowers and Cones

Lesson 2 What Are Some Animal Life Cycles? 495
Inquiry Flipchart p. 62—Model a Life Cycle/Plan a Life Cycle Observation

Inquiry Lesson 3 How Do Living Things Change? 507
Inquiry Flipchart p. 63—How Do Living Things Change?

Lesson 4 What Are Structural Adaptations? 509
Inquiry Flipchart p. 64—Show and Tell/Adapted to Survive

People in Science: Miriam Rothschild and Charles Henry Turner 521

Inquiry Lesson 5 How Can We Model a Physical Adaptation? 523
Inquiry Flipchart p. 65—How Can We Model a Physical Adaptation?

Lesson 6 What Are Behavioral Adaptations? 525
Inquiry Flipchart p. 66—Instinct or Learned Behavior?/Plan a Lesson

S.T.E.M. **Engineering & Technology:** Save It for Later:
Food Preservation 537
Inquiry Flipchart p. 67—Solve It: Helping Animals Migrate

Unit 11 Review 539

Now I Get the Big Idea!

Science Notebook
Before you begin each lesson, be sure to write your thoughts about the Essential Question.

Lesson 1

Essential Question

What Are Some Plant Life Cycles?

Engage Your Brain!

Find the answer to the following question in this lesson and record it here.

How is this hummingbird part of the plant's life cycle?

_____

_____

_____

_____

Active Reading

Lesson Vocabulary

List the terms. As you learn about each one, make notes in the Interactive Glossary.

_____ _____

_____ _____

_____ _____

_____ _____

Compare and Contrast

Many ideas in this lesson are connected because they explain comparisons and contrasts—how things are alike and different. Active readers stay focused on comparisons and contrasts when they ask themselves, How are these things alike? How are they different?

Inquiry Flipchart p. 61—Make It Germinate!/Flowers and Cones

The Cycle of a Plant's Life

Most plants come from seeds. How? Where do seeds come from? Investigate and compare the life cycles of plants.

Active Reading As you read these two pages, find and underline the definitions of *life cycle*, *germinate*, *flower*, *reproduce*, and *cone*.

Plants go through many stages in their lives. These stages form a *cycle*, or pattern, that repeats again and again. The stages an *organism*, or living thing, goes through during its life is its **life cycle**.

Most plants come from seeds. A seed **germinates** when it breaks open and a small plant grows out of it. The plant grows into an adult, which forms flowers in some types of plants. A **flower** is the part of some plants that enables them to **reproduce**, or make more plants similar to themselves.

Flowers can be colorful, dull, big, or small! Flowers have male parts and female parts that are involved in reproduction.

Seedling

When a seed is watered, it begins to germinate. A *seedling* is the tiny new plant that comes out of the seed.

Seed

Inside each seed is a plant in an early stage of its development. The hard outer covering of the seed protects it. These seeds will grow into large tomato plants.

Adult Plant

The seedling grows into an adult plant. The adult tomato plant makes flowers. In flowering plants, seeds are produced in the flowers.

▶ Compare the life cycle of the tomato plant with the pine tree.

_____

_____

_____

Fruit

The flowers fall off the plant, and the plant makes fruit. The fruit holds the seeds.

Some plants make seeds without flowers. Their seeds form in cones. **Cones** are the parts of some seed plants where reproduction occurs. Unlike flowers, cones do not develop into fruit. This pinecone has seeds in it that will grow into new pine trees.

Small Wonders

Did you know that even the tallest trees began as small seeds? Read to learn more.

Active Reading As you read these two pages, draw two lines under each main idea.

Plants that make seeds also make pollen. **Pollen** is a powder-like material involved in plant reproduction. **Pollination** happens when pollen is moved from the male plant part to the female plant part. The environment around a plant helps in pollination. Wind, water, and animals help move pollen from plant to plant. After a plant is pollinated, seeds form in the female parts of the flowers. The part of the flower that surrounds the seeds grows into a fruit. If a flower is not pollinated, it will not form seeds or grow fruit. Animals that eat these plants would need to find another source of food.

Plants make a sweet liquid called nectar. This plant function attracts insects and birds that drink the nectar. They then move from plant to plant carrying pollen with them.

Many seeds have parts that float on the wind. Wind carries these lightweight dandelion seeds to new ground.

Seeds come in many shapes and sizes. When seeds are released from a plant, they are often carried to new areas. Water, wind, and animals carry seeds to new ground. When a seed lands in a good place, it grows into a new plant.

▶ Predict how an ecosystem would be affected if all the bees in a field disappeared.

_____

_____

_____

_____

_____

This fruit has seeds in it. If the bird eats the fruit, the seeds will pass through its body. The seeds may be left in a new place. This is one way seeds are spread.

More and More Spores

Plants with flowers make seeds. Plants with cones make seeds. Do all plants make seeds? Investigate more plant life cycles to find out!

Active Reading As you read this page, draw a circle around a clue word that signals a comparison. Draw a box around a clue word that signals a contrast.

Some plants do not make flowers, cones, or seeds. Instead, they reproduce only with spores. Like seeds, **spores** are reproductive structures that can grow into new plants.

Ferns are one type of plant that reproduces using only spores. Ferns have leaves called *fronds.* Each frond has smaller leaves that branch off from the stem.

Spores form in small groups on the underside of the fern fronds. Each group contains hundreds of spores.

Moss is another type of plant that reproduces using only spores. Mosses are small, soft plants. Groups of moss often grow together in damp places without much light. Sometimes moss looks like a green blanket covering rocks and trees. This blanket is actually made up of many tiny moss plants.

Mosses make spores in little capsules at the end of stalks. The capsules keep the spores dry, while the moss remains damp. When the capsules dry out, they release the spores into the air. These tiny spores float away to make new plants where they land.

Do the Math!
Estimate and Answer

If one fern releases 1,312 spores and one moss plant releases 782 spores, estimate how many more spores the fern plant released.

Sum It Up!

When you're done, use the answer key to check
and revise your work.

Write the vocabulary term that matches each photo and caption.

1 _____

This is what it's called when a
seed starts to grow.

2 _____

Some plants do not have flowers
to help them reproduce. Instead,
they have this plant part.

3 _____

This is what plants do to make
more plants.

4 _____

This is what helps flowering
plants produce seeds.

Summarize

Fill in the missing words to tell about the life cycles of plants.

The different stages that a plant goes through in its life make up its

(5) _____ . After a seed germinates, it becomes a

(6) _____ . Insects are one way that (7) _____

moves from a male plant part to a female plant part. In a flowering plant, the

(8) _____ contains the seeds that will grow into a new plant. Water,

wind, and (9) _____ carry seeds to new ground. Plants like mosses

make (10) _____ but do not make seeds when they reproduce.

Answer Key: 1. germinate 2. cone 3. reproduce 4. pollination
5. life cycle 6. seedling 7. pollen 8. fruit 9. animals 10. spores

Brain Check

Name _____

Word Play

1 Use the words in the box to complete the puzzle.

Across

3. The stages that a plant goes through in its life are called its _____.

5. The colorful part of a plant that helps it reproduce is called a _____.

7. When a seed _____, it breaks open and a small plant grows out of it.

Down

1. _____ happens when pollen moves from the male part of a plant to a female part.

2. The powder-like material that helps plants reproduce is called _____.

4. Plants that make seeds but do not produce a fruit produce a _____.

6. When a seed plant _____, it makes seeds that will grow into new plants.

8. A_____ is the only structure that ferns use when they reproduce.

life cycle*   flower*   reproduces*   germinates*   pollination*   pollen*

cone*   spore*   *Key Lesson Vocabulary

Apply Concepts

2 Draw the life cycle of a peach tree. The first stage is already done.

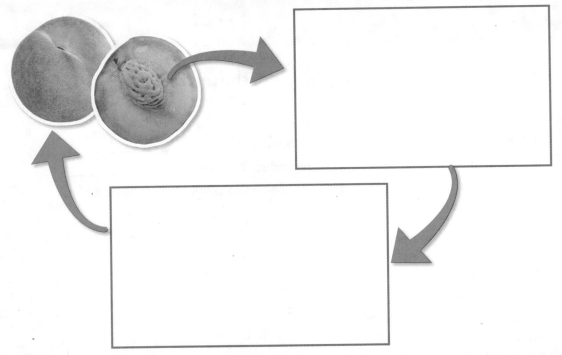

3 In each picture tell whether seeds or pollen are being moved.

_____   _____   _____

Take It Home! Find out more about different types of seeds. Try planting three different types of seeds at home and observing the length of time they take to germinate. Also, pay attention to the amount of water and sunlight that the different seeds need.

sential Question

What Are Some Animal Life Cycles?

Engage Your Brain!

Find the answer to the following question in this lesson and record it here.

Why does this young koala look similar to its mother?

_____

_____

_____

Active Reading

esson Vocabulary

st the terms. As you learn about ach one, make notes in the teractive Glossary.

_____ _____

_____ _____

Sequence

Many ideas in this lesson are connected by a sequence, or order, that describes the steps in a process. Active readers stay focused on sequence when they mark the transition from one step in a process to another.

Life Cycles

Robins hatch from eggs. Dogs give birth to live puppies. What do dogs and robins have in common?

Active Reading As you read these two pages, circle words that show differences between animal life cycles.

Most animals have male and female parents. But not all animals *reproduce*, or have young, in the same way. You can investigate how animals go through changes in their life cycles. Birds and some fish, reptiles, and amphibians lay eggs. Other animals, such as mammals, give birth to live young. These early stages are part of each animal's life cycle. The offspring have the same number of limbs as their parents.

Newborn lynx
A mother lynx gives birth to live cubs. There can be one to four cubs in a litter.

Ostrich egg
The ostrich is the largest bird. It's not surprising that ostriches lay very large eggs.

Horses are mammals and give birth to live young. This foal looks like its mother, only smaller. Both horses have a tail, brown hair, two eyes, and four legs.

Lynx cub

A young lynx grows up in the protection of its mother. A young lynx looks much like its parents, only smaller.

Adult lynx

A young lynx grows into an adult and finds a mate. The two adult lynxes reproduce.

Newborn lynx

The cycle begins again with a new litter of lynx cubs.

Ostrich chick

An ostrich chick depends on its mother to bring it food.

Adult ostrich

All grown up, an adult female can find a mate and reproduce.

What's Next?

Draw the next stage in the ostrich life cycle.

▶ Investigate and compare the changes that the lynx and ostrich go through in their diverse life cycles.

_____

_____

_____

_____

Frog Life Cycle

A frog sits beside a pond, croaking loudly. How did it get there? Let's investigate the changes in a frog's life cycle!

Active Reading As you read these two pages, circle words that name stages in the frog's life cycle.

Early in the spring, many frogs wake from hibernation and begin to croak. They are looking for mates. Before long, the pond's water is filled with eggs. Look closely at the photo of a clump of frog eggs. You will see tiny black specks. One day, each speck will grow into a frog as big and green as the one on this page. As a frog develops, its entire appearance changes. **Metamorphosis** [met•uh•MAWR•fuh•sis] is a major change in the body form of an animal during its life cycle.

Leopard frog

The leopard frog goes through a series of changes after it hatches as a tadpole.

Egg mass

Frog eggs are found all stuck together. They look like a cloud of eggs. They are usually in the water of a pond or marsh.

Tadpole

A tadpole is an immature frog that must live in the water. It hatches from an egg. It has gills and a long tail. It breathes and swims like a fish. It looks very different from its parents.

▶ Compare the series of orderly changes a frog and an ostrich go through in their diverse life cycles.

_____

_____

_____

_____

_____

_____

After about five weeks, the tadpole starts to change. Tiny buds beside the tadpole's tail grow into little hind legs.

Still a tadpole, this young frog has four legs. Its tail will soon disappear. Its lungs are almost completely developed.

Adult frog

This frog has fully developed legs and lungs. There are no gills and no tail. It's an adult!

Insect Life Cycles

Ladybugs crawl up a brick wall. Grasshoppers hop along the ground. Investigate the changes these insects go through during their life cycles!

Active Reading As you read this page, circle a signal word that tells when something happens.

Most insects undergo metamorphosis as they develop into adults. Ladybugs, like butterflies, go through complete metamorphosis. This means that they go through two stages of development between the egg and the adult. In both of these stages, the insect looks very different from the adult.

Some insects, such as grasshoppers and dragonflies, go through incomplete metamorphosis. After hatching, these insects look very much like adult insects. They also go through changes as they grow, but the way they look does not change much.

Complete Metamorphosis

Ladybug eggs

An adult ladybug lays her eggs on a leaf. The egg is the first stage in complete metamorphosis.

Incomplete Metamorphosis

Grasshopper eggs

A grasshopper lays her eggs in the soil. The egg is the first stage of incomplete metamorphosis.

As part of its life cycle, the adult grasshopper grows bigger and gains wings.

Ladybug larva

In the second stage, a ladybug larva hatches from each egg. The larva looks different from the adult.

Ladybug pupa

The larva becomes a pupa. During this third stage, the insect does not move as it slowly changes into an adult.

Adult ladybug

An adult ladybug emerges. The adult stage is the last of the four stages of complete metamorphosis.

Grasshopper nymph

Young grasshoppers, called *nymphs* [NIMFS], hatch from the eggs. A nymph looks like an adult grasshopper, but it doesn't have wings.

Grasshopper nymph

As a nymph grows, it sheds its outer body covering several times. Each time, its wings become larger and more fully formed.

Adult grasshopper

The last shedding produces an adult grasshopper. This is the third and last stage of incomplete metamorphosis.

Do the Math!
Measure in Millimeters

A grasshopper nymph can be 20 millimeters long. Draw a nymph that is that length.

An adult grasshopper can be 45 millimeters long. Draw an adult grasshopper that is that length.

Inherited Traits

Young plants and animals often look like their parents. Why is that?

Active Reading As you read these two pages, underline the main idea.

Imagine a family of dogs. The mother has brown fur. The father has black fur. What color fur will the puppies have? The answer may be different for every single puppy. The puppies get different features from each parent.

All living things share *traits*, or similar characteristics, with their parents. Some traits are the same for both parent and young. For example, dogs have four legs. When puppies are born, they also have four legs. Birds have two legs and two wings. When new birds hatch, they also have two legs and two wings. Traits that are passed from parents to their young are called *inherited traits*.

Plants also inherit traits from their parent plants. Look at the bluebonnet flowers on the next page. What characteristics have been passed on to the offspring?

Explore how this elephant calf looks like its mother. What traits did the calf inherit from its parent?

This bluebonnet is the parent plant. It has blue flowers and large green leaves.

The young bluebonnet looks just like the parent plant. It is the same color as the parent plant. What other traits did it inherit?

▶ Select one plant or animal. Tell which one you picked. Then tell what its offspring might look like.

_____

_____

_____

Sum It Up!

When you're done, use the answer key to check and revise your work.

The blue part of each statement is incorrect. Write words to replace the blue parts.

1 Most reptiles have live births.

_____

2 Ostriches and other birds lay puppies.

_____

3 Tadpoles look exactly like adult frogs.

_____

4 Nymphs hatch from frog eggs.

_____

5 Ladybugs go through incomplete metamorphosis.

_____

6 The stages of the ladybug life cycle are egg, larva, tadpole, adult.

_____

7 A young grasshopper is called a larva.

_____

8 A young pelican inherits four legs from its parents.

_____

Answer Key: 1. mammals 2. eggs 3. very little 4. Tadpoles 5. complete 6. pupa 7. nymph 8. two

504

Name _____

Word Play

1 Use the words in the box to complete the puzzle.

Across

4. A ladybug egg hatches and a _____ comes out.

6. Through _____, a tadpole becomes an adult frog.

8. During complete metamorphosis, a larva becomes a _____.

9. A _____ cycle includes many stages in an organism's life.

Down

1. After the pupa stage, a ladybug is an _____.

2. A _____ is an immature form of a frog.

3. Most birds and reptiles _____ by laying eggs.

5. _____ allow a tadpole to breathe under water.

7. Birds lay an _____ as part of their life cycle.

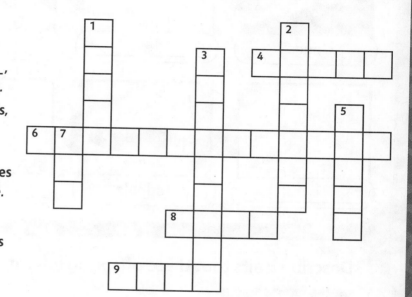

metamorphosis*   larva*   tadpole*   pupa*   gills   life

egg   reproduce   adult

*Key Lesson Vocabulary

Apply Concepts

2 Investigate and compare the life cycles of these animals by filling in the missing stages. Draw or write your answer in the boxes provided.

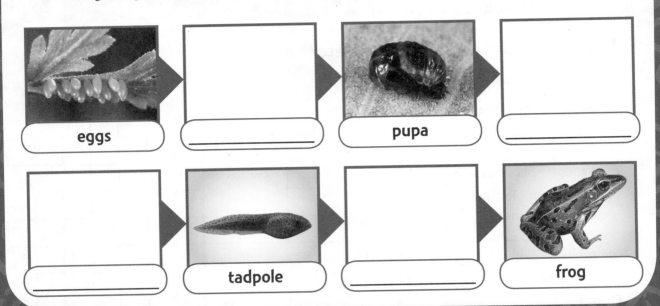

eggs → _____ → pupa → _____

_____ → tadpole → _____ → frog

3 Describe traits that these offspring inherited from their parents.

pelican

_____

_____

_____

orchid

_____

_____

_____

Take It Home! With your family, talk about animal life cycles. Walk in your neighborhood. For one animal you see, tell the stages of its life cycle. If you do not know, investigate it.

TEKS 3.3A in all fields of science, analyze, evaluate, and critique scientific explanations by using empirical evidence, logical reasoning, and experimental and observational testing, including examining all sides of scientific evidence of those scientific explanations, so as to encourage critical thinking by the student

Name _____

Essential Question

How Do Living Things Change?

Set a Purpose

In this activity, you will observe plant seeds several times. Why do you think scientists make many observations?

_____

_____

_____

Think About the Procedure

Why do you think that placing the seeds on a sunny windowsill and watering them is part of the procedure?

_____

_____

_____

_____

How can you make sure you are measuring the growth of the plant accurately?

_____

_____

_____

_____

Record Your Data

Use your simple table to construct a line graph below that shows how your plant grew over time.

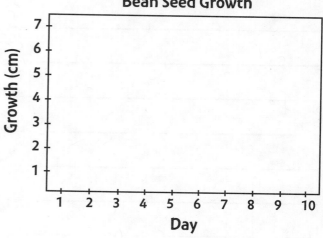

Bean Seed Growth

Draw Conclusions

What did you observe? Infer why the seeds responded this way.

_____

_____

_____

_____

_____

Analyze and Extend

1. Compare your observations with those of classmates. How do others explain different results? Critique explanations using empirical evidence, logical reasoning, and additional observational or experimental testing as needed.

_____

_____

_____

_____

_____

_____

2. What do you think will happen to the plants if you do not water them for the next 10 days? What if you move the plants off the sunny windowsill?

_____

_____

_____

_____

_____

_____

_____

3. Think of other questions you would like to ask about the way seeds grow.

_____

_____

_____

_____

_____

_____

Essential Question

What Are Structural Adaptations?

Engage Your Brain!

Find the answer to the following question in this lesson and record it here.

Why is the pelican's beak so large?

_____

_____

_____

_____

Active Reading

Lesson Vocabulary

List the terms. As you learn about each one, make notes in the Interactive Glossary.

_____

_____

_____

Visual Aids

Pictures and their captions add information to the text on a page. Active readers pause their reading to review pictures and captions, then decide how the information in the pictures and captions adds to what is provided in the text.

Staying Alive

Life in the wild isn't easy. Animals must survive in their particular environment. Explore how adaptations help!

Active Reading As you read these two pages, draw a line from the adaptation shown in each picture to the words that describe it.

An **adaptation** is any trait that helps a living thing survive. Structural adaptations are body parts that help animals survive in their specific environment. Dolphins have blowholes on their heads. This allows them to come to the surface and breathe air without having to come out of the water. Look at the other adaptations on these pages.

What animal is this? It has flat teeth. The flat teeth allow it to grind grass.

The tiger eats animals such as wild boar and deer. The tiger's sharp teeth help it tear meat.

The arctic hare lives in snow and ice. Less heat escapes from its small ears than from the larger ears of other hares. Its small ears help it stay warm in the cold.

The jackrabbit lives in the desert. Its long ears contain many tiny blood vessels that help remove heat from its body. This helps the jackrabbit keep cool in the heat.

Guess Who?

A finch has a beak that it uses to crack seeds and nuts. An eagle uses its beak to tear meat for food. Which bird's beak is shown in photo 1? In photo 2?

1. _____

2. _____

Staying Safe

Look out! It's a predator! Some structural adaptations help animals defend themselves without fighting.

Active Reading As you read these two pages, find and underline examples of defense adaptations.

Defense adaptations may attack a predator's sense of sight, smell, taste, touch, or hearing. A bad taste, loud noise, or nasty odor is often enough to make the predator go away.

A porcupine raises its quills. It swings its tail. One good strike pokes the quills into the attacker's skin. Ouch!

A skunk's spray has a bad odor. Even skunks dislike the smell! The spray also burns the eyes. It's a powerful defense against predators.

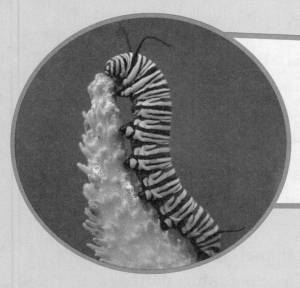

This caterpillar eats milkweed. The milkweed makes the caterpillar taste bad to birds. The pattern of stripes on the caterpillar is a warning to birds. It tells the birds that they don't want to eat it.

The frilled lizard hisses with open jaws. Its frill opens wide. It's a scary sight that frightens some predators away.

Sound the Alarm!

Like pet dogs, prairie dogs bark when they sense danger. How does the ability to bark help them survive?

_____

_____

Creature Costumes

Now you see it. Now you don't. Now you see it—but it looks like something else!

Active Reading As you read these two pages, find and underline the names of two adaptations that involve an animal's appearance.

Some animals can hide without trying. These animals are hidden by their shapes, colors, or patterns. Such disguises are called **camouflage** [KAM•uh•flazh].

Some harmless animals look a lot like animals that are harmful to predators or that taste bad. Since predators don't know which animal is harmful, neither animal gets eaten. Imitating the look of another animal is called **mimicry**.

Look at the color of this snow leopard's fur. Look at its spots. Its camouflage helps it blend into its environment of snow and rock. This helps it sneak up on prey.

This orchid mantis is the same color as the flower it's sitting on. The insect is perfectly camouflaged!

◄ **Monarch butterfly**

Eating monarch butterflies makes birds sick. Birds avoid eating them. The viceroy looks like the monarch, so birds leave them alone, too.

◄ **Viceroy butterfly**

The frogfish can look like a rock or a sponge. It can look like algae. Animals try to rest on the "rock." Others try to eat the "algae." The frogfish traps and eats them!

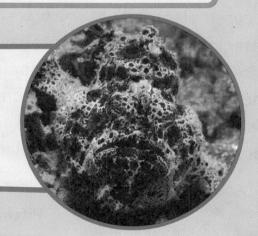

Make It Blend!

Color the lizard so that it is hidden on the leaf. On the line below, identify whether this is camouflage or mimicry.

_____

Plant Facts

Plants' structures help them survive in their environments, too. Explore to find out more!

Active Reading As you read these two pages, draw a line from the pictures to the words that tell how an adaptation helps a plant.

Plants need water. There isn't much water in a desert, so desert plants are adapted to hold moisture. Desert plants such as cactuses have thick stems that store water. The leaves of desert plants also have a waxy coating that helps prevent water loss. Most desert plants have spines, not leaves. Narrow spines help prevent water vapor from escaping from the plant. The spines also keep animals from eating the plants. Other plants have different structural adaptations that help them survive. Explore the different plants on these pages.

Pitcher plants can't get the nutrients they need from soil. The plants' pitchers hold water and trap insects for food. The sides are slippery, so when insects fall into the pitchers, they can't get out! The insects are digested, providing nutrients to the plant.

Blackberries taste bitter until they are ripe. Their bitter taste is an adaptation. It stops animals from eating the berries before the seeds are old enough to produce new plants.

The stone plant blends into the background of rocks and stones. Grazing animals don't see it. Camouflage keeps it from being eaten.

Do the Math!
Solve a Word Problem

A red pitcher plant catches 3 insects each week. A green pitcher plant catches 2 insects each week. How many more insects does the red plant catch in four weeks than the green plant? Show your work.

_____

_____

_____

_____

Sum It Up!

When you're done, use the answer key to check and revise your work.

Complete the summary. Use it to complete the graphic organizer.

Summarize

(1) _____ are characteristics that help living things survive.

(2) _____ is a kind of adaptation. It helps the frogfish blend into algae and catch prey. An adaptation called

(3) _____ makes the harmless viceroy butterfly look like the harmful monarch butterfly.

Main Idea: Living things have adaptations that help them survive in their environments.

(4) Detail:	(5) Detail:	Detail: A horse has flat teeth to help it grind grass.

© Houghton Mifflin Harcourt Publishing Company   (t) ©Eclectic Images/Alamy Images; (b) ©Nathan Allred/Alamy Images

Name _____

Word Play

1 Unscramble the letters to complete each clue.

1. _____ help living things survive in their environments.	p i d t a t a n a o s
2. Some plants have adaptations that help _____ them against animals that eat them.	f e d d e n
3. _____ helps an animal blend into its surroundings.	f a m a l o g c u e
4. An adaptation that makes one organism look like another is called _____.	y i m r m c i
5. A porcupine's _____ protect it from other animals.	s i l u q l
6. Animals do not eat the _____ butterfly because it looks like the monarch butterfly.	c o i r e y v

Apply Concepts

2 Look at each picture. Write the kind of adaptation that it shows.

_____   _____

3 Draw two pictures. Show a structural adaptation of a plant. Show a structural adaptation of an animal. Write captions to describe each.

Plant Adaptation

Animal Adaptation

_____   _____

_____   _____

_____   _____

Take It Home!

Observe a plant or animal in its natural habitat. What is one of its adaptations? How does the adaptation help it survive?

People in Science

Meet the Insect Scientists

Miriam Rothschild 1908–2005

As a child, Miriam Rothschild collected beetles and caterpillars. Later, she studied fleas and other parasites. Parasites are living things that live on or in other living things. Rothschild studied fleas on rabbits' fur. She discovered how fleas jump. In 1952, she wrote her first book. It was called *Fleas, Flukes and Cuckoos*. In 1973, she finished a book about 30,000 different fleas.

Rothschild studied the life cycle of the flea and how it reproduces.

Charles Henry Turner 1867–1923

Charles Turner was an entomologist, a scientist who studies insects. He studied many kinds of insects, including ants and honeybees. In 1910, he proved that honeybees can see color. The next year he proved they could also see patterns. Turner found that some ants move in circles toward their home. To honor his work with ants, scientists call this behavior "Turner's circling."

Turner showed that honeybees can see a flower's color.

The Insect Scientists

Connect science concepts with the history of science by using what you read about Rothschild and Turner to fill in each box.

_____
_____
_____
_____

1952 Rothschild writes her first book.

1910 Turner proves that honeybees can see color.

1908 Miriam Rothschild is born.

1907 Charles Turner writes about his study of ants.

_____
_____
_____
_____

Think About It!

After what year on the timeline should you add the following?

A scientist names the circles that ants make when returning home "Turner's circling."

_____

TEKS **3.2E** demonstrate that repeated investigations may increase the reliability of results **3.2F** communicate valid conclusions supported by data in writing, by drawing pictures, and through verbal discussion

Name _____

Essential Question

How Can We Model a Physical Adaptation?

Set a Purpose
What will you learn from this experiment?

_____

_____

_____

Think About the Procedure
How do you think the stickiness of the tongue will affect the number of insects the frog catches? State your prediction.

_____

_____

_____

Why do you think the pieces of paper are all the same size?

_____

_____

_____

_____

_____

Record Your Data
Record the number of insects caught with a sticky tongue and with a wet tongue for each of your five trials.

Trial	1	2	3	4	5
Sticky tongue					
Wet tongue					

Draw Conclusions

Which is better at catching insects: a sticky tongue or a wet tongue? Communicate your conclusion in writing.

_____

_____

What did you demonstrate by repeating your investigation?

_____

_____

Analyze and Extend

1. How is a sticky tongue an example of an adaptation?

_____

_____

_____

_____

_____

2. How would this experiment change if the insects were inside a test tube instead of on the flat desktop?

_____

_____

_____

3. Suppose you were an insect that lived in an area with many sticky-tongued frogs. What adaptation might help you survive?

_____

_____

_____

_____

_____

4. What kind of tongue is better for catching insects? What other animals do you think might have this kind of tongue?

_____

_____

_____

_____

_____

5. What other questions do you have about adaptations for eating?

_____

_____

_____

_____

_____

TEKS 3.10A explore how structures and functions of plants and animals allow them to survive in a particular environment **3.10B** explore that some characteristics of organisms are inherited such as the number of limbs on an animal or flower color and recognize that some behaviors are learned in response to living in a certain environment such as animals using tools to get food

Lesson 6

Essential Question

What Are Behavioral Adaptations?

Engage Your Brain!

Find the answer to the following question in this lesson and record it here.

Migrating geese often fly in a V formation. How do they know when it is time to migrate?

_____

_____

_____

Active Reading

Lesson Vocabulary

List the terms. As you learn about each one, make notes in the Interactive Glossary.

_____   _____

_____   _____

_____

Compare and Contrast

Many ideas in this lesson are connected because they show comparisons and contrasts—how things are alike and how things are different. Active readers stay focused on comparisons and contrasts by asking themselves, How are these things alike? How are these things different?

Know It or Learn It?

Eating, sleeping, finding shelter, and moving from place to place. How do animals know what to do?

Active Reading As you read these two pages, recognize and circle words that tell how instinct and learned behaviors are different. Underline examples of each.

A **behavior** is anything an organism does. **Learned behaviors** are behaviors that come from watching other animals or through experience. These behaviors are learned in response to the animal's environment.

There are other behaviors. An **instinct** is a behavior that an animal knows without learning it. Animals are born with instincts. Behaviors are adaptations that may help an animal survive in its environment.

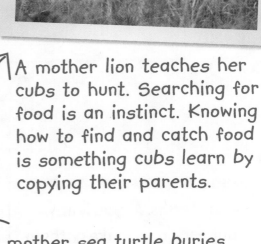

A mother lion teaches her cubs to hunt. Searching for food is an instinct. Knowing how to find and catch food is something cubs learn by copying their parents.

A mother sea turtle buries her eggs in the sand. Most young sea turtles hatch at night. Their instinct is to go toward the brightest area. This instinct helps the hatchlings find the ocean.

A chimpanzee isn't born knowing how to use a tool. It learns this behavior by watching others. Sometimes, a chimp may figure it out on its own.

It is an instinct for some birds to sing, but sometimes the songs they sing are learned from other birds.

A spider's web helps it survive. The web is sticky, so it traps insects. But how does a spider know how to spin a web? This is an instinctive behavior.

A moth's instinct is to use moonlight to find its way. That is why moths are attracted to porch lights.

▶ How are instincts and learned behaviors alike?

_____

_____

_____

_____

Finding Food

Hungry. Cold. Wet. That's what animals would be without the instinct to find food and shelter.

Active Reading As you read these two pages, underline details that tell ways animals find food. Circle ways animals find shelter.

Every animal looks for food when it's hungry. It's an instinctual behavior. But actually finding food can be a learned behavior. Some animals learn from watching their parents or other adults. But some animals can learn by themselves, too.

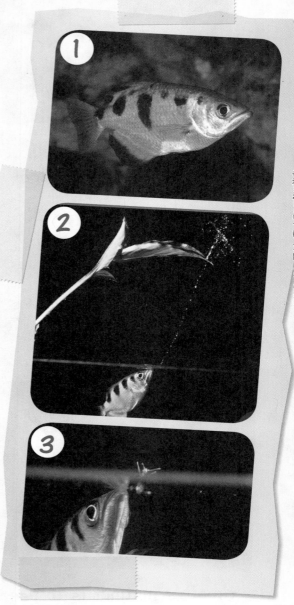

Bears come to this stream to catch salmon. The bears wait for the fish to swim upstream. This is a learned behavior.

How did this archerfish know how to get food from above the water? The fish instinctively shoots water at insects in the air to catch them.

Finding Shelter

These birds learned to build nests on buildings when trees were cut down.

A gopher uses what it has—soil and claws—to make a shelter in the ground.

How Animals Survive

How does the function of building an anthill help the group of ants?

_____

_____

_____

_____

_____

_____

Ants work together to make an anthill. They use the soil around them. The hill hides a tunnel system that provides shelter and storage space for food.

Hibernation

Some animals live in environments that get cold. Let's explore how some animals survive.

Active Reading As you read these two pages, draw a line under the words that describe what is happening to the animals in the photos.

Animals respond to cold winter weather in different ways. Some animals stay active during winter. They find food or eat food they have hidden. Some animals **hibernate**, or go into a deep, sleeplike state that helps them survive the cold winter conditions. Normal body activities slow down. The heart beats slowly, and breathing almost stops. Hibernating is an instinctive behavior.

A hibernating animal doesn't use much energy, because its body is barely working. There is enough fat stored in the animal's body to keep it alive through the winter.

This ground squirrel spent the fall eating and gaining weight. It stored up enough energy to survive winter hibernation. The squirrel's heart rate and breathing have become slower.

© Houghton Mifflin Harcourt Publishing Company (b) ©James Simon/Photo Researchers, Inc.

Many bats like this one hibernate in the winter. In the spring when the weather warms up, there is more food for the bat. It will come out of hibernation.

Some plants also have a functional adaptation that helps them survive the winter. Many trees go dormant in the winter. They lose their leaves and stop growing. When the temperatures begin to warm up in the springtime, the trees produce new leaves and begin growing again.

These snakes are all hibernating together. When spring arrives, they will leave this den.

Function of Hibernation

Explain how the function of hibernation allows an animal to survive in its environment.

_____

_____

_____

_____

Migration

Some animals are travelers. Explore how some animals use the function of migration to survive in their environments.

Active Reading As you read, compare the different reasons animals migrate. Circle each reason an animal might migrate.

Animals **migrate** when they move a long distance as a group from one region to another and back. Whales swim to a warm place to mate. They swim to a different spot to give birth. Then they swim back to where they were to find food.

Many animals, including birds and fish, migrate. Whales and some other animals teach their young the way to go. The path the animals take is learned, but knowing when to migrate is an instinct.

Gray whales have one of the longest migration routes of any mammal. They travel up to 21,000 kilometers each year. Gray whales swim from the cold Arctic to warm Mexico to have their young.

In the winter, when the land freezes over in the Arctic, tundra swans fly to the warmer south. When the weather warms up, the swans return to the Arctic. There, they mate and wait for their eggs to hatch.

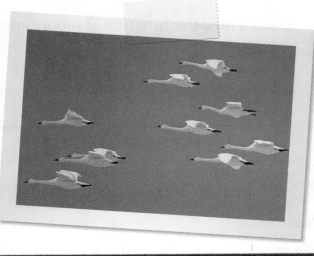

Migration Routes of Gray Whales and Tundra Swans

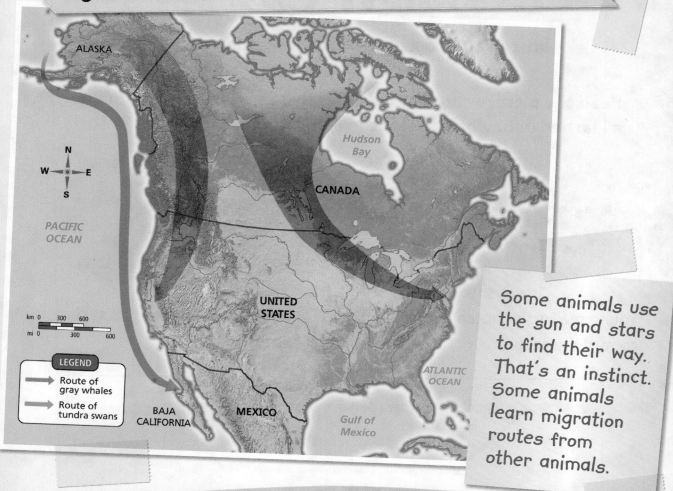

Some animals use the sun and stars to find their way. That's an instinct. Some animals learn migration routes from other animals.

Do the Math!
Make a Graph

Many animals migrate. The gray whale may travel over 10,000 kilometers each way as it migrates. The tundra swan may travel over 3,000 kilometers each way as it migrates. Draw a bar graph to compare the distances.

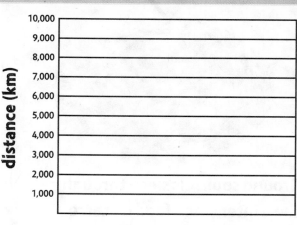

Sum It Up!

When you're done, use the answer key to check and revise your work.

Read the picture clues. Decide if each behavior is an instinct or a learned behavior. Label the graphic organizer.

1

Young sea turtles hatch and walk toward the ocean.

_____

2

Chimps use tools like this stick to get food.

_____

Behavioral Adaptations

3

Ground squirrels sleep through the winter when food is scarce.

_____

4

Grizzly bears wait in the water to catch fish.

_____

Answer Key: 1. instinct 2. learned behavior 3. instinct 4. learned behavior

Name _____

Word Play

1 Use the words in the box to complete the puzzle.

| adaptations | behavior* | instinct* | learn |
| migrate* | parent | shelter | hibernate* |

* Key Lesson Vocabulary

Across

4. Behaviors are _____ that help organisms survive.

7. Animals that _____ take a long winter's rest.

8. Animals _____ to hunt by watching other animals.

Down

1. A young animal learns behaviors by watching its _____.

2. Animals that need a warm place out of the rain seek _____.

3. Looking for food and shelter is an _____.

5. Each year, gray whales _____ thousands of miles.

6. Migration and hibernation are two examples of animal _____.

Apply Concepts

2 How are instincts and learned behaviors the same? What is the difference between them?

_____

_____

_____

_____

3 Look at the photos. Write how each function helps the animal survive.

_____ _____ _____ _____

_____ _____ _____ _____

_____ _____ _____ _____

_____ _____ _____ _____

Take It Home! Talk to your family about the things you do every day. Which things have you learned? Which are instincts?

S.T.E.M.
Engineering and Technology

Save It for Later:
Food Preservation

Long ago, people learned to save, or preserve, food. First, people used nature to help them preserve food. Then, people made tools and processes to help. Follow the timeline to see how food preservation has changed over time.

5,000 Years Ago

Salt preserved meat. Ice kept food from spoiling. People dried meat and fruit.

1795

Heating foods in glass jars kept them fresh. Preserving foods in glass jars and metal cans became common.

1855

In an icebox, air flowed around a block of ice like this one. The cool air kept food fresh.

What types of food preservation are still used today? Why are older ways still used even though we have newer tools?

_____

_____

_____

Frozen dinners last about six months.

Analyze a Product

Grocery stores are filled with products that are preserved for freshness. Think about a favorite product you buy in the grocery store.

1900s

Refrigerators became common in the 1940s. Before the 1990s, most refrigerators used gases that harmed the atmosphere.

How is your favorite product preserved? How does the package help it stay fresh? How long does it last after you open it?

_____

_____

_____

Build On It!

DESIGN PROCESS STEPS

Rise to the engineering design challenge—complete **Solve It: Helping Animals Migrate** on the Inquiry Flipchart.

Vocabulary Review

Use the terms in the box to complete the sentences.

> adaptation
> behavior
> germinate
> life cycle
> metamorphosis

TEKS 3.10C

1. A frog develops front and back legs during

   _____.

TEKS 3.10B

2. A bird building a nest is an example of a(n)

   _____.

TEKS 3.10C

3. Before a new plant can grow, the seed must

   _____.

TEKS 3.10C

4. Snakes lay eggs as part of their _____.

TEKS 3.10A

5. The quill of a porcupine is a structural _____.

Science Concepts

Fill in the letter of the choice that best answers the question.

TEKS 3.10C

6. Which stage of a butterfly's life cycle is being shown at step 3?

   Ⓐ adult   Ⓒ larva
   Ⓑ egg   Ⓓ pupa

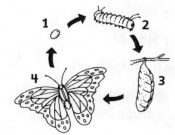

TEKS 3.10B

7. Some animal behaviors are learned in response to living in a certain environment. Some come from instinct. Which of the following behaviors is based on instinct?

Ⓐ a chimpanzee using a tool to dig up insects

Ⓑ bats hibernating in the winter months

Ⓒ lion cubs imitating the hunting behaviors of their mother

Ⓓ a dog responding to its owner's commands

TEKS 3.10A

8. Oscar enjoys bird watching. His favorite bird is a warbler, but he can see them only until September. Then the warblers head south in search of food. What is the warbler's behavior an example of?

Ⓐ camouflage   Ⓒ migration

Ⓑ hibernation   Ⓓ mimicry

TEKS 3.10C

9. What is the main difference between the life cycles of ferns and of tomato plants?

Ⓐ Only ferns reproduce by seeds.

Ⓑ Only ferns reproduce by spores.

Ⓒ Only tomato plants reproduce by cones.

Ⓓ Only tomato plants reproduce by spores

TEKS 3.10A

10. Animals have body structures that help them find food and shelter or defend themselves from predators. Look at the picture below.

What adaptation helps the cheetah compete with other animals for food?

Ⓐ climbing ability

Ⓑ a long life cycle

Ⓒ fur to maintain body heat

Ⓓ strong legs for high-speed hunting

TEKS 3.10A

11. Flowers come in many shapes, sizes, and colors. How do these structures allow plants to survive in their particular environments?

Ⓐ The different flowers help make a garden look attractive.

Ⓑ The different flowers help the plant get the most sunlight.

Ⓒ The different flower types help the plant survive in different climates.

Ⓓ The different flower types attract different kinds of insects to pollinate them.

TEKS 3.10C

12. Tanisha is making a chart about the life cycle of a pine tree. Place the stages of the tree's life cycle below in the correct sequence.

> 1. A seed forms inside a cone.
>
> 2. A plant grows into an adult pine tree.
>
> 3. A cone is pollinated.
>
> 4. A seed germinates and a new plant sprouts.

Ⓐ 1, 2, 3, 4

Ⓑ 3, 1, 4, 2

Ⓒ 2, 1, 4, 3

Ⓓ 4, 3, 2, 1

TEKS 3.10C

13. Sara is studying how animals undergo a series of orderly changes in their different life cycles. She sees the insect shown below. How does the life cycle of this insect differ from that of a frog?

Ⓐ It undergoes hibernation in the winter.

Ⓑ It undergoes migration in the summer.

Ⓒ It does not have legs when it hatches.

Ⓓ It breathes air when it hatches.

TEKS 3.10A

14. A scientist is studying the behavior of chipmunks. She records the information below.

Month	Average Body Temperature (°F)
January	55
April	90
June	99
October	95

Which adaptation is shown in the table above?

Ⓐ camouflage

Ⓑ hibernation

Ⓒ migration

Ⓓ mimicry

TEKS 3.10A

15. Which function of a cactus allows it to survive long dry periods in its environment?

Ⓐ It produces green stems.

Ⓑ It absorbs water from the air.

Ⓒ It stores water in its thick stems.

Ⓓ It produces sharp spines.

TEKS 3.10B

16. An organism has six legs and two wings. What characteristics of this organism would you expect its offspring to inherit?

Ⓐ six legs and two wings

Ⓑ six legs and four wings

Ⓒ four legs and two wings

Ⓓ two legs and two wings

Apply Inquiry and Review the Big Idea

Write the answers to these questions.

TEKS 3.2A

17. Matt is investigating the life cycle of plants. He wants to find out how fruit forms. Plan a descriptive investigation that he can do to find out. Identify the question he should ask, how he can find the answer, and any inferences he might make. Select the equipment or technology that will be needed. Describe ways he could communicate his conclusion.

_____

_____

_____

_____

_____

_____

TEKS 3.10C

18. Katerina is doing a project on the life cycles of a frog and a peach tree. Explain how she could compare the changes that each undergoes as part of its life cycle.

_____

_____

_____

_____

_____

TEKS 3.10C

19. The life cycles of plants vary. Redwood trees live several hundred years. Suppose in 2014, a scientist finds out that a redwood tree is 650 years old. Based on her findings, in what year would the redwood tree have germinated?

_____

Interactive Glossary

As you learn about each term, add notes, drawings, or sentences in the extra space. This will help you remember what the terms mean. Here are some examples.

Fungi [FUHN•jeye] A kingdom of organisms that have a nucleus and get nutrients by decomposing other organisms

A mushroom is from the kingdom Fungi.

physical change [FIZ•i•kuhl CHAYNJ] Change in the size, shape, or state of matter with no new substance being formed

When I cut paper, the paper has a physical change.

Glossary Pronunciation Key

With every glossary term, there is also a phonetic respelling. A phonetic respelling writes the word the way it sounds, which can help you pronounce new or unfamiliar words. Use this key to help you understand the respellings.

Sound	As in	Phonetic Respelling	Sound	As in	Phonetic Respelling
a	bat	(BAT)	oh	over	(OH•ver)
ah	lock	(LAHK)	oo	pool	(POOL)
air	rare	(RAIR)	ow	out	(OWT)
ar	argue	(AR•gyoo)	oy	foil	(FOYL)
aw	law	(LAW)	s	cell	(SEL)
ay	face	(FAYS)		sit	(SIT)
ch	chapel	(CHAP•uhl)	sh	sheep	(SHEEP)
e	test	(TEST)	th	that	(THAT)
	metric	(MEH•trik)		thin	(THIN)
ee	eat	(EET)	u	pull	(PUL)
	feet	(FEET)	uh	medal	(MED•uhl)
	ski	(SKEE)		talent	(TAL•uhnt)
er	paper	(PAY•per)		pencil	(PEN•suhl)
	fern	(FERN)		onion	(UHN•yuhn)
eye	idea	(eye•DEE•uh)		playful	(PLAY•fuhl)
i	bit	(BIT)		dull	(DUHL)
ing	going	(GOH•ing)	y	yes	(YES)
k	card	(KARD)		ripe	(RYP)
	kite	(KYT)	z	bags	(BAGZ)
ngk	bank	(BANGK)	zh	treasure	(TREZH•er)

Interactive Glossary

A

absorb [ab•SAWRB] Take in by an object (p. 179)

adaptation [ad•uhp•TAY•shuhn] Trait or characteristic that helps an organism survive (p. 510)

atmosphere [AT•muhs•feer] The layer of gases that surround Earth (p. 358)

axis [AK•sis] The imaginary line around which Earth rotates (p. 381)

B

bar graph [BAR GRAF] A graph using parallel bars of varying lengths to show comparison (p. 35)

behavior [bi•HAYV•yer] The way that an organism usually acts in a certain situation (p. 526)

C

camouflage [KAM•uh•flazh] The coloring, marking, or other physical appearance of an organism that helps it blend in with its surroundings (p. 514)

canyon [KAN•yuhn] A valley with steep sides (p. 260)

chart [CHART] A display that organizes data into rows and columns (p. 35)

compound machine [KAHM•pownd muh•SHEEN] A machine that is made up of two or more simple machines (p. 229)

chemical change [KEM•i•kuhl CHAYNJ] A change in one or more substances that forms new and different substances (p. 134)

condensation [kahn•duhn•SAY•shuhn] The process by which a gas changes into a liquid (pp. 123, 348)

clay [KLAY] The smallest particles of rock that make up soil (p. 324)

cone [KOHN] A part of some nonflowering plants where seeds form (p. 487)

community [kuh•MYOO•ni•tee] All the populations of organisms that live and interact in an area (p. 436)

conservation [kahn•ser•VAY•shuhn] The use of less of something to make its supply last longer. (p. 307)

Interactive Glossary

consumer [kuhn·SOOM·er] A living thing that cannot make its own food and must eat other living things (p. 452)

design process [di·ZYN PRAWS·es] The process of applying basic principles of engineering to solve problems (p. 56)

D

data [DAY·tuh] Individual facts, statistics, and items of information (p. 33)

dissolve [di·ZAWLV] To completely and evenly mix one substance in another (p. 131)

data table [DAY·tuh TAY·buhl] A kind of chart used for recording number data (p. 35)

drought [DROWT] A long period of time with very little rain (p. 467)

E

decomposer [dee·kuhm·POHZ·er] A living thing that gets energy by breaking down dead organisms and animal wastes (p. 452)

earthquake [ERTH·kwayk] A shaking of Earth's surface that can cause land to rise and fall (p. 284)

ecosystem [EE•koh•sis•tuhm] A community of organisms and the physical environment in which they live (p. 434)

environment [en•VY•ruhn•muhnt] All the living and nonliving things that surround and affect an organism (p. 434)

electrical energy [ee•LEK•tri•kuhl EN•er•jee] A form of energy that can move through wires (p. 152)

erosion [i•ROH•zhuhn] The process of moving weathered rock and soil from one place to another (pp. 272, 466)

empirical evidence [em•PEER•i•kuhl ev•uh•duhns] Data collected during an investigation (p. 33)

evaporation [ee•vap•uh•RAY•shuhn] The process by which a liquid changes into a gas (pp. 122, 348)

energy [EN•er•jee] The ability to make something move or change (pp. 150, 162)

experiment [ek•SPAIR•i•muhnt] A test done to see whether a hypothesis is correct (p. 11)

Interactive Glossary

F

flood [FLUHD] A large amount of water that covers normally dry land (pp. 288, 467)

flower [FLOW•er] The part of a flowering plant that produces seeds (p. 486)

food chain [FOOD CHAYN] A series of organisms that depend on one another for food (p. 454)

force [FAWRS] A push or a pull (p. 241)

fossil fuel [FAHS•uhl FYOO•uhl] Fuel formed from the remains of once-living things. Coal, oil, and natural gas are fossil fuels. (p. 307)

fresh water [FRESH WAW•ter] Water that has very little salt in it (p. 344)

fulcrum [FUHL•kruhm] The balance point of a lever that supports the arm but does not move (p. 212)

G

gas [GAS] The state of matter that does not have a definite shape or volume (p. 116)

germinate [JER•muh•nayt] To start to grow (a seed) (p. 486)

habitat [HAB•i•tat] The place where an organism lives and can find everything it needs to survive (p. 434)

glacier [GLAY•sher] A large, thick sheet of slow-moving ice (p. 272)

heat [HEET] Energy that moves from warmer to cooler objects (p. 190)

graduated cylinder [GRAJ•oo•ay•tid sil•in•der] A container marked with a graded scale used for measuring liquids (p. 21)

hibernate [HY•ber•nayt] To go into a deep, sleeplike state for winter (p. 530)

gravity [GRAV•i•tee] A force that pulls two objects toward each other. (p. 241)

humus [HYOO•muhs] The remains of decayed plants or animals in the soil (p. 320)

Interactive Glossary

hypothesis [hy•PAHTH•uh•sis] A possible answer to a question that can be tested to see if it is correct (p. 10)

investigation [in•ves•tuh•GAY•shuhn] Procedure carried out to carefully observe, study, or test something in order to learn more about it (p. 9)

I

inclined plane [in•KLYND PLAYN] A simple machine that is a slanted surface (p. 224)

K

kinetic energy [ki•NET•ik EN•er•jee] The energy of motion (p. 150)

infer [in•FER] To draw a conclusion about something (p. 6)

L

landform (LAND•fawrm] A natural shape or feature on Earth's surface (p. 259)

instinct [IN•stinkt] An inherited behavior of an animal that helps it meet its needs (p. 526)

larva [LAR•vuh] The stage between egg and pupa in complete metamorphosis in insects (p. 501)

learned behavior [LERND bee•HAYV•yer] A behavior that an animal doesn't begin life with but develops as a result of experience or by observing other animals (p. 526)

M

map [MAP] A picture that shows the locations of things (p. 35)

lever [LEV•er] A simple machine made up of a bar that pivots, or turns, on a fixed point (p. 212)

mass [MAS] The amount of matter in an object (p. 96)

life cycle [LYF SY•kuhl] The stages that a living thing passes through as it grows and changes (p. 486)

matter [MAT•er] Anything that takes up space and has mass (p. 95)

liquid [LIK•wid] The state of matter that has a definite volume but no definite shape (p. 116)

mechanical energy [muh•KAN•i•kuhl EN•er•jee] The total potential and kinetic energy of an object (p. 150)

Interactive Glossary

metamorphosis [met•uh•MAWR•fuh•sis] A phase in the life cycle of many animals during which they undergo major changes in body form (p. 498)

mixture [MIKS•cher] A combination of two or more different substances that keep their identities (p. 130)

microscope [MY•kruh•skohp] A tool that makes an object look several times bigger than it is (p. 19)

model [MOD•uhl] A representation of something real that is too big, too small, or that has too many parts to be studied directly (p. 34)

migrate [MY•grayt] To travel from one place to another and back again (p. 532)

mountain [MOWNT•uhn] The highest kind of land, with sides that slope toward its top (p. 262)

mimicry [MIM•i•kree] An adaptation in which a harmless animal looks like an animal that is poisonous or tastes bad, so that predators avoid it (p. 514)

N

natural resource [NACH•er•uhl REE•sawrs] Anything from nature that people can use (p. 304)

nonrenewable resource
[nahn•ri•NOO•uh•buhl REE•sawrs] A resource that, once used, cannot be replaced in a reasonable amount of time (p. 307)

nutrients [NOO•tree•uhnts] Substances in soil that plants need to grow and stay healthy (p. 326)

P

photosynthesis [foh•toh•SIN•thuh•sis] The process in which plants use energy from the sun to change carbon dioxide and water into sugar and oxygen (p. 450)

physical change [FIZ•i•kuhl CHAYNJ] A change in which a new substance is not formed (p. 128)

O

observe [uhb•ZERV] To use your senses to gather information (p. 6)

physical property [FIZ•i•kuhl PRAHP•er•tee] A characteristic of matter that you can observe or measure directly (p. 95)

oxygen [OK•si•jen] A gas in the air and water, which most living things need to survive (p. 358)

pitch [PICH] How high or low a sound is (p. 167)

Interactive Glossary

plain [PLAYN] Flat land that spreads out a long way (p. 264)

pollination [pawl•uh•NAY•shuhn] The transfer of pollen from the male structures to the female structures of seed plants (p. 488)

planet [PLAN•it] A large, round body that revolves around a star in a clear orbit (p. 410)

pollution [puh•LOO•shuhn] Any harmful substance in the environment (p. 310)

plateau [pla•TOH] A flat area higher than the land around it (p. 264)

population [pahp•yuh•LAY•shuhn] All the organisms of the same kind that live together in an ecosystem (p. 436)

pollen [PAHL•uhn] A powder-like material that plants need to make seeds (p. 488)

potential energy [poh•TEN•shuhl EN•er•jee] Stored energy (p. 150)

© Houghton Mifflin Harcourt Publishing Company   HMH Credits

precipitation [pri•sip•uh•TAY•shuhn] Water that falls from clouds to Earth's surface (p. 350)

pupa [PYOO•puh] The stage of complete metamorphosis in which an insect changes from a larva to an adult (p. 501)

predict [pri-DIKT] Use observations and data to form an idea of what will happen under certain conditions (p. 8)

R

reflect [ri•FLEKT] To bounce off (p. 180)

producer [pruh•DOOS•er] A living thing, such as a plant, that can make its own food (p. 450)

refract [ri•FRAKT] To bend light as it moves from one material to another (p. 182)

pulley [PUHL•ee] A simple machine made of a wheel with a rope, cord, or chain around it (p. 216)

renewable resource [ri•NOO•uh•buhl REE•sawrs] A resource that can be replaced within a reasonable amount of time (p. 304)

Interactive Glossary

reproduce [ree•pruh•DOOS] To make more living things of the same kind (p. 486)

sand [SAND] The largest particles of rock that make up soil (p. 324)

revolution [rev•uh•LOO•shuhn] The movement of Earth one time around the sun (p. 382)

screw [SKROO] A simple machine made of a post with an inclined plane wrapped around it (p. 226)

rotation [ro•TAY•shuhn] The turning of Earth on its axis (p. 381)

shadow [SHAD•oh] A dark area that forms when an object blocks the path of light (p. 179)

S

salt water [SAWLT WAW•ter] Water found in oceans and seas; makes up 97% of Earth's water (p. 344)

silt [SILT] Particles of rock that are smaller than sand but larger than clay. (p. 324)

R14

simple machine [SIM•puhl muh•SHEEN] A machine with few or no moving parts that you apply just one force to (p. 212)

solution [suh•LOO•shuhn] A mixture in which all the parts are evenly mixed (p. 131)

soil [SOYL] A mixture of water, air, tiny pieces of rock, and humus (p. 320)

sound [SOWND] Energy that travels in waves you can hear (p. 162)

solar system [SOH•ler SIS•tuhm] The sun, and the planets, and the planets' moons that move around the sun. (p. 410)

spore [SPAWR] A reproductive structure made by seedless plants, including mosses and ferns (p. 490)

solid [SAHL•id] A state of matter that has a definite volume and shape (p. 116)

star [STAR] A hot ball of glowing gases that gives off energy (p. 399)

Interactive Glossary

sun [SUHN] The star closest to Earth (p. 398)

temperature [TEM•per•uh•cher] A measure of how hot or cold something is (pp. 23, 102, 191, 360)

T

tadpole [TAD•pohl] A young frog that comes out of an egg and has gills to take in oxygen from the water (p. 499)

tide [TYD] The regular rise and fall of the ocean's surface, caused mostly by the moon's gravitational pull on Earth's oceans (p. 388)

V

technology [tek•NAWL•uh•jee] Anything that people make or do that changes the natural world (p. 70)

valley [VAL•ee] The low land between mountains or hills (p. 260)

telescope [TEL•uh•skohp] A device people use to observe distant objects with their eyes (p. 404)

variable [VAIR•ee•uh•buhl] The one thing that changes in an experiment (p. 11)

vibrate [VY•brayt] To move back and forth very quickly (p. 164)

weather [WETH•er] What is happening in the atmosphere at a certain place and time (p. 358)

volcano [vahl•KAY•noh] A mountain made of lava, ash, or other materials from eruptions (p. 286)

weathering [WETH•er•ing] The breaking down of rocks on Earth's surface into smaller pieces (p. 270)

volume [VAHL•yoom] The amount of space that matter takes up (p. 98)

wedge [WEJ] A simple machine composed of two inclined planes back to back (p. 225)

water cycle [WAW•ter SY•kuhl] The movement of water from Earth's surface to the air and back again (p. 350)

weight [WAYT] A measure of the force of gravity on an object (p. 241)

Interactive Glossary

wheel-and-axle [WEEL-AND-AK•suhl] A simple machine made of a wheel and an axle that turn together (p. 214)

work [WERK] The use of a force to move an object over a distance (p. 210)

Note: Page numbers in **boldface** type show where terms are highlighted and defined.

Index

A

absorb, 179
absorption of light, 179, 180
Active Reading. *See* **Reading Skills**
adaptations, 509–517, **510**
  by animals, 509–515
  behavioral, 525–533
  camouflage and mimicry,
    514–515, 517
  defense, 512–513
  plants, 516–517
  for survival, 510–511
advertising, 76–77
air. *See also* **wind**
  pollution of, 310–311
  water vapor in, 347
aluminum recycling, 335
amphibians
  frog, 434, 498–499
  leopard frog, 498
  reproduction, 498–499
  tadpoles, 499
analyze, critical thinking,
  38–39, 41
Analyze and Extend, 16, 28, 46,
  68, 84, 108, 112, 114, 174, 202,
  236, 282, 318, 370, 396, 424,
  446, 462, 508, 524
animals. *See also* **amphibians;**
  birds; fish and ocean
  animals; insects; reptiles
  adaptations, 509–515
  antelope, 436–437
  arctic hare, 511
  bats, 531
  bear, 528
  beaver, 468

  behavioral adaptations,
    526–527
  bison, 436–437
  camouflage and mimicry,
    514–515
  cheetah, 449
  chicken, 456–457
  chimpanzee, 527
  as consumers, 452–453,
    456–457
  coyote, 465
  dolphin, 510
  ecosystems, 434–435,
    464–465
  elephant, 503
  environmental change,
    468–469
  giraffe, 452
  gopher, 529
  gray whale, 532–533
  habitat, 434–435
  hibernation, 530–531
  horse, 496, 510
  instinct, 526–530, 532
  jackrabbit, 511
  jaguar, 453
  kangaroo rat, 438, 455
  koala, 495
  life cycles, 495–503
  lion, 526
  lynx, 496–497
  migration, 532–533
  porcupine, 512
  prairie dog, 463, 513
  as predators, 454
  as prey, 454
  reproduction, 496–497
  river otter, 441
  skunk, 512
  snake, 29, 437
  snow leopard, 514
  snow monkey, 190–191

  squirrel, 530
  tiger, 510
  traits and inheritance,
    502–503
  wolf, 437
Armstrong, Neil, 393
ask questions, in investigation,
  10
atmosphere, 358
  clouds, 359
  of Earth, 358–359, 418
auger, 227
automobiles. *See* **cars**
axis of Earth, 381
axle (shaft), 215

B

bagels, 136–137
balance (tool), 20, 97
Barboursville, Virginia (hill),
  263
bar graph, 35, 36, 37
basketball, 240–241
beach erosion, 273, 279
bedrock, 322
behavior, 526
behavioral adaptations,
  525–533
  finding food, 528
  finding shelter, 529
  hibernation, 530–531
  instinct and learned behavior,
    526–527
  migration, 532–533
bell, ringing, 165
bending matter, 128
bicycles
  as compound machine,
    214–215, 229
  manufacturing, 142

Index

bike helmet, 142
binoculars, 184–185
birds
    elf owl, 439
    feather, 29
    hummingbird, 485
    instinct, 527, 529
    ostrich, 496–497
    pelicans, 509
    roadrunner, 455
    seeds and, 489
    Steller's jay, 439
    tundra swan, 532–533
    woodpecker, 433
blizzards, 364–365
boiling, 121
bridges, 56–57, 60–61
brightness of stars, 401
brooms, 213
build, in design process, 60–61
burning wood, 135

cameras, 79
camouflage, 514
    as adaptation, 514–515, 517
    plants, 517
canyons, 260, 260–261
carbon dioxide in
    photosynthesis, 450–451
Careers in Science
    civil engineer, 85–86
    geologist, 333–334
    hydrologist, 355–356
    metallurgist, 109–110
    meteorologist, 47–48
carnivores, 452–453
cars
    changes in technology, 79
    natural resources in
        manufacturing, 141

cause and effect, 115, 177, 209, 239, 463
cell phones, 62–63, 78, 79
Celsius scale
    boiling, 121
    freezing, 118
    measuring temperature, 23, 102–103, 360
chart, 35
chemical changes to matter, 134, 134–135
circular motion
    screws, 226–227
    wheel-and-axle, 214–215
cirrus clouds, 359
civil engineers, 85–86
classify, 8
clay, 324, 324–325
clock, 22, 71
clothing, seasonal, 362–363, 371–372
clouds
    atmosphere of Earth, 358–359
    types of, 359
    water cycle, 350–351
    weather, 357–359
coal, 306
color
    as property of matter, 91–92, 94
    of soil, 324–325
    of stars, 401
comet, 410
communicate
    data, 34–35
    in design process, 61
communities, 436, 436–437
Compare and Contrast, 17, 93, 127, 223, 257, 303, 319, 343, 409, 485, 525
compost, 328–329

compound machines, 228–229
computers, 79, 309
condensation, 123, 348
    as state of matter, 123, 348–349
    water cycle, 350–351
cones, 487
conservation, 307
    of natural resources, 312–313
consumers, 452
    animals as, 452–453, 456–457
contrast, 161
cooking and baking, 136–137, 192–193
Cooper, Martin, 62–63
copper, 308
coral, 91–92
core of Earth, 258
corn, 456–457
cotton, 309
cranes (construction), 221–222
crescent moon, 387
critical thinking, 38–41
critique, critical thinking, 38–39, 41
crops, 456–457
crust of Earth, 258–259, 284, 286
cube, volume of, 98
cubic centimeters, 99
cumulonimbus clouds, 358
cumulus clouds, 359
cutting matter, 128

dam, 301–302
dams and reservoirs, 470
data, 31–41, 33
    communicating, 34–35
    display, 35, 36–37

evidence, 32–33
  record and display, 34–35
data tables, 35, 36, 155
day-and-night cycle, 377–378,
  380–381
decomposer, 452, 452–453
decomposition, 135, 321
defense adaptations, 512–513
deltas, 274–275
desert ecosystems, 438–439
design process, 55–63, 56
  communicate, 61
  finding a problem, 58–59
  improve, 60, 62–63
  plan and build, 60–61
  prototypes, 60–61
  test, 60
diesel train engine, 73
disaster planning, 290–291
display data, 34–35
dissolve, 131
dissolved substance, 131
doorknob, 215
Do the Math!
  calculate distance, 413
  calculate force, 225
  estimate and answer, 491
  estimate the difference, 263
  find the fraction, 345
  find the volume, 98
  interpret a graph, 469
  interpret a table, 73, 241
  make a bar graph, 37, 437
  make a graph, 37, 533
  make bar and line graphs, 37
  measure in millimeters, 501
  multiply whole numbers, 185
  read a table, 63, 193
  skip count by 5s, 289
  solve a story problem, 119, 313
  solve a two-step problem, 137
  solve a word problem, 217,
    273, 361, 405, 457, 517

subtract, 329
subtract units, 21
  understand data tables, 155
  use a data table, 385
  use subtraction, 329
Draw Conclusions, 16, 28, 46,
  84, 108, 112, 114, 202, 236,
  282, 318, 396, 424, 446, 462,
  508, 524
draw conclusions, 11
dropper, 18
drought, 467
drum, 169

Earth

  atmosphere of, 358–359
  composition of, 412, 414
  crust of, 258–259, 284, 286
  day-and-night cycle, 377–378,
    380–381
  earthquakes, 284–285,
    295–296
  erosion, 272–273, 466
  fire and flood, 288
  frozen water, 344–345
  gravity, 242–243
  landslides and mudslides, 289
  layers of, 258–259
  phases of the moon, 386–387
  as planet, 410, 412, 415
  radiant energy of the sun,
    402–403
  revolution of, 382–383
  rotation of, 377–378, 380–381
  satellite images of, 415
  seasons, 382–383
  in solar system life zone,
    418–419
  tides, 388–389
  volcanoes, 286–287, 295–296

weathering, 270–271
earthquake magnitude scale,
  296
earthquakes, 284, 284–285,
  295–296
earth scientists, 295–296
Earth's surface
  changes in, 269–275, 283–289
  landforms, 255–265
eating. *See* **food**
ecosystems, 434. *See also*
  environment
  animals and plants in,
    434–435, 468–469
  communities, 436–437
  environmental change
    impacts, 463–473
  fire, 288, 464–465
  food chains, 449–457
  fragility of, 464–465
  land, 438–439
  ocean, 434–435, 440–441
  populations, 436–437
  study of, 447–448
  water, 440–441, 466–467
egg mass, amphibian, 498
eggs
  amphibian, 496, 498
  bird, 496
electrical energy, 152, 159–160
electricity, 159
emergency checklist, 291
emergency planning, 290–291
empirical evidence, 33, **33**
energy, 147–155, **150, 162.** *See*
  also **light**
  described, 150–151
  electrical, 152, 159–160
  forms of, 149–155, 163
  fossil fuels, 307–310
  heat, 153, 189–197
  light, 153, 177–185

Index

location of, 152–153

nonrenewable natural resources, 306–307

radiant energy of the sun, 402–403

solar cells, 309

sound, 152, 154–155, 161–169

using, 154–155

engineering

design process, 55–63

tools, 59

Engineering and Technology. *See also* **STEM (Science, Technology, Engineering, and Mathematics)**

cranes, 221–222

erosion technology, 279–280

firefighting, 477–478

food preservation, 537–538

natural resources in bicycles, 142

natural resources in cars, 141

raincoats, 371–372

recycling and pollution, 335–336

telephone developments, 175–176

engineers and technology, 69–79

environment, 434

adaptations, 509–517

animals and plants in, 434, 468–469

changes in, ecosystem impacts, 463–473

hibernation, 530–531

people and, 470–473

pollution, 470

water, 466–467

erosion, 272, 466

beach, 273, 279

plants, 274

soil, 274–275, 280

water, wind, and ice, 272–273

evaluate, critical thinking, 38–39, 41

evaporation, 122, 348

to create salt, 133

to separate mixtures, 133

of water, 122, 133, 348–349

water cycle, 350–351

evidence, 32–33

experiment, 11

explore, 8

Fahrenheit scale

boiling, 121

freezing, 118

measuring temperature, 23, 102–103, 360

fall season, 382–383

farmers, 456–457

fertile soil, 321

filters to separate mixtures, 133

find a problem, design process, 58–59

fire

burning wood, 135

in ecosystems, 288, 464–465

heat and light from, 195

firefighting, 477–478

fire hose, 128

fish and ocean animals

archer fish, 528

clownfish, 440

coral, 91–92, 440

dolphin, 510

frogfish, 515

gray whale, 532–533

hermit crab, 434

mantis shrimp, 483–484

mussel, 435

as renewable resource, 305

sea anemone, 435

sea star, 435

sea turtle, 1–2

whale shark, 447

fishing pole reel, 207–208

flashlights, 178–179

flatlands, 264–265

float, objects that, 100–101

flood, 288, 466

flowers, 486

folding matter, 128

food

finding, as instinct, 528

food chains, 449–457

preservation techniques, 537–538

food chains, 449–457, **454**

consumers and decomposers, 452–453

photosynthesis, 450–451

predator and prey interactions, 454–455

force, 241

change position of object, 210–211

gravity, 239–247

pull or push, 210–211, 240–241

simple machines, 209–217, 223–231

forceps, 18

forest ecosystems, 438

fork (tuning), 165

fork (utensil), 212

fossil fuels, 307, 307–310

freezing, 348

water, 118–119, 120, 270–271, 344–345

waterfalls, 341–342

weathering, 270–271

freight trains, 75
fresh water, 344, 344–345
friction, 196–197
fronds, 490
fruit, 487
fruit salad, 130–131
fulcrum, 212, 212–213

garden clippers, 228–229
gases, 116
    boiling, 121
    condensation, 123, 348
    water as, 346–349
gas giants, 416
gemstones, 307
geologists, 333–334
germinates, 486
glaciers, 346–347
glass recycling, 313
Glenn, John, 393
graduated cylinder, 21, 99
grams (g), 97
Granados, Hugo Delgado, 295
Grand Canyon, 260
graphs
    bar graph, 35, 36, 37
    line graph, 37
grassland ecosystems, 436–437
gravity, 239–247, 241
    downward movement,
       240–243
    of Earth, 242–243
    in space, 246–247
    at work and play, 244–245
Great Plains, 265
Great Red Spot, Jupiter, 416
Greiner, Helen, 237
groundwater, 350
guitars, 166–167

habitats, 434, 434–435
hail, 119
hand lens, 18–19
hardness, as property of
    matter, 95
hay bales, to control erosion,
    280
headings, 3, 357, 397
heat, 189–197, 190
    as energy, 153, 191
    from friction (rubbing),
       196–197
    light and, 194–195
    lightning, 162
    movement of, 190–193
    sources of, 189–197
    temperature and, 190–191
helicopter hovers, 245
herbivores, 452–453
hibernation, 530, 530–531
hills, 262–263
home, cooking and baking at,
    192–193
humus, 320, 322
hurricanes, 364–365
hydrologists, 355–356
hypothesis, 10, 10–11

ice, 342, 346–347
icebergs, 345
inclined planes, 224, 224–227
    screws, 226–227, 229
    wedge as, 225
indoor science safety rules,
    xxiii
infer, 6, 6–7

inheritance and traits,
    502–503
inner core of Earth, 258
inner planets, 410–412,
    414–415
Inquiry Skills
    Analyze and Extend, 16, 28, 46,
       68, 84, 108, 112, 114, 174,
       202, 236, 282, 318, 370,
       396, 424, 446, 462, 508, 524
    Draw Conclusions, 16, 28, 46,
       84, 108, 112, 114, 174, 202,
       236, 282, 318, 370, 396,
       424, 446, 462, 508, 524
    Record Your Data, 68, 83, 107,
       111, 113, 173, 201, 235,
       317, 423, 445, 461, 507, 523
    Record Your Observations,
       281, 395
    Record Your Results, 15, 27
    Set a Purpose, 15, 27, 45, 67,
       83, 107, 111, 113, 173, 201,
       235, 281, 317, 369, 395,
       423, 445, 461, 507, 523
    State Your Hypothesis, 15, 45,
       67, 173
    Think About the Procedure,
       15, 27, 45, 67, 83, 107, 111,
       113, 173, 201, 235, 281,
       317, 369, 395, 423, 445,
       461, 507, 523
insects
    acacia ant, 431–432
    ant, 431–432, 529
    bees, 488, 521
    butterfly, 513, 515
    fleas, 521
    grasshopper, 500–501
    honeybee, 521
    housefly, 165, 167
    ladybug beetle, 29, 500–501
    life cycles, 500–501
    Monarch butterfly, 515

Index

Monarch caterpillar, 513
moth, 527
orchid mantis, 514
pollination, 488
reproduction, 500–501
spider, 527
study of, 521–522
termite, 468
Viceroy butterfly, 515
instinct, 526
in animals, 526–530, 532
finding food, 528
hibernation, 530
learned behavior and,
526–527
migration, 532
investigation, 3–11, 9
irrigation, 457

jackhammer, 164
jetty, to control erosion, 279
Johnson, Katherine, 393, 394
Jupiter, 411, 413, 416

Kamen, Dean, 237
Keck Observatory, Hawaii,
425–426
kinetic energy, 150, 151
knives, 225

labels, product, 76–77
lakes, 345
land, pollution of, 310–311
land ecosystems, 436–437,
438–439
landforms, 259, 257–265

canyons and valleys, 260–261
crust of Earth, 258–259
flatlands, 264–265
mountains and hills, 262–263
plains and plateaus, 264–265
landslides, 289
larva, 501
lava, 286
learned behaviors, 526
leaves, changing seasons, 135
lemonade, 130–131
length, measuring, 21
lenses, 185
levers, 212, 212–213, 228–229
life cycles, 486. *See also* **eggs;**
reproduction
of amphibians, 498–499
of animals, 495–503
of birds, 496–497
of insects, 500–501
of plants, 485–491
traits and inheritance,
502–503
life zone in solar system,
418–419
light, 177–185
absorption of, 179, 180
as energy, 153, 177–185
heat and, 194–195
lightning, 162
movement of, 177–185
reflected, 180–181, 182–183,
184–185
refracted (bent), 182–183,
184–185
shadows, 179
straight path of, 178–179
light bulb, 194
light energy, sun, 402–403
lightning, 162, 163, 365
line graphs, 37
liquids, 116

boiling, 121
condensation, 123, 348
freezing (*see* **freezing**)
melting, 120–121, 286, 346,
348
temperature of liquid water,
120
water as, 120, 346–349
livestock, 456
living things. *See* **animals;**
plants
loam, 326
logical reasoning, 33

machine engineers, 237
maglev train, 73
magma, 286
magnets, to separate
mixtures, 133
magnification tools, 18–19
magnifying box, 19
Main Idea and Details, 31, 69,
149, 189, 433
mantle of Earth, 258
maps, 35
Mars, 410, 412, 415, 418, 419
Mars *Spirit* **rover (probe), 415**
mass, 96
gravity and, 246
measuring, 21, 96–97
as property of matter, 96–97
materials. *See* **natural**
resources
matter, 95. *See also* **freezing;**
gases; liquids; solids
changes in, 127–137
chemical changes in, 134–135,
136–137
described, 94–95

melting, 120–121, 286, 348
mixtures, 130–131, 132–133
physical changes in, 128–129
physical properties, 93–103
properties of, 91–92, 132–133
sink or float, 100–101
solutions, 131
states of, 115–123
temperature, 102–103
McKinley, Mount, 263
measurement
design process and, 59
of length, 21
of mass, 21, 96–97
of temperature, 23, 102–103
of time, 22
tools for, 20–21
of volume, 21, 98–99
of weather, 360–361
of weight, 241
measuring cup, 21
measuring tape, 20
mechanical energy, 150, 151
melting, 120–121, 286, 346, 348
Mercury, 410, 412, 414
Messenger **(probe),** 414
metallurgists, 109–110
metals, bronze, 110
metamorphosis, 498
of amphibians, 498–499
of insects, 500–501
meteorologists, 47–48
methane clouds, Neptune,
417
microscope, 18–19, **19**
migrate, 532
migration, 532–533
milliliters (mL), 99
mimicry, 514
mirrors, 181
mixtures, 130, 130–131,
132–133

models, 9
moon (of Earth)
craters of, 393
gravity, 246–247
phases of, 386–387
tides on Earth, 388–389
moons of Jupiter, 416
motion
circular, 214–215, 226–227
force and, 210
in space, 246–247
Mottarone, Mount, 263
mountain ecosystems, 438
mountains, 262, 262–263
Mount McKinley, Alaska, 263
Mount Mottarone, Italy, 263
Mount St. Helens, Washington,
287
movement
of Earth, 379–389
gravity, 239–247
of heat, 190–193
of light, 177–185
of moon, 386–389
phases of moon, 386–387
rotation of Earth, 380–381
mudslides, 289
music
pitch and volume, 166–167,
168–169
sound compared to, 168–169
sounds from vibrations, 165,
166–167
music concerts, 147–148

Nahm, Amanda, 393, 394
Nashville flood, Tennessee, 288
natural resources, 303–313,
304

bicycle manufacture, 142
car manufacture, 141
conservation, 307, 312–313
nonrenewable, 306–307
pollution and, 310–311
renewable, 304–305
soil, 319–329
types of, 308–309
uses for, 308–309
water, 305
nectar, 488
Neptune, 411, 413, 416–417
Niagara Falls, 255–256
Nichols, Cassandra, 447
night and day cycle, 377–378,
380–381
nonrenewable resources,
306–307, **307**
nutrients, 326
consumers and decomposers,
452–453
for plants, in soil, 326–327
nymph, 501

O

objects, moving, and mass, 96
observational testing, 9
observe, 6, 6–7, 18–19
oceans. *See also* **fish and ocean**
animals
ecosystems, 434–435,
440–441
salt water, 344–345
tides, 388–389
water cycle, 350–351
oil rig, 308
omnivores, 452–453
order. *See* **sequence**
order, in measuring, 21

Index

organism, 486
outdoor science safety rules, xxiv
outer core of Earth, 258
outer planets, 412–413, 416–417
oxygen, 358
   from photosynthesis, 450–451

pan balance, 20, 97
pencil sharpener, 215
people, environment and, 470–473
People in Science
   Franklin, Benjamin, 159–160
   Granados, Hugo Delgado, 295
   Greiner, Helen, 237
   Johnson, Katherine, 393, 394
   Kamen, Dean, 237
   Nahm, Amanda, 393, 394
   Nichols, Cassandra, 447
   Person, Waverly, 295
   Ramírez, Dení, 447
   Rothschild, Miriam, 521–522
   Turner, Charles Henry, 521–522
Person, Waverly, 295
phases of moon, 386–387
photography, 163
photosynthesis, 450, 450–451
physical changes to matter, 128, 128–129, 136–137
physical properties of matter, 93–103, 95
   color, 94
   hardness, 95
   mass, 96–97
   sink or float, 100–101
   size and shape, 95
   temperature, 102–103

   texture, 94
   volume, 98–99
pinecones, 465
pitch (sound), 167, 168–169
plains (landform), 264, 264–265
plan
   an investigation, 10
   in design process, 60–61
planets, 409–419, 410. See also Earth
   inner planets, 410–412, 414–415
   in life zone, 418–419
   outer planets, 412–413, 416–417
plants. See also trees
   adaptations, 516–517
   algae, 469
   blackberries, 517
   bluebonnet, 503
   cabbage, 327
   cactus, 438–439
   camouflage, 517
   compost, 328–329
   as crops, 456–457
   dandelion, 489
   desert, 516
   ecosystems, 434–435
   environmental change, 468–469
   erosion and, 274
   fern, 490
   habitat, 434–435
   hemlock tree cone, 29
   life cycles, 485–491
   milkweed, 513
   moss, 491
   mushrooms, 453
   nutrients in soil for, 326–327
   parts of, 486–487
   photosynthesis, 450–451
   pitcher plant, 516

   as producers, 450, 456
   radiant energy of the sun, 402–403
   reproduction, 486–491
   sea grapes and sea oats, 327
   seeds, 486–487, 489
   stone plant, 517
   tomato, 486–487
   traits and inheritance, 502–503
plateaus, 264, 264–265
pollen, 488
pollination, 488
pollution, 310
   people and environment, 470
   recycling, 335–336
   reduce, reuse, recycle, 312–313
Popocatépetl volcano, Mexico, 295
populations, 436, 436–437
porometer, 447
position, changed by force, 210–211
potential energy, 150, 151
precipitation, 350
   measuring, 360–361
   in water cycle, 350–351
predators, 454, 512–514
predict, 8, 8–9, 10
prey, 454, 514
producers, 450, 456
product labels, 76–77
promotion, technology for, 76–77
prototypes, in design process, 60–61
pull, 210–211, 240–241
pulleys, 216–217, 229
pupa, 501
push, 210–211, 240–241

Q

questions, in investigation, 10

R

radiant energy, sun, 402–403
raincoats, 362–363, 371–372
rainforest, 438, 447
rain gauge, 360–361
rakes, 213
Ramírez, Dení, 447
Reading Skills
    Cause and Effect, 115, 177, 209, 239, 463
    Compare and Contrast, 17, 93, 127, 223, 257, 303, 319, 343, 409, 485, 525
    Main Idea and Details, 31, 69, 149, 189, 433
    Problem-Solution, 55
    Sequence, 10, 36, 283, 379, 449, 495
    Signal Words (clue words), 69, 223, 257
    Using Headings, 3, 357, 397
    Visual Aids, 509
record data, in design process, 59
Record Your Data, 68, 83, 107, 111, 113, 173, 201, 235, 317, 369, 423, 461, 507, 523
Record Your Observations, 281, 395
Record Your Results, 15, 27
rectangular solid, volume of, 98
recycle, 312–313, 335–336
reduce, 312–313

reflect, 180
reflected light, 180–181, 182–183, 184–185
refract, 182
refracted (bent) light, 182–183, 184–185
renewable resources, 304, 304–305
reproduce, 486
reproduction
    of amphibians, 498–499
    of animals, 496–497
    of insects, 500–501
    of plants, 486–491
reptiles
    bull snake, 437
    frilled lizard, 513
    rattlesnake, 438
    sea turtle, 1–2, 453, 526
    snake, 437, 438, 455, 531
reservoirs, 470
resources. See natural resources
reuse, 312–313
revolution (of Earth), 382
rings of Saturn, 417
river ecosystems, 440–441
rivers, 274–275
robots, 237
rock
    geologists, 333–334
    soil composition, 322–325
    weathering, 270–271, 272
Rocky Mountain plateaus, 265
rotation (of Earth), 377–378, 380–381, 381
Rothschild, Miriam, 521–522
ruby (gemstone), 307
ruler, 20
rust, 134

S

safety
    emergency planning, 290–291
    in science, xxiii–xxiv
    weather awareness, 364–365
sail boat, raise/lower sails, 217
salt, 133
salt water, 100, 344, 344–345
sand, 324
    in soil, 324–325
Saturn, 411, 413, 416–417
science, 4–11. See also Inquiry Skills
    critical thinking, 38–41
    data and evidence, 31–33
    described, 4–5
    draw conclusions, 11
    experiments and variables, 10–11
    explore, 8
    hypothesis, 10–11
    investigate, 9
    investigation, 3–11
    models, 9
    observation and inference, 6–7
    predict, 8
    safety in, xxiii–xxiv
    testing, 10–11
science tools, 17–23
    to magnify, 18–19
    to measure, 20–21
    for temperature, 23
    for time, 22
screwdriver, 226
screws, 226, 226–227, 229
seasons, 382–383
seedling, 486

Index

seeds, in plant life cycle, 486–487, 489

seesaw, 213

Segway® Human Transporter, 237, 238

separating mixtures, 132–133

Sequence, 10, 36, 283, 379, 449, 495

Set a Purpose, 15, 27, 45, 67, 83, 107, 111, 113, 173, 201, 235, 281, 317, 369, 395, 423, 445, 461, 507, 523

shadow, 179

shaft, in wheel-and-axle, 215

shape, as property of matter, 95

shelter, 529

Shepard, Alan, 393

sieve, to separate mixtures, 133

Signal Words (Clue Words), 69, 223, 257

silt, 324, 324–325

silt fence, to control erosion, 280

simple machines, 209–217, 212, 223–231
  compound machines, 228–229
  inclined plane, 224–227
  levers, 212–213, 228–229
  pulleys, 216–217, 229
  screw, 226–227, 229
  types described, 229
  wedge, 225, 228–229
  wheel-and-axle, 214–215, 229
  work, 210–211

sink, objects that, 100–101

sinkholes, 243

size of stars, 401

sky. See space; weather

skydivers, 245

sliding downhill, 245

snow, 364–365

society, technology and, 74–75

soil, 320
  composition of, 322–323
  composting, 328–329
  erosion, 272–275, 280
  as fertile, 321
  formation of, 322–323
  importance of, 320
  as natural resource, 319–329
  plants and, 326–327
  types of, 324–325

solar cells, 309

solar system, 410
  planets, 409–419
  planets in life zone, 418–419

solids, 116. See also freezing
  melting, 120–121, 294, 348
  water as, 346–349

solutions, 131

sound, 161–169, 162
  as energy, 152, 154–155
  explained, 162–163
  music, 165–169
  pitch and volume, 166–167, 168–169
  producing, 164–165
  telephones, 175–176
  from vibrations, 165, 166–167

space
  gravity, 246–247
  motion in, 246–247
  planets in our solar system, 409–419
  sun and stars, 397–405

space scientists, 393–394

sponge, 129

spores, 490, 490–491

springs, potential vs. kinetic energy in, 151

spring scale, 241

spring season, 382–383

star, 399
  stargazing, 404–405
  sun as, 398–401

State Your Hypothesis, 15, 45, 67, 173

STEM (Science, Technology, Engineering, and Mathematics). See also Engineering and Technology
  Call Me! Telephone Timeline, 175–176
  Firefighting Tools: Controlling Forest Fires, 477–478
  How It Works: Keck Observatory, 425–426
  Keeping Dry: Raincoat vs. Poncho, 371–372
  Reach for the Sky: Building with Cranes, 221–222
  Resources on the Road, 141–142
  Sand and Surf: Erosion Technology, 279–280
  Save It for Later: Food Preservation, 537–538
  Technology at Work: Problems and Fixes, 335–336

St. Helens, Mount, 287

storms, 364–365

stratus clouds, 359

subsoil, 322–323

suitcase, as technology, 70

summer season, 382–383

sun, 398
  Earth's revolution around, 382–383
  gravity and, 247
  heat and light from, 195
  radiant energy of, 402–403

rotation of Earth, 380–381
as star, 398–401
sunlight and photosynthesis, 450–451
water cycle, 350–351
survival, adaptations for, 510–511
Swiss Alps, trains through, 75

technology, 70
for advertising, 76–77
changes in, 78–79
design process, 55–63
engineers and, 69–79
erosion control, 279–280
product labels, 76–77
recycling, 335–336
society and, 74–75
telescopes, 185, 404–405, 425–426
through time, 72–73
trains, 72–75
telephones, 175–176
telescopes, 185, **404,** 404–405, 425–426
temperature, 23, 102, 191, 360
boiling, 121
on Earth, 419
evaporation, 122
freezing, 118–119, 120
of liquid water, 120
measuring, 23, 102–103
melting, 120–121
movement of heat, 192–193
as property of matter, 102–103
testing
in design process, 60
observational, 9
in science, 10–11

texture
as property of matter, 94
of soil, 324–325
thermometers, 23, 102–103, 360
Think About the Procedure, 15, 27, 45, 67, 83, 111, 113, 173, 201, 235, 281, 317, 369, 395, 423, 461, 507, 523
thinking, critical, 38–41
thunder, 162, 163
thunderstorms, 364–365
tides, 388, 388–389
time, 22
tools
engineering, 59
for measuring, 20–21
science tools, 17–23
topsoil, 322–323
tornadoes, 364
torn matter, 128
trains, 72–75
train schedule board, as technology, 71
traits and inheritance, 502–503
trees
acacia, 431–432
dormancy, 531
forest ecosystems, 438
mesquite trees, 454–455
as renewable resource, 304
trombone, 168
trumpet, 169
tuning fork, 165
tunnels, trains through, 75
Turner, Charles Henry, 521–522

United States map of earthquake risk, 285

Uranus, 411, 413, 416–417
Using Headings, 3, 357, 397

valleys, 260, 260–261
variables, in investigation, 10–11
Venus, 410, 412, 414, 418
Venus Express **(probe),** 414
vibrate, 164
vibrations
in music, 166, 168–169
in sound, 164–165, 166
violin, 168
Visual Aids, 509
volcanic explosivity index, 296
volcano, 286
Earth's crust, 286–287
light and heat from, 194
study of, 295–296
volume, 98, 167
measuring, 21, 98–99
in music, 168–169

waning moon, 387
water, 343–351. *See also* freezing
boiling, 121
condensation, 123, 348–349
dams and reservoirs, 470
drought, 467
on Earth, 418
environmental change, 466–467
erosion, 272–273, 466
evaporation, 122, 133, 348–349
fresh and salt, 344–345
frozen, 344–345

Index

gravity and, 243

hydrologists, 355–356

irrigation, to raise crops, 457

as liquid, 120, 346–349

magnified, 19

melting, 120–121, 270–271, 348

as natural resource, 305

photosynthesis, 450–451

pollution of, 310–311

precipitation, 350–351

rivers and deltas, 274–275

states of, 346–349

water cycle, 350–351

weathering, 270–271, 272

water cycle, 350, 350–351

water ecosystems, 440–441, 466–467

waterfalls, 341–342, 345

water vapor, 346

  condensation, 348–349

  precipitation, 350–351

  as water state, 346–347

waxing moon, 387

weather, 357–365, 358

  atmosphere of Earth, 358–359

  awareness and safety, 364–365

  clouds, 359

  dressing for, 362–363, 371–372

  measuring, 360–361

  meteorologists, 47–48

  precipitation, 350–351

  severe, 364–365

weathering, 270, 270–271, 272

wedge, 225, 228–229

weight, 241

wheel-and-axle, 214, 214–215, 229

Why It Matters, 62–63, 78–79, 136–137, 154–155, 184–185, 192–193, 230–231, 274–275, 290–291, 362–363, 384–385, 456–457, 472–473

William H. Natcher Bridge, 56–57, 60–61

wind, for seed dispersal, 489

wind meter, 360–361

wind vane, 360–361

winter season, 382–385

wood

  burning, 135

  wedge to split, 225, 228

work, 210

  simple machines, 209–217, 223–231

wrecking ball, 244

Y

Yellowstone National Park, 436–437